Mike Holt's Illustrated Guide to

Essential Rules of the
NATIONAL
ELECTRICAL CODE®

What You Need to Know for Safe Electrical Installations

Based on the 2014 NEC®

Mike Holt Enterprises, Inc.
888.NEC.CODE (632.2633) • www.MikeHolt.com

NOTICE TO THE READER

Mike Holt's Illustrated Guide to Essential Rules of the National Electrical Code®, based on the 2014 NEC®

First Printing: July 2014

Author: Mike Holt
Technical Illustrator: Mike Culbreath
Cover Design: Madalina Iordache-Levay
Layout Design and Typesetting: Cathleen Kwas

COPYRIGHT © 2014 Charles Michael Holt
ISBN 978-1-932685-66-4

Produced and Printed in the USA

 This logo is a registered trademark of Mike Holt Enterprises, Inc.

If you are an instructor and would like to request an examination copy of this or other Mike Holt Publications:

Call: 888.NEC.CODE (632.2633) • Fax: 352.360.0983
E-mail: Info@MikeHolt.com • Visit: www.MikeHolt.com

You can download a sample PDF of all our publications by visiting www.MikeHolt.com

I dedicate this book to the
Lord Jesus Christ, my mentor and teacher

Mike Holt

Our Commitment

We are committed to serving the electrical industry with integrity and respect by always searching for the most accurate interpretation of the NEC® and creating the highest quality instructional material that makes learning easy.

We are invested in the idea of changing lives, and build our products with the goal of not only helping you meet your licensing requirements, but also with the goal that this knowledge will improve your expertise in the field and help you throughout your career.

We are committed to building a life-long relationship with you, and to helping you in each stage of your electrical career. Whether you are an apprentice just getting started in the industry, or an electrician preparing to take an exam, we are here to help you. When you need Continuing Education credits to renew your license, we will do everything we can to get our online courses and seminars approved in your state. Or if you are a contractor looking to train your team, we have a solution for you. And if you have advanced to the point where you are now teaching others, we are here to help you build your program and provide tools to make that task easier.

We genuinely care about providing quality electrical training that will help you take your skills to the next level.

Thanks for choosing Mike Holt Enterprises for your electrical training needs. We are here to help you every step of the way and encourage you to contact us so we can be a part of your success.

God bless,

TABLE OF CONTENTS

ABOUT THIS TEXTBOOK

Mike Holt's Illustrated Guide to Essential Rules of the National Electrical Code®

This book is extracted from *Mike Holt's Illustrated Guide Understanding the National Electrical Code®* series, based on the 2014 *NEC®*, for the purpose of creating a publication that specifically addresses safe electrical installations. Anyone who has any connection with electricity (inspectors, contractors, engineers, electricians or tradesmen) should have this book.

Every day people are shocked, injured and in some cases electrocuted due to electrical installations that do not adhere to the *National Electrical Code*. Nowhere is this more evident than in the deaths of U.S. service personnel who served in Iraq and Afghanistan and were shocked at military bases due to installations not compliant with the *NEC*. These deaths were preventable with proper training, and this book was written in an effort to help prevent further deaths and injuries by bringing together the most essential *Code* rules that specifically address safe installations as they relate to electric shock and fire.

The writing style of this textbook is meant to be informative, practical, useful, easy to read, and applicable for everyday use. Just like all of Mike Holt's textbooks, this one contains hundreds of full-color illustrations showing the safety requirements of the *National Electrical Code* in practical use, helping you visualize the *Code* in today's electrical installations.

This illustrated textbook contains cautions regarding possible conflicts or confusing *NEC* requirements, tips on proper electrical installations, and warnings of dangers related to improper electrical installations. In spite of this effort, some rules may still seem unclear or need additional editorial improvement.

We can't eliminate confusing, conflicting, or controversial *Code* requirements, but we do try to put them into sharper focus to help you understand their intended purpose. Sometimes a requirement is confusing and it might be hard to understand its actual application. When this occurs, this textbook will point the situation out in an upfront and straightforward manner. We apologize in advance if that ever seems disrespectful, but our intention is to help the industry understand the current *NEC* as best as possible, point out areas that need refinement, and encourage *Code* users to be a part of the change process that creates a better *NEC* for the future.

The Scope of this Textbook

This textbook is written with the following stipulations:

1. **Power Systems and Voltage.** All power-supply systems are assumed to be one of the following, unless identified otherwise:

   - 2-wire, single-phase, 120V
   - 3-wire, single-phase, 120/240V
   - 4-wire, three-phase, 120/240V Delta
   - 4-wire, three-phase, 120/208V or 277/480V Wye

2. **Electrical Calculations.** Unless the questions or examples specify three-phase, they're based on a single-phase power supply. In addition, all amperage calculations are rounded to the nearest ampere in accordance with Section 220.5(B).

3. **Conductor Material.** Conductors are assumed to be copper, unless aluminum is identified or specified.

4. **Conductor Sizing.** Conductors are sized based on a THHN/THWN-2 copper conductor terminating on a 75°C terminal in accordance with 110.14(C), unless the question or example indicates otherwise.

5. **Overcurrent Device.** The term "overcurrent device" refers to a molded-case circuit breaker, unless specified otherwise. Where a fuse is specified, it's a single-element type fuse, also known as a "one-time fuse," unless the text specifies otherwise.

This textbook is to be used along with the *NEC*, not as a replacement for it. Be sure to have a copy of the 2014 *National Electrical Code* handy. Compare what's being explained in this textbook to what the *Code* book says, and discuss with others any topics that you find difficult to understand.

You'll notice that we've paraphrased a great deal of the *NEC* wording, and some of the article and section titles appear different from the text in the actual *Code* book. We believe doing so makes it easier to understand the content of the rule, so keep this in mind when comparing this textbook to the actual *NEC*.

This textbook follows the *NEC* format, but it doesn't cover every *Code* requirement. For example, it doesn't include every article, section, subsection, exception, or Informational Note. So don't be concerned if you see that the textbook contains Exception 1 and Exception 3, but not Exception 2.

We hope that as you read through this textbook, you'll allow sufficient time to review the text along with the outstanding graphics and examples, which are invaluable to your understanding.

How to Use This Textbook

The layout of this textbook incorporates special features designed not only to help you navigate easily through the material but to enhance your understanding as well.

Bulleted Author's Comments are intended to help you understand the *NEC* material and background information.

Danger, Caution, and Warning icons highlight areas of concern.

Framed white notes contain examples and practical application questions and answers. **Formulas** are easily identifiable in green text in the gray bar.

2014 CC **Graphics with an icon and green border** contain a 2014 *Code* change, with *NEC* text changes underlined in green. Green-bordered graphics with no green underlined text most likely indicate that the change is the removal of some text. Graphics without a colored border support the concept being discussed, and nothing in the graphic was affected by a change for 2014.

A QR code in the corresponding text can be scanned with a smartphone app to take you to a sample video clip so you can watch Mike and the DVD panel discuss this topic.

Light gray sections with a border in the chapter color contain additional background information.

Text that's underlined in the chapter color denotes a change in the *Code* for 2014.

Color coding and a modular format make it easy to navigate through each section of the textbook.

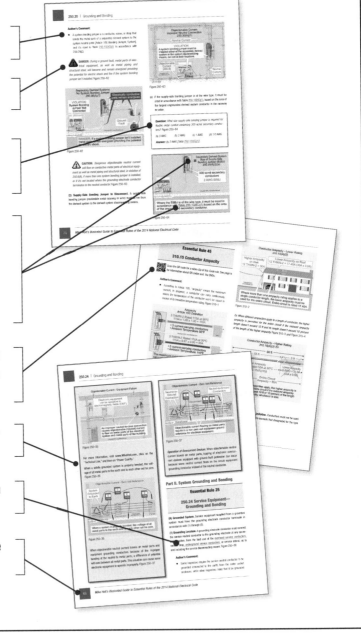

Cross-References, Notes, and Exceptions

Cross-References. This textbook contains several *NEC* cross-references to other related *Code* requirements to help you develop a better understanding of how the *NEC* rules relate to one another. These cross-references are indicated by *Code* section numbers in brackets, an example of which is "[90.4]."

Informational Notes. Informational Notes contained in the *NEC* will be identified in this textbook as "Note."

Exceptions. Exceptions contained in this textbook will be identified as "Ex" and not spelled out.

QR Codes

What's this symbol? It's a QR code and gives you the ability to use your smartphone to scan the image (using a barcode reader app) and be directed to a website. For example, the QR code to the right (when captured) will direct your smartphone to the Mike Holt Enterprises website. We've included these in various places in our textbook to make it easier for you to go directly to the website page referenced.

Follow the QR Code! When you see a QR code next to a section in the text, scan it with your smartphone to bring it to life. You will be able to watch a video clip that shows Mike and his panel of experts discussing this topic.

These video clips are samples from the DVDs that were created for *Mike Holt's Illustrated Guide to Understanding the National Electrical Code, Volumes 1 and 2* textbooks. Whether you're a visual or an auditory learner, watching the DVDs will enhance your knowledge and understanding as you read through the textbook.

Mike's Detailed *Code* Library includes these textbooks and DVDs. To order this library, visit www.mikeholt.com/14DECO or call our office at 888.632.2633.

Textbook Corrections

We're committed to providing you the finest product with the fewest errors. We take great care in proofreading and researching the *NEC* requirements to ensure this textbook is correct, but we're realistic and know that there may be errors found and reported after this textbook is printed. This can occur because the *NEC* is dramatically changed each *Code* cycle; new articles are added, some are deleted, some are relocated, and many are renumbered.

The last thing we want is for you to have problems finding, communicating, or accessing this information. Any errors found after printing are listed on our website, so if you find an error, first check to see if it's already been corrected by going to www.MikeHolt.com, click on "Books," and then click on "Corrections" (www.MikeHolt.com/book-corrections.htm).

If you believe that there's an error (typographical, grammatical, technical, or anything else) in this textbook or in the Answer Key and it isn't already listed on the website, e-mail Corrections@MikeHolt.com. Be sure to include the textbook title, page number, and any other pertinent information.

If you have adopted Mike Holt textbooks for use in your classroom you can register for up-to-date Answer Keys that can be downloaded from our website. To register and receive a log-in password, go to our web site www.MikeHolt.com, click on "Instructors" in the sidebar of links, and then click on "Answer Keys." On this same page you'll also find instructions for accessing and downloading these Answer Keys. Please note that this feature will only work after you've received a log-in password.

Technical Questions

As you progress through this textbook, you might find that you don't understand every explanation, example, calculation, or comment. Don't become frustrated, and don't get down on yourself. Remember, this is the *National Electrical Code*, and sometimes the best attempt to explain a concept isn't enough to make it perfectly clear. If you're still confused, visit www.MikeHolt.com, and post your question on our free Code Forum for help. The forum is a moderated community of electrical professionals where you can exchange ideas and post technical questions that will be answered by your peers.

Additional Products to Help You Learn

Electrical Theory DVD Library

Only when you truly know electrical theory can you have confidence in the practical aspects of your electrical work. Build your electrical foundation with Mike's Electrical Theory Library. When you finish this program you will understand: basics of electricity, how electricity is made, circuit types, electrical formulas, magnetism and electromagnetism, and practical applications of electricity.

This program includes the *Basic Electrical Theory* textbook and the following DVDs:

- Electrical Fundamentals and Basic Electricity
- Electrical Circuits, Systems and Protection
- Alternating Current, Motors, Generators, and Transformers

To order, visit www.MikeHolt.com/Theory, scan this QR code, or call 888.NEC.CODE (632.2633).

Grounding vs. Bonding DVD Library, based on the 2014 *NEC*

Grounding and Bonding is the most important and least understood article in the *NEC*, and surveys have repeatedly shown that the majority of electrical shocks and power quality problems are due to improper grounding or bonding. This illustrated textbook is informative and practical, and includes all articles that relate to Grounding and Bonding in one single place. The full-color illustrations help break down the concepts and make them easier to understand. This book focuses on Article 250 but also addresses Grounding rules throughout the *Code* Book.

The DVDs give you a 360° view of each topic with specialized commentary from Mike and his panel of industry experts.

To order, visit www.MikeHolt.com/14Code or call 888.632.2633.

Detailed *Code* Library

When you really need to understand the *NEC*, there's no better way to learn it than with Mike's Detailed *Code* Library. It takes you step-by-step through the *NEC*, in *Code* order with detailed illustrations, great practice questions, and in-depth DVD analysis. This library is perfect for engineers, electricians, contractors, and electrical inspectors.

- *Understanding the National Electrical Code—Volume 1*
- *Understanding the National Electrical Code—Volume 2*
- *NEC Exam Practice Questions* workbook
- General Requirements DVD
- Wiring and Protection DVD
- Grounding versus Bonding DVDs (2)
- Wiring Methods and Materials DVDs (2)
- Equipment for General Use DVD
- Special Occupancies DVD
- Special Equipment DVD
- Limited Energy and Communications Systems DVD.

To order, visit www.MikeHolt.com/14DECO, scan the QR code, or call us at 888.632.2633.

2014 *Code* Book and Tabs

Whether you prefer the softbound, spiral bound, or the loose-leaf version, everyone should have an updated *Code* book for accurate reference. Placing tabs on *Code* articles, sections, and tables will make it easier for you to use the *NEC*. However, too many tabs will defeat the purpose. Mike's best-selling tabs make organizing your *Code* book easy.

To order your *Code* book and set of tabs visit www.MikeHolt.com/14Code, or call 1.888.NEC.CODE (632.2633).

ABOUT THE
NATIONAL ELECTRICAL CODE

The *National Electrical Code* is written for persons who understand electrical terms, theory, safety procedures, and electrical trade practices. These individuals include electricians, electrical contractors, electrical inspectors, electrical engineers, designers, and other qualified persons. The *Code* isn't written to serve as an instructional or teaching manual for untrained individuals [90.1(A)].

Learning to use the *NEC* can be likened to learning the strategy needed to play the game of chess well; it's a great game if you enjoy mental warfare. When learning to play chess, you must first learn the names of the game pieces, how they're placed on the board, and how each one is moved.

Once you understand the fundamentals, you're ready to start playing the game. Unfortunately, at this point all you can do is make crude moves, because you really don't understand how all the information works together. To play chess well, you'll need to learn how to use your knowledge by working on subtle strategies before you can work your way up to the more intriguing and complicated moves.

The *Code* is updated every three years to accommodate new electrical products and materials, changing technologies, improved installation techniques, and to make editorial refinements to improve readability and application. While the uniform adoption of each new edition of the *NEC* is the best approach for all involved in the electrical industry, many inspection jurisdictions modify the *Code* when it's adopted. To further complicate this situation, the *NEC* allows the authority having jurisdiction, typically the "Electrical Inspector," the flexibility to waive specific *Code* requirements, and to permit alternative methods. This is only allowed when he or she is assured the completed electrical installation is equivalent in establishing and maintaining effective safety [90.4].

Keeping up with requirements of the *Code* should be the goal of everyone involved in the safety of electrical installations. This includes electrical installers, contractors, owners, inspectors, engineers, instructors, and others concerned with electrical installations.

About the 2014 *NEC*

The actual process of changing the *Code* takes about two years, and it involves hundreds of individuals making an effort to have the *NEC* as current and accurate as possible. Let's review how this process worked for the 2014 *NEC*:

Step 1. Proposals—November, 2011. Anybody can submit a proposal to change the *Code* before the proposal closing date. Thousands of proposals were submitted to modify the 2011 *NEC* and create the 2014 *Code*. Of these proposals, several hundred rules were revised that significantly affect the electrical industry. Some changes were editorial revisions, while others were more significant, such as new articles, sections, exceptions, and Informational Notes.

Step 2. *Code*-Making Panel(s) Review Proposals—January, 2012. All *Code* change proposals were reviewed by *Code*-Making Panels. There were 19 panels in the 2014 revision process who voted to accept, reject, or modify proposals.

Step 3. Report on Proposals (ROP)—July, 2012. The voting of the *Code*-Making Panels on the proposals was published for public review in a document called the "Report on Proposals," frequently referred to as the "ROP."

Step 4. Public Comments—October, 2012. Once the ROP was available, public comments were submitted asking the *Code*-Making Panel members to revise their earlier actions on change proposals, based on new information. The closing date for "Comments" was October, 2012.

Step 5. Comments Reviewed by *Code* Panels—December, 2012. The *Code*-Making Panels met again to review, discuss, and vote on public comments.

Step 6. Report on Comments (ROC)—March, 2013. The voting on the "Comments" was published for public review in a document called the "Report on Comments," frequently referred to as the "ROC."

Step 7. Electrical Section—June, 2013. The NFPA Electrical Section discussed and reviewed the work of the *Code*-Making Panels. The Electrical Section developed recommendations on last-minute motions to revise the proposed *NEC* draft that would be presented at the NFPA's annual meeting.

Step 8. NFPA Annual Meeting—June, 2013. The 2014 *NEC* was voted by the NFPA members to approve the action of the *Code*-Making Panels at the annual meeting, after a number of motions (often called "floor actions" or "NITMAMs") were voted on.

Step 9. Standards Council Review Appeals and Approves the 2014 *NEC*—July, 2013. The NFPA Standards Council reviewed the record of the *Code*-making process and approved publication of the 2014 *NEC*.

Step 10. 2014 *NEC* Published—September, 2013. The 2014 *National Electrical Code* was published, following the NFPA Board of Directors review of appeals.

Author's Comment:

■ Proposals and comments can be submitted online at the NFPA website (www.nfpa.org). From the homepage, click on "Codes and Standards", then find NFPA 70 (*National Electrical Code*). From there, follow the on screen instructions to download the proposal form. The deadline for proposals to create the 2017 *National Electrical Code* will be around November of 2014. If you would like to see something changed in the *Code*, you're encouraged to participate in the process.

Not a Game

Electrical work isn't a game, and it must be taken very seriously. Learning the basics of electricity, important terms and concepts, as well as the basic layout of the *NEC* gives you just enough knowledge to be dangerous. There are thousands of specific and unique applications of electrical installations, and the *Code* doesn't cover every one of them. To safely apply the *NEC*, you must understand the purpose of a rule and how it affects the safety aspects of the installation.

NEC Terms and Concepts

The *NEC* contains many technical terms, so it's crucial for *Code* users to understand their meanings and their applications. If you don't understand a term used in a *Code* rule, it will be impossible to properly apply the *NEC* requirement. Be sure you understand that Article 100 defines the terms that apply to two or more *Code* articles. For example, the term "Dwelling Unit" is found in many articles; if you don't know what a dwelling unit is, how can you apply the requirements for it?

In addition, many articles have terms unique for that specific article and definitions of those terms are only applicable for that given article. For example, Section 250.2 contains the definitions of terms that only apply to Article 250—Grounding and Bonding.

Small Words, Grammar, and Punctuation

It's not only the technical words that require close attention, because even the simplest of words can make a big difference to the application of a rule. The word "or" can imply alternate choices for wiring methods, while "and" can mean an additional requirement. Let's not forget about grammar and punctuation. The location of a comma can dramatically change the requirement of a rule.

Slang Terms or Technical Jargon

Electricians, engineers, and other trade-related professionals use slang terms or technical jargon that isn't shared by all. This makes it very difficult to communicate because not everybody understands the intent or application of those slang terms. So where possible, be sure you use the proper word, and don't use a word if you don't understand its definition and application. For example, lots of electricians use the term "pigtail" when describing the short conductor for the connection of a receptacle, switch, luminaire, or equipment. Although they may understand it, not everyone does.

NEC Style and Layout

Before we get into the details of the *NEC*, we need to take a few moments to understand its style and layout. Understanding the structure and writing style of the *Code* is very important before it can be used and applied effectively. The *National Electrical Code* is organized into ten major components.

1. Table of Contents
2. Article 90 (Introduction to the *Code*)
3. Chapters 1 through 9 (major categories)
4. Articles 90 through 840 (individual subjects)
5. Parts (divisions of an article)
6. Sections and Tables (*NEC* requirements)
7. Exceptions (*Code* permissions)
8. Informational Notes (explanatory material)
9. Annexes (information)
10. Index

1. Table of Contents. The Table of Contents displays the layout of the chapters, articles, and parts as well as the page numbers. It's an excellent resource and should be referred to periodically to observe the interrelationship of the various *NEC* components. When attempting to locate the rules for a particular situation, knowledgeable *Code* users often go first to the Table of Contents to quickly find the specific *NEC* Part that applies.

2. Introduction. The *NEC* begins with Article 90, the introduction to the *Code*. It contains the purpose of the *NEC*, what's covered and what isn't covered along with how the *Code* is arranged. It also gives information on enforcement and how mandatory and permissive rules are written as well as how explanatory material is included. Article 90 also includes information on formal interpretations, examination of equipment for safety, wiring planning, and information about formatting units of measurement.

3. Chapters. There are nine chapters, each of which is divided into articles. The articles fall into one of four groupings: General Requirements (Chapters 1 through 4), Specific Requirements (Chapters 5 through 7), Communications Systems (Chapter 8), and Tables (Chapter 9).

Chapter 1—General
Chapter 2—Wiring and Protection
Chapter 3—Wiring Methods and Materials
Chapter 4—Equipment for General Use
Chapter 5—Special Occupancies
Chapter 6—Special Equipment
Chapter 7—Special Conditions
Chapter 8—Communications Systems (Telephone, Data, Satellite, Cable TV and Broadband)
Chapter 9—Tables–Conductor and Raceway Specifications

4. Articles. The *NEC* contains approximately 140 articles, each of which covers a specific subject. For example:

Article 110—General Requirements
Article 250—Grounding and Bonding
Article 300—General Requirements for Wiring Methods and Materials
Article 430—Motors and Motor Controllers
Article 500—Hazardous (Classified) Locations
Article 680—Swimming Pools, Fountains, and Similar Installations
Article 725—Remote-Control, Signaling, and Power-Limited Circuits
Article 800—Communications Circuits

5. Parts. Larger articles are subdivided into parts. Because the parts of a *Code* article aren't included in the section numbers, we have a tendency to forget what "part" the *NEC* rule is relating to. For example, Table 110.34(A) contains working space clearances for electrical equipment. If we aren't careful, we might think this table applies to all electrical installations, but Table 110.34(A) is located in Part III, which only contains requirements for "Over 600 Volts, Nominal" installations. The rules for working clearances for electrical equipment for systems 600V, nominal, or less are contained in Table 110.26(A)(1), which is located in Part II—600 Volts, Nominal, or Less.

6. Sections and Tables.

Sections. Each *NEC* rule is called a "*Code* Section." A *Code* section may be broken down into subsections by letters in parentheses (A), (B), and so on. Numbers in parentheses (1), (2), and so forth, may further break down a subsection, and lowercase letters (a), (b), and so on, further break the rule down to the third level. For example, the rule requiring all receptacles in a dwelling unit bathroom to be GFCI protected is contained in Section 210.8(A)(1). Section 210.8(A)(1) is located in Chapter 2, Article 210, Section 8, Subsection (A), Sub-subsection (1).

Many in the industry incorrectly use the term "Article" when referring to a *Code* section. For example, they say "Article 210.8," when they should say "Section 210.8." Section numbers in this textbook are shown without the word "Section," unless they begin a sentence. For example, Section 210.8(A) is shown as simply 210.8(A).

Tables. Many *NEC* requirements are contained within tables, which are lists of *Code* rules placed in a systematic arrangement. The titles of the tables are extremely important; you must read them carefully in order to understand the contents, applications, limitations, and so forth, of each table in the *NEC*. Many times notes are provided in or below a table; be sure to read them as well since they're also part of the requirement. For example, Note 1 for Table 300.5 explains how to measure the cover when burying cables and raceways, and Note 5 explains what to do if solid rock is encountered.

7. Exceptions. Exceptions are *Code* requirements or permissions that provide an alternative method to a specific rule. There are two types of exceptions—mandatory and permissive. When a rule has several exceptions, those exceptions with mandatory requirements are listed before the permissive exceptions.

Mandatory Exceptions. A mandatory exception uses the words "shall" or "shall not." The word "shall" in an exception means that if you're using the exception, you're required to do it in a particular way. The phrase "shall not" means it isn't permitted.

Permissive Exceptions. A permissive exception uses words such as "shall be permitted," which means it's acceptable (but not mandatory) to do it in this way.

8. Informational Notes. An Informational Note contains explanatory material intended to clarify a rule or give assistance, but it isn't a *Code* requirement.

9. Annexes. Annexes aren't a part of the *NEC* requirements, and are included in the *Code* for informational purposes only.

Annex A. Product Safety Standards

Annex B. Application Information for Ampacity Calculation

Annex C. Raceway Fill Tables for Conductors and Fixture Wires of the Same Size

Annex D. Examples

Annex E. Types of Construction

Annex F. Critical Operations Power Systems (COPS)

Annex G. Supervisory Control and Data Acquisition (SCADA)

Annex H. Administration and Enforcement

Annex I. Recommended Tightening Torques

Annex J. ADA Standards for Accessible Design

10. Index. The Index at the back of the *Code* book is helpful in locating a specific rule.

Changes to the *NEC* since the previous edition(s), are identified by shading, but rules that have been relocated aren't identified as a change. A bullet symbol "•" is located on the margin to indicate the location of a rule that was deleted from a previous edition. New articles contain a vertical line in the margin of the page.

Different Interpretations

Some electricians, contractors, instructors, inspectors, engineers, and others enjoy the challenge of discussing the *NEC* requirements, hopefully in a positive and productive manner. This give-and-take is important to the process of better understanding the *Code* requirements and application(s). However, if you're going to participate in an *NEC* discussion, please don't spout out what you think without having the actual *Code* book in your hand. The professional way of discussing an *NEC* requirement is by referring to a specific section, rather than talking in vague generalities.

How to Locate a Specific Requirement

How to go about finding what you're looking for in the *Code* book depends, to some degree, on your experience with the *NEC*. *Code* experts typically know the requirements so well they just go to the correct rule without any outside assistance. The Table of Contents might be the only thing very experienced *NEC* users need to locate the requirement they're looking for. On the other hand, average *Code* users should use all of the tools at their disposal, including the Table of Contents and the Index.

Table of Contents. Let's work out a simple example: What *NEC* rule specifies the maximum number of disconnects permitted for a service? If you're an experienced *Code* user, you'll know Article 230 applies to "Services," and because this article is so large, it's divided up into multiple parts (actually eight parts). With this knowledge, you can quickly go to the Table of Contents and see it lists the Service Equipment Disconnecting Means requirements in Part VI.

Author's Comment:

■ The number 70 precedes all page numbers because the *NEC* is NFPA Standard Number 70.

Index. If you use the Index, which lists subjects in alphabetical order, to look up the term "service disconnect," you'll see there's no listing. If you try "disconnecting means," then "services," you'll find that the Index indicates that the rule is located in Article 230, Part VI. Because the *NEC* doesn't give a page number in the Index, you'll need to use the Table of Contents to find it, or flip through the *Code* book to Article 230, then continue to flip through pages until you find Part VI.

Many people complain that the *NEC* only confuses them by taking them in circles. As you gain experience in using the *Code* and deepen your understanding of words, terms, principles, and practices, you'll find the *NEC* much easier to understand and use than you originally thought.

Customizing Your *Code* Book

One way to increase your comfort level with the *Code* book is to customize it to meet your needs. You can do this by highlighting and underlining important *NEC* requirements, and by attaching tabs to important pages. Be aware that if you're using your *Code* book to take an exam, some exam centers don't allow markings of any type.

Highlighting. As you read through this textbook, be sure you highlight those requirements in the *Code* that are the most important or relevant to you. Use one color for general interest and a different one for important requirements you want to find quickly. Be sure to highlight terms in the Index and the Table of Contents as you use them.

Underlining. Underline or circle key words and phrases in the *NEC* with a red pen (not a lead pencil) and use a short ruler or other straightedge to keep lines straight and neat. This is a very handy way to make important requirements stand out. A short ruler or other straightedge also comes in handy for locating specific information in the many *Code* tables.

ABOUT THE AUTHOR

Mike Holt—Author

Founder and President
Mike Holt Enterprises
Groveland, FL
www.MikeHolt.com

Mike Holt worked his way up through the electrical trade. He began as an apprentice electrician and became one of the most recognized experts in the world as it relates to electrical power installations. He's worked as a journeyman electrician, master electrician, and electrical contractor. Mike's experience in the real world gives him a unique understanding of how the *NEC* relates to electrical installations from a practical standpoint. You'll find his writing style to be direct, nontechnical, and powerful.

Did you know Mike didn't finish high school? So if you struggled in high school or didn't finish at all, don't let it get you down. However, realizing that success depends on one's continuing pursuit of education, Mike immediately attained his GED, and ultimately attended the University of Miami's Graduate School for a Master's degree in Business Administration.

Mike resides in Central Florida, is the father of seven children, has five grandchildren, and enjoys many outside interests and activities. He's a nine-time National Barefoot Water-Ski Champion (1988, 1999, 2005–2009, 2012–2013). He's set many national records and continues to train year-round at a World competition level (www.barefootwaterskier.com).

What sets him apart from some is his commitment to living a balanced lifestyle; placing God first, family, career, then self.

Special Acknowledgments—First, I want to thank God for my godly wife who's always by my side and my children, Belynda, Melissa, Autumn, Steven, Michael, Meghan, and Brittney.

A special thank you must be sent to the staff at the National Fire Protection Association (NFPA), publishers of the *NEC*—in particular Jeff Sargent for his assistance in answering my many *Code* questions over the years. Jeff, you're a "first class" guy, and I admire your dedication and commitment to helping others understand the *NEC*. Other former NFPA staff members I would like to thank include John Caloggero, Joe Ross, and Dick Murray for their help in the past.

A personal thank you goes to Sarina, my long-time friend and office manager. It's been wonderful working side-by-side with you for over 25 years nurturing this company's growth from its small beginnings.

ABOUT THE ILLUSTRATOR

Mike Culbreath—Illustrator

Graphic Illustrator
Alden, MI
www.MikeHolt.com

Mike Culbreath devoted his career to the electrical industry and worked his way up from an apprentice electrician to master electrician. He started in the electrical field doing residential and light commercial construction. He later did service work and custom electrical installations. While working as a journeyman electrician, he suffered a serious on-the-job knee injury. As part of his rehabilitation, Mike completed courses at Mike Holt Enterprises. and then passed the exam to receive his Master Electrician's license. In 1986, with a keen interest in continuing education for electricians, he joined the staff to update material and began illustrating Mike Holt's textbooks and magazine articles.

He started with simple hand-drawn diagrams and cut-and-paste graphics. When frustrated by the limitations of that style of illustrating, he took a company computer home to learn how to operate some basic computer graphic software. Becoming aware that computer graphics offered a lot of flexibility for creating illustrations, Mike took every computer graphics class and seminar he could to help develop his computer graphic skills. He's now worked as an illustrator and editor with the company for over 25 years and, as Mike Holt has proudly acknowledged, has helped to transform his words and visions into lifelike graphics.

Originally from South Florida, Mike now lives in northern lower Michigan where he enjoys kayaking, photography, and cooking, but his real passion is his horses.

Mike loves spending time with his children Dawn and Mac and his grandchildren Jonah and Kieley.

Special Acknowledgments—I would like to thank Ryan Jackson, an outstanding and very knowledgeable *Code* guy, and Eric Stromberg, an electrical engineer and super geek (and I mean that in the most complimentary manner, this guy is brilliant), for helping me keep our graphics as technically correct as possible.

I also want to give a special thank you to Cathleen Kwas for making me look good with her outstanding layout design and typesetting skills and Toni Culbreath who proofreads all of my material. I would also like to acknowledge Belynda Holt Pinto, our Chief Operations Officer and the rest of the outstanding staff at Mike Holt Enterprises, for all the hard work they do to help produce and distribute these outstanding products.

And last but not least, I need to give a special thank you to Mike Holt for not firing me over 25 years ago when I "borrowed" one of his computers and took it home to begin the process of learning how to do computer illustrations. He gave me the opportunity and time needed to develop my computer graphic skills. He's been an amazing friend and mentor since I met him as a student many years ago. Thanks for believing in me and allowing me to be part of the Mike Holt Enterprises family.

ARTICLE

90

INTRODUCTION TO THE
NATIONAL ELECTRICAL CODE

Introduction to Article 90—Introduction to the *National Electrical Code*

Many *NEC* violations and misunderstandings wouldn't occur if people doing the work simply understood Article 90. For example, many people see *Code* requirements as performance standards. In fact, the *NEC* requirements are bare minimums for safety. This is exactly the stance electrical inspectors, insurance companies, and courts take when making a decision regarding electrical design or installation.

Article 90 opens by saying the *NEC* isn't intended as a design specification or instruction manual. The *National Electrical Code* has one purpose only, and that's the "practical safeguarding of persons and property from hazards arising from the use of electricity." The necessity of carefully studying the *NEC* rules can't be overemphasized, and the role of textbooks such as this one is to help in that undertaking. Understanding where to find the rules in the *Code* that apply to the installation is invaluable. Rules in several different articles often apply to even a simple installation.

Article 90 then describes the scope and arrangement of the *NEC*. The balance of this article provides the reader with information essential to understanding the *Code* rules.

Typically, electrical work requires you to understand the first four chapters of the *NEC* which apply generally, plus have a working knowledge of the Chapter 9 tables. That understanding begins with Article 90. Chapters 5, 6, and 7 make up a large portion of the *Code*, but they apply to special occupancies, special equipment, or other special conditions. They build on, modify, or amend the rules in the first four chapters. Chapter 8 contains the requirements for communications systems, such as telephone systems, antenna wiring, CATV, and network-powered broadband systems. Communications systems aren't subject to the general requirements of Chapters 1 through 4, or the special requirements of Chapters 5 through 7, unless there's a specific reference in Chapter 8 to a rule in Chapters 1 through 7.

Essential Rule 1

90.1 Purpose of the *NEC*

(A) Practical Safeguarding. The purpose of the *NEC* is to ensure that electrical systems are installed in a manner that protects people and property by minimizing the risks associated with the use of electricity. It isn't a design specification standard or instruction manual for the untrained and unqualified. Figure 90–1

Author's Comment:

■ The *Code* is intended to be used by those skilled and knowledgeable in electrical theory, electrical systems, construction, and the installation and operation of electrical equipment.

(B) Adequacy. The *Code* contains requirements considered necessary for a safe electrical installation. If an electrical system is installed in compliance with the *NEC*, it'll be essentially free from electrical hazards. The *Code* is a safety standard, not a design guide.

Figure 90–1

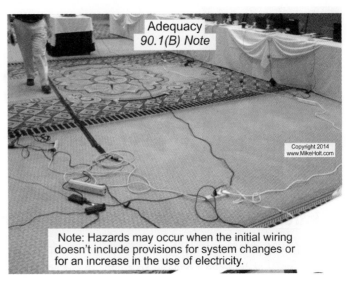

Figure 90–3

NEC requirements aren't intended to ensure the electrical installation will be efficient, convenient, adequate for good service, or suitable for future expansion. Specific items of concern, such as electrical energy management, maintenance, and power quality issues aren't within the scope of the *Code*. Figure 90–2

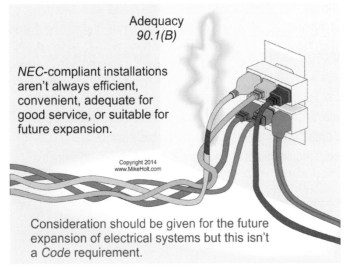

Figure 90–2

Note: Hazards in electrical systems often occur because circuits are overloaded or not properly installed in accordance with the *NEC*. These often occur if the initial wiring didn't provide reasonable provisions for system changes or for the increase in the use of electricity. Figure 90–3

Author's Comment:

■ See the definition of "Overload" in Article 100.

■ The *NEC* doesn't require electrical systems to be designed or installed to accommodate future loads. However, the electrical designer (typically an electrical engineer) is concerned with not only ensuring electrical safety (*Code* compliance), but also with ensuring the system meets the customers' needs, both of today and in the near future. To satisfy customers' needs, electrical systems are often designed and installed above the minimum requirements contained in the *NEC*. But just remember, if you're taking an exam, licensing exams are based on your understanding of the minimum *Code* requirements.

(C) Relation to International Standards. The requirements of the *NEC* address the fundamental safety principles contained in the International Electrotechnical Commission (IEC) standards, including protection against electric shock, adverse thermal effects, overcurrent, fault currents, and overvoltage. Figure 90–4

Author's Comment:

■ The *NEC* is used in Chile, Ecuador, Peru, and the Philippines. It's also the *Electrical Code* for Colombia, Costa Rica, Mexico, Panama, Puerto Rico, and Venezuela. Because of these adoptions, it's available in Spanish from the National Fire Protection Association, 617.770.3000, or www.NFPA.org.

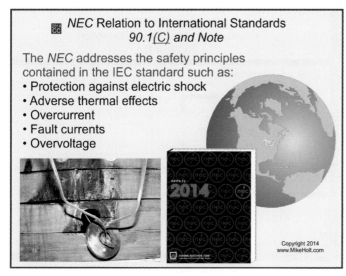

Figure 90–4

Essential Rule 2

90.2 Scope of the *NEC*

(A) What Is Covered. The *NEC* contains requirements necessary for the proper installation of electrical conductors, equipment, cables, and raceways for power, signaling, fire alarm, optical cable, and communications systems for: Figure 90–5

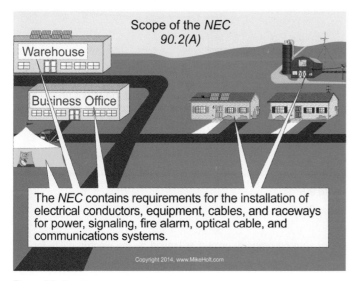

Figure 90–5

(1) Public and private premises, including buildings, mobile homes, recreational vehicles, and floating buildings. Figure 90–6

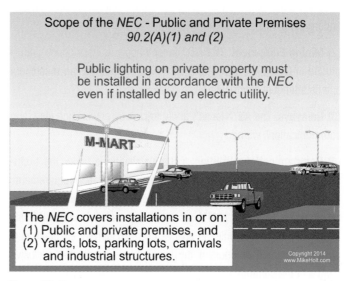

Figure 90–6

(2) Yards, lots, parking lots, carnivals, and industrial substations.

(3) Conductors and equipment connected to the utility supply.

(4) Installations used by an electric utility, such as office buildings, warehouses, garages, machine shops, recreational buildings, and other electric utility buildings that aren't an integral part of a utility's generating plant, substation, or control center. Figure 90–7

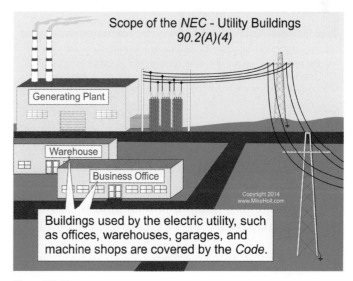

Figure 90–7

(B) What Isn't Covered. The *NEC* doesn't apply to:

(1) Transportation Vehicles. The *NEC* doesn't apply to installations in cars, trucks, boats, ships and watercraft, planes, electric trains, or underground mines.

(2) Mining Equipment. The *NEC* doesn't apply to installations underground in mines and self-propelled mobile surface mining machinery and its attendant electrical trailing cables.

(3) Railways. The *NEC* doesn't apply to railway power, signaling, and communications wiring.

(4) Communications Utilities. If the installation is under the exclusive control of the communications utility, the installation requirements of the *NEC* don't apply to the communications (telephone), Community Antenna Television (CATV), or network-powered broadband utility equipment located in building spaces used exclusively for these purposes, or located outdoors if the installation is under the exclusive control of the communications utility. Figure 90–8 and Figure 90–9

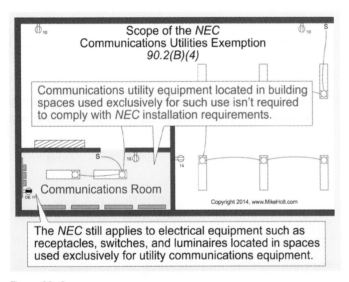

Figure 90–8

Author's Comment:

- Interior wiring for communications systems, not in building spaces used exclusively for these purposes, must be installed in accordance with the following Chapter 8 Articles:

  □ Telephone and Data, Article 800

  □ CATV, Article 820

  □ Network-Powered Broadband, Article 830

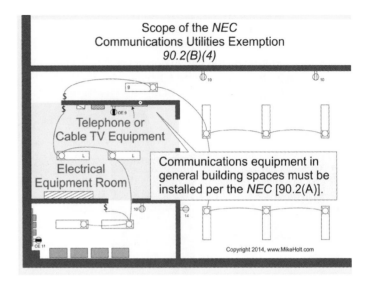

Figure 90–9

(5) Electric Utilities. The *NEC* doesn't apply to electrical installations under the exclusive control of an electric utility where such installations:

   a. Consist of utility installed service drops or service laterals under their exclusive control. Figure 90–10

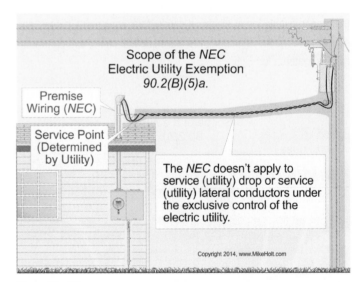

Figure 90–10

   b. Are on property owned or leased by the electric utility for the purpose of generation, transformation, transmission, distribution, or metering of electric energy. Figure 90–11

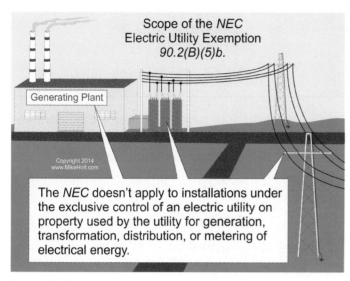

Figure 90–11

Author's Comment:

- Luminaires located in legally established easements, or rights-of-way, such as at poles supporting transmission or distribution lines, are exempt from the *NEC*. However, if the electric utility provides site and public lighting on private property, then the installation must comply with the *Code* [90.2(A)(4)].

c. Are located on legally established easements, or rights-of-way. Figure 90–12

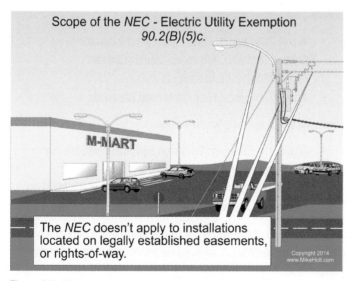

Figure 90–12

d. Are located by other written agreements either designated by or recognized by public service commissions, utility commissions, or other regulatory agencies having jurisdiction for such installations; limited to installations for the purpose of communications, metering, generation, control, transformation, transmission, or distribution of electric energy where legally established easements or rights-of-way can't be obtained. These installations are limited to federal lands, Native American reservations through the U.S. Department of the Interior Bureau of Indian Affairs, military bases, lands controlled by port authorities and state agencies and departments, and lands owned by railroads.

Note to 90.2(B)(4) and (5): Utilities include entities that install, operate, and maintain communications systems (telephone, CATV, Internet, satellite, or data services) or electric supply (generation, transmission, or distribution systems) and are designated or recognized by governmental law or regulation by public service/utility commissions. Utilities may be subject to compliance with codes and standards covering their regulated activities as adopted under governmental law or regulation.

Essential Rule 3

90.3 *Code* Arrangement

The *Code* is divided into an introduction and nine chapters. Figure 90–13

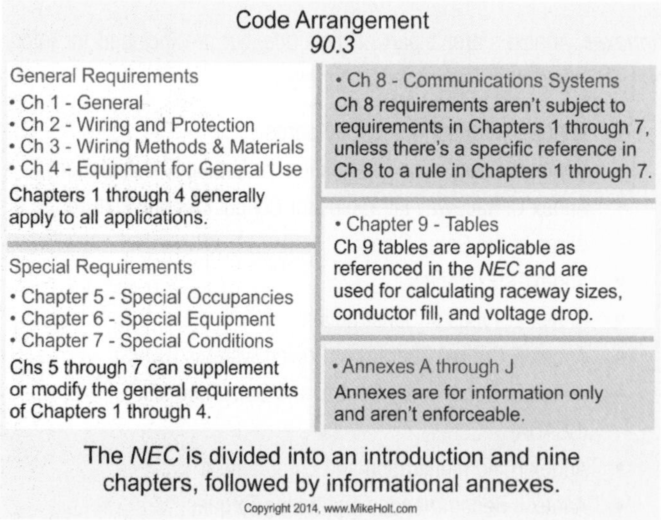

Code Arrangement
90.3

General Requirements
- Ch 1 - General
- Ch 2 - Wiring and Protection
- Ch 3 - Wiring Methods & Materials
- Ch 4 - Equipment for General Use

Chapters 1 through 4 generally apply to all applications.

Special Requirements
- Chapter 5 - Special Occupancies
- Chapter 6 - Special Equipment
- Chapter 7 - Special Conditions

Chs 5 through 7 can supplement or modify the general requirements of Chapters 1 through 4.

- Ch 8 - Communications Systems
Ch 8 requirements aren't subject to requirements in Chapters 1 through 7, unless there's a specific reference in Ch 8 to a rule in Chapters 1 through 7.

- Chapter 9 - Tables
Ch 9 tables are applicable as referenced in the *NEC* and are used for calculating raceway sizes, conductor fill, and voltage drop.

- Annexes A through J
Annexes are for information only and aren't enforceable.

The *NEC* is divided into an introduction and nine chapters, followed by informational annexes.

Copyright 2014, www.MikeHolt.com

Figure 90–13

General Requirements. The requirements contained in Chapters 1, 2, 3, and 4 apply to all installations.

Author's Comment:

■ These first four chapters may be thought of as the foundation for the rest of the *Code*, and are the main focus of this textbook.

Special Requirements. The requirements contained in Chapters 5, 6, and 7 apply to special occupancies, special equipment, or other special conditions. These chapters can supplement or modify the requirements in Chapters 1 through 4.

Communications Systems. Chapter 8 contains the requirements for communications systems, such as telephone systems, antenna wiring, CATV, and network-powered broadband systems. Communications systems aren't subject to the general requirements of Chapters 1 through 4, or the special requirements of Chapters 5 through 7, unless there's a specific reference in Chapter 8 to a rule in Chapters 1 through 7.

Author's Comment:

■ An example of how Chapter 8 works is in the rules for working space about equipment. The typical 3 ft working space isn't required in front of communications equipment, because Table 110.26(A)(1) isn't referenced in Chapter 8.

Tables. Chapter 9 consists of tables applicable as referenced in the *NEC*. The tables are used to calculate raceway sizing, conductor fill, the radius of raceway bends, and conductor voltage drop.

Annexes. Annexes aren't part of the *Code*, but are included for informational purposes. There are ten Annexes:

- Annex A. Product Safety Standards
- Annex B. Application Information for Ampacity Calculation
- Annex C. Raceway Fill Tables for Conductors and Fixture Wires of the Same Size
- Annex D. Examples
- Annex E. Types of Construction
- Annex F. Critical Operations Power Systems (COPS)
- Annex G. Supervisory Control and Data Acquisition (SCADA)
- Annex H. Administration and Enforcement
- Annex I. Recommended Tightening Torques
- Annex J. ADA Standards for Accessible Design

Essential Rule 4

90.4 Enforcement

The *Code* is intended to be suitable for enforcement by governmental bodies that exercise legal jurisdiction over electrical installations for power, lighting, signaling circuits, and communications systems, such as: Figure 90–14

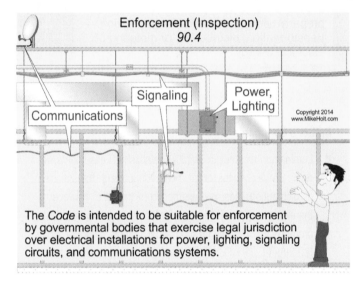

The *Code* is intended to be suitable for enforcement by governmental bodies that exercise legal jurisdiction over electrical installations for power, lighting, signaling circuits, and communications systems.

Figure 90–14

Signaling circuits which include:

- Article 725 Class 1, Class 2, and Class 3 Remote-Control, Signaling, and Power-Limited Circuits
- Article 760 Fire Alarm Systems
- Article 770 Optical Fiber Cables and Raceways

Communications systems which include:

- Article 810 Radio and Television Equipment (satellite dish and antenna)
- Article 820 Community Antenna Television and Radio Distribution Systems (coaxial cable)

The enforcement of the *NEC* is the responsibility of the authority having jurisdiction (AHJ), who is responsible for interpreting requirements, approving equipment and materials, waiving *Code* requirements, and ensuring equipment is installed in accordance with listing instructions.

Author's Comment:

- See the definition of "Authority Having Jurisdiction" in Article 100.

Interpretation of the Requirements. The authority having jurisdiction is responsible for interpreting the *NEC*, but his or her decisions must be based on a specific *Code* requirement. If an installation is rejected, the authority having jurisdiction is legally responsible for informing the installer of the specific *NEC* rule that was violated. Figure 90–15

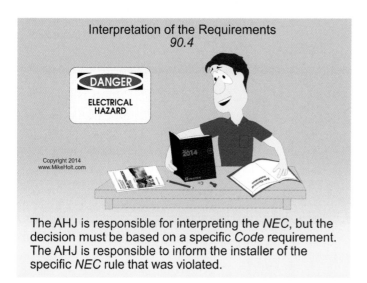

The AHJ is responsible for interpreting the *NEC*, but the decision must be based on a specific *Code* requirement. The AHJ is responsible to inform the installer of the specific *NEC* rule that was violated.

Figure 90–15

Author's Comment:

- The art of getting along with the authority having jurisdiction consists of doing good work and knowing what the *Code* actually says (as opposed to what you only think it says). It's also useful to know how to choose your battles when the inevitable disagreement does occur.

Approval of Equipment and Materials. Only the authority having jurisdiction has authority to approve the installation of equipment and materials. Typically, the authority having jurisdiction will approve equipment listed by a product testing organization, such as Underwriters Laboratories, Inc. (UL). The *NEC* doesn't require all equipment to be listed, but many state and local AHJs do. See 90.7, 110.2, 110.3, and the definitions for "Approved," "Identified," "Labeled," and "Listed" in Article 100. Figure 90–16

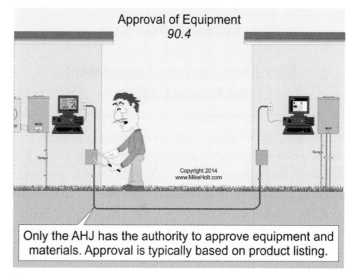

Only the AHJ has the authority to approve equipment and materials. Approval is typically based on product listing.

Figure 90–16

Author's Comment:

- According to the *NEC*, the authority having jurisdiction determines the approval of equipment. This means he or she can reject an installation of listed equipment and can approve the use of unlisted equipment. Given our highly litigious society, approval of unlisted equipment is becoming increasingly difficult to obtain.

Approval of Alternate Means. By special permission, the authority having jurisdiction may approve alternate methods where it's assured equivalent safety can be achieved and maintained.

Author's Comment:

- Special permission is defined in Article 100 as the written consent of the authority having jurisdiction.

Waiver of New Product Requirements. If the current *NEC* requires products that aren't yet available at the time the *Code* is adopted, the authority having jurisdiction can allow products that were acceptable in the previous *Code* to continue to be used.

Author's Comment:

- Sometimes it takes years before testing laboratories establish product standards for new *NEC* requirements, and then it takes time before manufacturers can design, manufacture, and distribute those products to the marketplace.

Essential Rule 5

90.7 Examination of Equipment for Product Safety

Product evaluation for safety is typically performed by a testing laboratory, which publishes a list of equipment that meets a nationally recognized test standard. Products and materials that are listed, labeled, or identified by a testing laboratory are generally approved by the authority having jurisdiction.

Author's Comment:

- See Article 100 for the definition of "Approved."

Except to detect alterations or damage, listed factory-installed internal wiring and construction of equipment needn't be inspected at the time of installation [300.1(B)]. Figure 90–17

Figure 90–17

ARTICLE 110

REQUIREMENTS FOR ELECTRICAL INSTALLATIONS

Introduction to Article 110—Requirements for Electrical Installations

Article 110 sets the stage for how you'll implement the rest of the *NEC*. This article contains a few of the most important and yet neglected parts of the *Code*. For example:

- How should conductors be terminated?
- What kinds of warnings, markings, and identification does a given installation require?
- What's the right working clearance for a given installation?
- What do the temperature limitations at terminals mean?
- What are the *NEC* requirements for dealing with flash protection?

It's critical that you master Article 110. As you read this article, you're building your foundation for correctly applying the *NEC*. In fact, this article itself is a foundation for much of the *Code*. The purpose for the *National Electrical Code* is to provide a safe installation, but Article 110 is perhaps focused a little more on providing an installation that's safe for the installer and maintenance electrician, so time spent in this article is time well spent.

Part I. General Requirements

Essential Rule 6

110.2 Approval of Conductors and Equipment

The authority having jurisdiction must approve all electrical conductors and equipment. Figure 110–1

Author's Comment:

- For a better understanding of product approval, review 90.4, 90.7, 110.3 and the definitions for "Approved," "Identified," "Labeled," and "Listed" in Article 100.

Figure 110–1

Essential Rule 7

110.3 Examination, Identification, Installation, and Use of Equipment

(A) Guidelines for Approval. The authority having jurisdiction must approve equipment. In doing so, consideration must be given to the following:

(1) Suitability for installation and use in accordance with the *NEC*

> **Note:** Suitability of equipment use may be identified by a description marked on or provided with a product to identify the suitability of the product for a specific purpose, environment, or application. Special conditions of use or other limitations may be marked on the equipment, in the product instructions, or appropriate listing and labeling information. Suitability of equipment may be evidenced by listing or labeling.

(2) Mechanical strength and durability

(3) Wire-bending and connection space

(4) Electrical insulation

(5) Heating effects under all conditions of use

(6) Arcing effects

(7) Classification by type, size, voltage, current capacity, and specific use

(8) Other factors contributing to the practical safeguarding of persons using or in contact with the equipment

(B) Installation and Use. Equipment must be installed and used in accordance with any instructions included in the listing or labeling requirements. Figure 110–2

Author's Comment:

- See the definitions of "Labeling" and "Listing" in Article 100.

- Failure to follow product listing instructions, such as the torquing of terminals and the sizing of conductors, is a violation of this *Code* rule. Figure 110–3

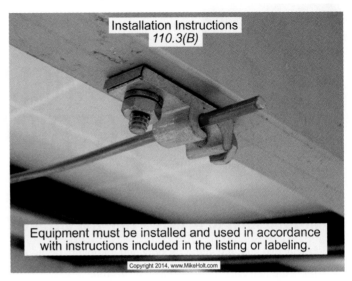

Installation Instructions
110.3(B)

Equipment must be installed and used in accordance with instructions included in the listing or labeling.

Copyright 2014, www.MikeHolt.com

Figure 110–2

- When an air conditioner nameplate specifies "Maximum Fuse Size," one-time or dual-element fuses must be used to protect the equipment. Figure 110–4

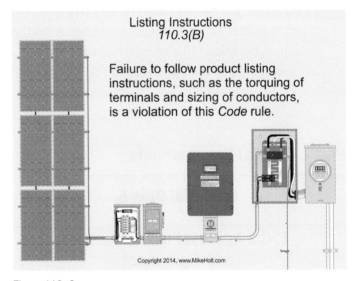

Listing Instructions
110.3(B)

Failure to follow product listing instructions, such as the torquing of terminals and sizing of conductors, is a violation of this *Code* rule.

Copyright 2014, www.MikeHolt.com

Figure 110–3

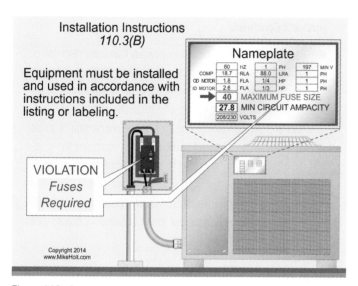

Figure 110–4

Essential Rule 8

110.14 Conductor Termination and Splicing

Conductor terminal and splicing devices must be identified for the conductor material and they must be properly installed and used. Figure 110–5

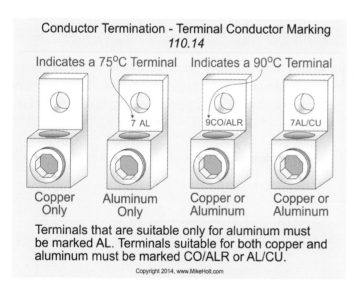

Figure 110–5

Author's Comment:

■ Switches and receptacles marked CO/ALR are designed to ensure a good connection through the use of a larger contact area and compatible materials. The terminal screws are plated with the element called "Indium." Indium is an extremely soft metal that forms a gas-sealed connection with the aluminum conductor.

Connectors and terminals for conductors more finely stranded than Class B and Class C, as shown in Table 10 of Chapter 9, must be identified for the use of finely stranded conductors. Figure 110–6

Figure 110–6

Author's Comment:

■ According to UL Standard 486 A-B, a terminal/lug/connector must be listed and marked for use with other than Class B stranded conductors. With no marking or factory literature/ instructions to the contrary, terminals may only be used with Class B stranded conductors.

■ See the definition of "Identified" in Article 100.

■ Conductor terminations must comply with the manufacturer's instructions as required by 110.3(B). For example, if the instructions for the device state "Suitable for 18-12 AWG Stranded," then only stranded conductors can be used with the terminating device. If the instructions state "Suitable for 18-12 AWG Solid," then only solid conductors are permitted, and if the instructions state "Suitable for 18-12 AWG," then either solid or stranded conductors can be used with the terminating device.

Copper and Aluminum Mixed. Copper and aluminum conductors must not make contact with each other in a device unless the device is listed and identified for this purpose.

Author's Comment:

■ Few terminations are listed for the mixing of aluminum and copper conductors, but if they are, that'll be marked on the product package or terminal device. The reason copper and aluminum shouldn't be in contact with each other is because corrosion develops between the two different metals due to galvanic action, resulting in increased contact resistance at the splicing device. This increased resistance can cause the splice to overheat and cause a fire.

Note: Many terminations and equipment are <u>either</u> marked with a tightening torque <u>or have the torque values included in the product's instructions.</u> Figure 110–7

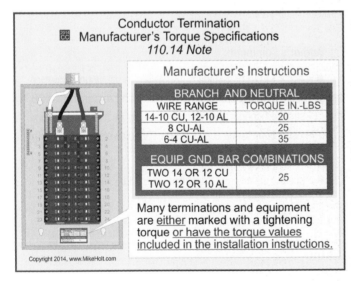

Conductor Termination
Manufacturer's Torque Specifications
110.14 Note

Manufacturer's Instructions

BRANCH AND NEUTRAL	
WIRE RANGE	TORQUE IN.-LBS
14-10 CU, 12-10 AL	20
8 CU-AL	25
6-4 CU-AL	35

EQUIP. GND. BAR COMBINATIONS	
TWO 14 OR 12 CU TWO 12 OR 10 AL	25

Many terminations and equipment are <u>either</u> marked with a tightening torque <u>or have the torque values included in the installation instructions.</u>

Copyright 2014, www.MikeHolt.com

Figure 110–7

Author's Comment:

■ Conductors must terminate in devices that have been properly tightened in accordance with the manufacturer's torque specifications included with equipment instructions. Failure to torque terminals can result in excessive heating of terminals or splicing devices due to a loose connection. A loose connection can also lead to arcing which increases the heating effect and may also lead to a short circuit or ground fault. Any of these can result in a fire or other failure, including an arc-flash event. In addition, this is a violation of 110.3(B), which requires all equipment to be installed in accordance with listing or labeling instructions.

> **Question:** *What do you do if the torque value isn't provided with the device?*
>
> **Answer:** *In the absence of connector or equipment manufacturer's recommended torque values, Table I.1, Table I.2, and Table I.3 contained in Annex I may be used to correctly tighten screw-type connections for power and lighting circuits.*

Author's Comment:

■ Terminating conductors without a torque tool can result in an improper and unsafe installation. If a torque screwdriver isn't used, there's a good chance the conductors aren't properly terminated.

(A) Terminations. Conductor terminals must ensure a good connection without damaging the conductors and must be made by pressure connectors (including set screw type) or splices to flexible leads. Figure 110–8

Author's Comment:

■ See the definition of "Connector, Pressure" in Article 100.

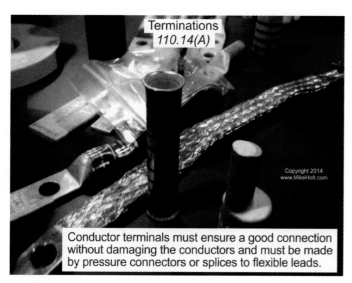

Figure 110–8

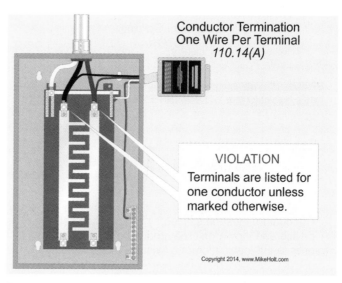

Figure 110–9

Question: What if the conductor is larger than the terminal device?

Answer: This condition needs to be anticipated in advance, and the equipment should be ordered with terminals that'll accommodate the larger conductor. However, if you're in the field, you should:

- Contact the manufacturer and have them express deliver you the proper terminals, bolts, washers, and nuts, or
- Order a terminal device that crimps on the end of the larger conductor and reduces the termination size.

Terminals for more than one conductor and terminals used for aluminum conductors must be identified for this purpose, either within the equipment instructions or on the terminal itself. Figure 110–9

Author's Comment:

■ Split-bolt connectors are commonly listed for only two conductors, although some are listed for three conductors. However, it's a common industry practice to terminate as many conductors as possible within a split-bolt connector, even though this violates the *NEC*. Figure 110–10

(B) Conductor Splices. Conductors must be spliced by a splicing device identified for the purpose or by exothermic welding.

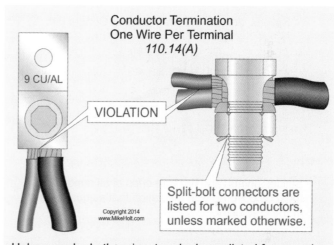

Unless marked otherwise, terminals are listed for one wire.

Figure 110–10

Author's Comment:

■ Conductors aren't required to be twisted together prior to the installation of a twist-on wire connector, unless specifically required in the installation instructions. Figure 110–11

Unused circuit conductors aren't required to be removed. However, to prevent an electrical hazard, the free ends of the conductors must be insulated to prevent the exposed end of the conductor from touching energized parts. This requirement can be met by the use of an insulated twist-on or push-on wire connector. Figure 110–12

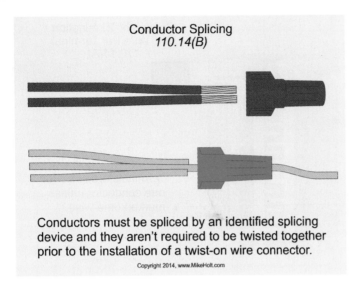

Figure 110–11

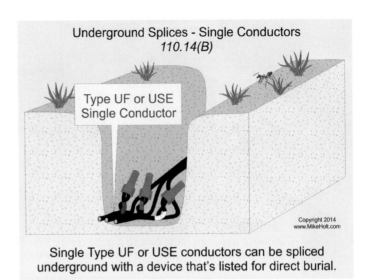

Figure 110–13

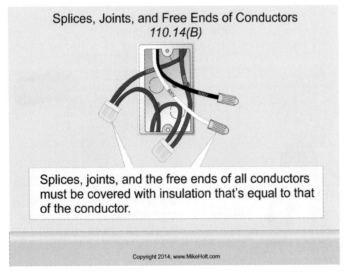

Figure 110–12

Author's Comment:

■ See the definition of "Energized" in Article 100.

Underground Splices:

Single Conductors. Single direct burial conductors of types UF or USE can be spliced underground without a junction box, but the conductors must be spliced with a device listed for direct burial [300.5(E) and 300.15(G)]. Figure 110–13

Multiconductor Cable. Multiconductor UF or USE cable can have the individual conductors spliced underground without a junction box as long as a listed splice kit that encapsulates the conductors as well as the cable jacket is used.

(C) Temperature Limitations (Conductor Size). Conductors are to be sized using their ampacity from the insulation temperature rating column of Table 310.15(B)(16) that corresponds to the lowest temperature rating of any terminal, device, or conductor of the circuit.

Author's Comment:

■ Conductors with insulation temperature ratings higher than the termination's temperature rating can be used for ampacity adjustment, correction, or both. Figure 110–14

(1) Equipment Temperature Rating Provisions. Unless the equipment is listed and marked otherwise, conductor sizing for equipment terminations must be based on Table 310.15(B)(16) in accordance with (a) or (b):

(a) Equipment Rated 100A or Less.

(1) Conductors must be sized using the 60°C temperature column of Table 310.15(B)(16). Figure 110–15

(3) Conductors terminating on terminals rated 75°C are sized in accordance with the ampacities listed in the 75°C temperature column of Table 310.15(B)(16). Figure 110–16

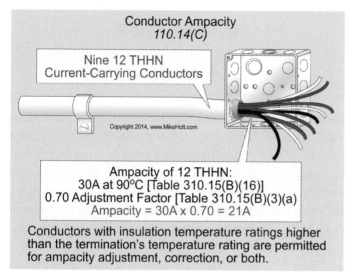

Figure 110–14

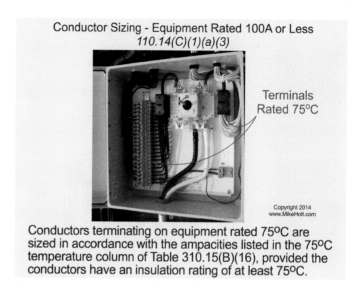

Figure 110–16

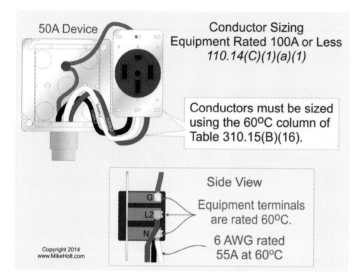

Figure 110–15

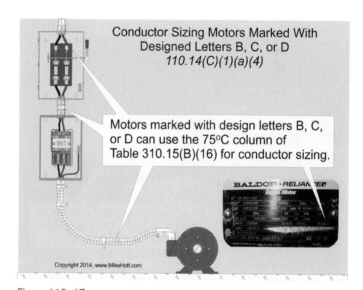

Figure 110–17

(4) Motors marked with design letters B, C, or D, conductors having an insulation rating of 75°C or higher can be used, provided the ampacity of such conductors doesn't exceed the 75°C ampacity. Figure 110–17

(b) Equipment Rated Over 100A.

(1) Conductors must be sized using the 75°C temperature column of Table 310.15(B)(16). Figure 110–18

(2) Separate Connector Provisions. Conductors can be sized to the 90°C column of Table 310.15(B)(16) if the conductors and pressure connectors are rated at least 90°C. Figure 110–19

Note: Equipment markings or listing information may restrict the sizing and temperature ratings of connected conductors.

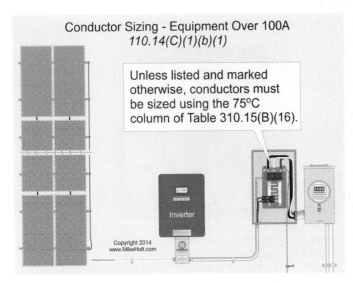

Conductor Sizing - Equipment Over 100A
110.14(C)(1)(b)(1)

Unless listed and marked otherwise, conductors must be sized using the 75°C column of Table 310.15(B)(16).

Inverter

Copyright 2014
www.MikeHolt.com

Figure 110–18

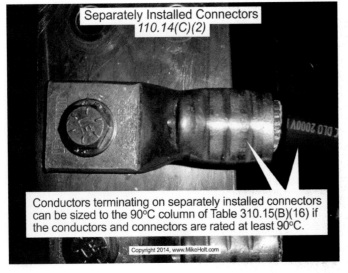

Separately Installed Connectors
110.14(C)(2)

Conductors terminating on separately installed connectors can be sized to the 90°C column of Table 310.15(B)(16) if the conductors and connectors are rated at least 90°C.

Copyright 2014, www.MikeHolt.com

Figure 110–19

Essential Rule 9

110.16 Arc-Flash Hazard Warning

Electrical equipment such as switchboards, switchgear, panelboards, industrial control panels, meter socket enclosures, and motor control centers in other than dwelling units that are likely to require examination, adjustment, servicing, or maintenance while energized must be marked to warn qualified persons of the danger associated with an arc flash from short circuits or ground faults. The marking can be made in the field or the factory, must not be handwritten, must be permanently affixed, be of sufficient durability to withstand the environment involved [110.21(B)], and be clearly visible to qualified persons before they examine, adjust, service, or perform maintenance on the equipment. Figure 110–20

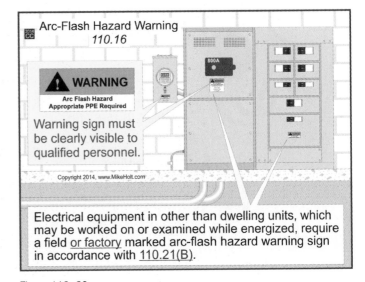

Arc-Flash Hazard Warning
110.16

⚠ **WARNING**
Arc Flash Hazard
Appropriate PPE Required

Warning sign must be clearly visible to qualified personnel.

800A

Copyright 2014, www.MikeHolt.com

Electrical equipment in other than dwelling units, which may be worked on or examined while energized, require a field or factory marked arc-flash hazard warning sign in accordance with 110.21(B).

Figure 110–20

Author's Comment:

- See the definition of "Qualified Person" in Article 100.

- This rule is meant to warn qualified persons who work on energized electrical systems that an arc flash hazard exists so they'll select proper personal protective equipment (PPE) in accordance with industry accepted safe work practice standards.

Note 1: NFPA 70E, *Standard for Electrical Safety in the Workplace*, provides assistance in determining the severity of potential exposure, planning safe work practices, arc-flash labeling, and selecting personal protective equipment.

Essential Rule 10

110.24 Available Fault Current

(A) Field Marking. Service equipment in other than dwelling units must be legibly field marked with the maximum available fault current, including the date the fault current calculation was performed, and be of sufficient durability to withstand the environment involved. Figure 110–21

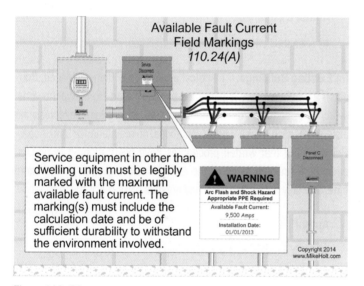

Available Fault Current Field Markings
110.24(A)

Service equipment in other than dwelling units must be legibly marked with the maximum available fault current. The marking(s) must include the calculation date and be of sufficient durability to withstand the environment involved.

⚠ WARNING
Arc Flash and Shock Hazard
Appropriate PPE Required
Available Fault Current:
9,500 Amps
Installation Date:
01/01/2013

Copyright 2014
www.MikeHolt.com

Figure 110–21

Note: The fault current markings required by this section are to ensure compliance with 110.9 and 110.10. They're not intended to be used for arc flash analysis. Arc flash hazard information is available in NFPA 70E, *Standard for Electrical Safety in the Workplace.*

(B) Modifications. When modifications to the electrical installation affect the maximum available fault current at the service, the maximum available fault current must be recalculated to ensure the service equipment ratings are sufficient for the maximum available fault current at the line terminals of the equipment. The required field marking(s) in 110.24(A) must be adjusted to reflect the new level of maximum available fault current.

Ex: Field markings aren't required for industrial installations where conditions of maintenance and supervision ensure that only qualified persons service the equipment.

Part II. 600V, Nominal, or Less

Essential Rule 11

110.26 Spaces About Electrical Equipment

 Scan the QR code for a video clip of this *Code* rule. See page x for additional products to help you learn.

For the purpose of safe operation and maintenance of equipment, access and working space must be provided about all electrical equipment.

(A) Working Space. Equipment that may need examination, adjustment, servicing, or maintenance while energized must have working space provided in accordance with (1), (2), and (3):

Author's Comment:

- The phrase "while energized" is the root of many debates. As always, check with the AHJ to see what equipment he or she believes needs a clear working space.

(1) Depth of Working Space. The working space, which is measured from the enclosure front, must not be less than the distances contained in Table 110.26(A)(1). Figure 110–22

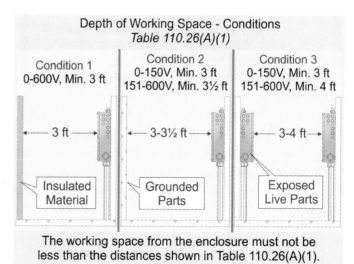

Depth of Working Space - Conditions
Table 110.26(A)(1)

Condition 1	Condition 2	Condition 3
0-600V, Min. 3 ft	0-150V, Min. 3 ft	0-150V, Min. 3 ft
	151-600V, Min. 3½ ft	151-600V, Min. 4 ft
← 3 ft →	← 3-3½ ft →	← 3-4 ft →
Insulated Material	Grounded Parts	Exposed Live Parts

The working space from the enclosure must not be less than the distances shown in Table 110.26(A)(1).

Copyright 2014, www.MikeHolt.com

Figure 110–22

Table 110.26(A)(1) Working Space			
Voltage–to–Ground	Condition 1	Condition 2	Condition 3
0–150V	3 ft	3 ft	3 ft
151–600V	3 ft	3½ ft	4 ft

- **Condition 1**—*Exposed live parts on one side of the working space and no live or grounded parts, including concrete, brick, or tile walls are on the other side of the working space.*

- **Condition 2**—*Exposed live parts on one side of the working space and grounded parts, including concrete, brick, or tile walls are on the other side of the working space.*

- **Condition 3**—*Exposed live parts on both sides of the working space.*

(a) Rear and Sides. Working space isn't required for the back or sides of assemblies where all connections and all renewable or adjustable parts are accessible from the front. Figure 110–23

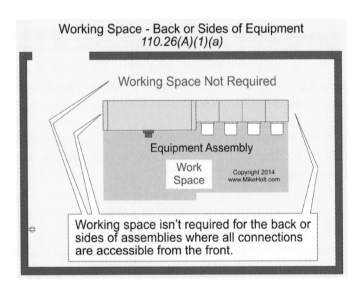

Figure 110–23

(b) Low Voltage. If special permission is granted in accordance with 90.4, working space for equipment that operates at not more than 30V ac or 60V dc can be less than the distance in Table 110.26(A)(1). Figure 110–24

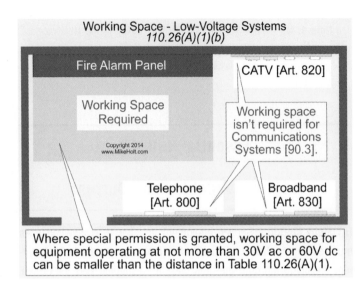

Figure 110–24

Author's Comment:

- See the definition of "Special Permission" in Article 100.

(c) Existing Buildings. If electrical equipment is being replaced, Condition 2 working space is permitted between dead-front switchboards, switchgear, panelboards, or motor control centers located across the aisle from each other where conditions of maintenance and supervision ensure that written procedures have been adopted to prohibit equipment on both sides of the aisle from being open at the same time, and only authorized, qualified persons will service the installation.

Author's Comment:

- The working space requirements of 110.26 don't apply to equipment included in Chapter 8—Communications Circuits [90.3].

(2) Width of Working Space. The width of the working space must be a minimum of 30 in., but in no case less than the width of the equipment. Figure 110–25

Author's Comment:

- The width of the working space can be measured from left-to-right, from right-to-left, or simply centered on the equipment, and the working space can overlap the working space for other electrical equipment. Figure 110–26

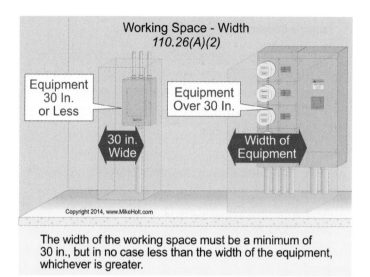

Figure 110–25

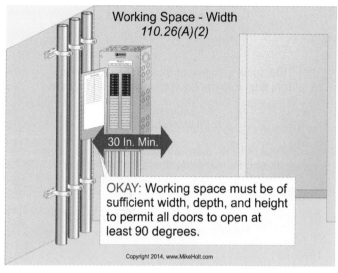

Figure 110–27

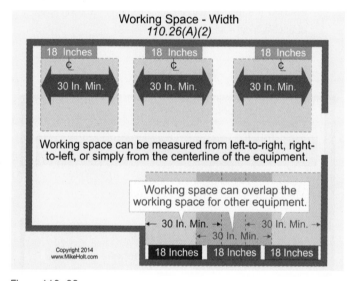

Figure 110–26

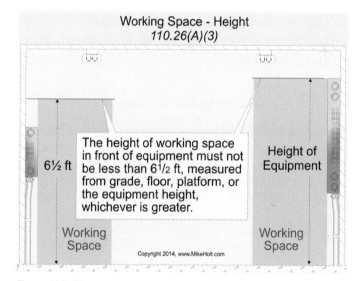

Figure 110–28

In all cases, the working space must be of sufficient width, depth, and height to permit all equipment doors to open 90 degrees. Figure 110–27

(3) Height of Working Space (Headroom). The height of the working space in front of equipment must not be less than 6½ ft, measured from the grade, floor, platform, or the equipment height, whichever is greater. Figure 110–28

Equipment such as raceways, cables, wireways, cabinets, panels, and so on, can be located above or below electrical equipment, but must not extend more than 6 in. into the equipment's working space. Figure 110–29

Ex 1: The minimum headroom requirement doesn't apply to service equipment or panelboards rated 200A or less located in an existing dwelling unit.

Author's Comment:

■ See the definition of "Dwelling Unit" in Article 100.

Ex 2: Meters are permitted to extend beyond the other equipment.

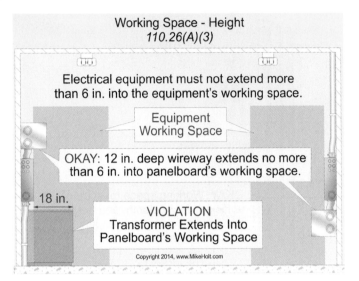

Figure 110–29

(B) Clear Working Space. The working space required by this section must be clear at all times. Therefore, this space isn't permitted for storage. Figure 110–30

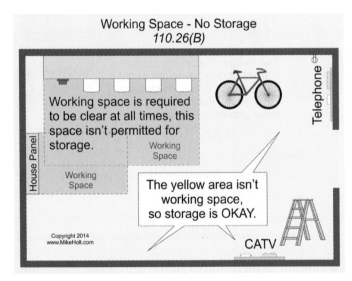

Figure 110–30

When normally enclosed live parts are exposed for inspection or servicing, the working space, if in a passageway or general open space, must be suitably guarded.

Author's Comment:

- When working in a passageway, the working space should be guarded from occupants using it. When working on electrical equipment in a passageway one must be mindful of a fire alarm evacuation with numerous occupants congregated and moving through the area.

⚠ **CAUTION:** *It's very dangerous to service energized parts in the first place, and it's unacceptable to be subjected to additional dangers by working around bicycles, boxes, crates, appliances, and other impediments.*

Author's Comment:

- Signaling and communications equipment must not be installed in a manner that encroaches on the working space of the electrical equipment. Figure 110–31

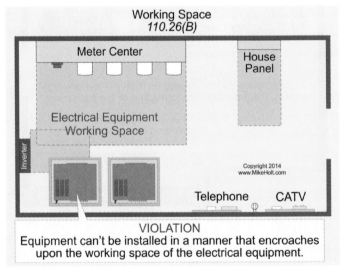

Figure 110–31

(C) Entrance to and Egress from Working Space.

(1) Minimum Required. At least one entrance of sufficient area must provide access to and egress from the working space.

Author's Comment:

- Check to see what the authority having jurisdiction considers "Sufficient Area." Building codes contain minimum dimensions for doors and openings for personnel travel.

(2) Large Equipment. An entrance to and egress from each end of the working space of electrical equipment rated 1,200A or more that's over 6 ft wide is required. The opening must be a minimum of 24 in. wide and 6½ ft high. Figure 110–32

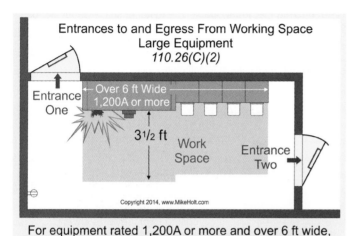

For equipment rated 1,200A or more and over 6 ft wide, an entrance to and egress from (2 ft wide x 6 ½ ft wide) is required at each end of the working space.

Figure 110–32

A single entrance to and egress from the required working space is permitted where either of the following conditions is met:

(a) Unobstructed Egress. Only one entrance is required where the location permits a continuous and unobstructed way of egress travel. Figure 110–33

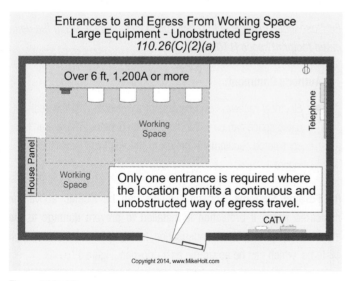

Figure 110–33

(b) Double Workspace. Only one entrance is required where the required working space depth is doubled, and the equipment is located so the edge of the entrance is no closer than the required working space distance. Figure 110–34

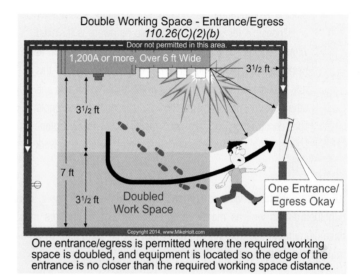

One entrance/egress is permitted where the required working space is doubled, and equipment is located so the edge of the entrance is no closer than the required working space distance.

Figure 110–34

(3) Personnel Doors. If equipment with overcurrent or switching devices rated 800A or more is installed, personnel door(s) for entrance to and egress from the working space located less than 25 ft from the nearest edge of the working space must have the door(s) open in the direction of egress and be equipped with listed panic hardware. Figure 110–35

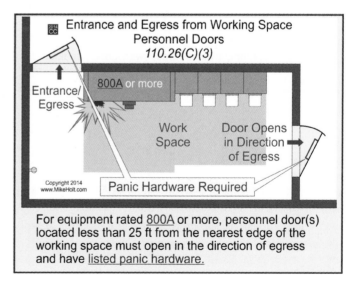

For equipment rated 800A or more, personnel door(s) located less than 25 ft from the nearest edge of the working space must open in the direction of egress and have listed panic hardware.

Figure 110–35

Author's Comment:

- History has shown that electricians who suffer burns on their hands in electrical arc flash or arc blast events often can't open doors equipped with knobs that must be turned.

- Since this requirement is in the *NEC*, the electrical contractor is responsible for ensuring that panic hardware is installed where required. Some electrical contractors are offended at being held liable for nonelectrical responsibilities, but this rule is designed to save the lives of electricians. For this and other reasons, many construction professionals routinely hold "pre-construction" or "pre-con" meetings to review potential opportunities for miscommunication—before the work begins.

(D) Illumination. Service equipment, switchboards, switchgear, and panelboards, as well as motor control centers located indoors must have illumination located indoors and must not be controlled by automatic means only. Figure 110–36

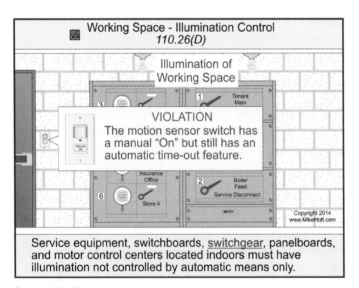

Figure 110–36

Author's Comment:

- The *Code* doesn't provide the minimum foot-candles required to provide proper illumination. Proper illumination of electrical equipment rooms is essential for the safety of those qualified to work on such equipment.

(E) Dedicated Equipment Space. Switchboards, switchgear, panelboards, and motor control centers must have dedicated equipment space as follows:

(1) Indoors.

(a) Dedicated Electrical Space. The footprint space (width and depth of the equipment) extending from the floor to a height of 6 ft above the equipment or to the structural ceiling, whichever is lower, must be dedicated for the electrical installation. Figure 110–37

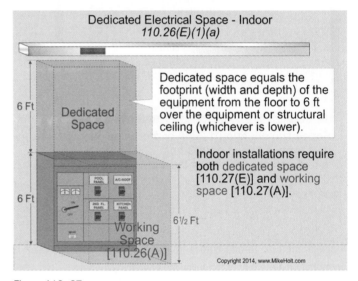

Figure 110–37

No piping, ducts, or other equipment foreign to the electrical installation can be installed in this dedicated footprint space. Figure 110–38

Ex: Suspended ceilings with removable panels can be within the dedicated footprint space [110.26(E)(1)(d)].

Author's Comment:

- Electrical raceways and cables not associated with the dedicated space can be within the dedicated space. These aren't considered "equipment foreign to the electrical installation." Figure 110–39

(b) Foreign Systems. Foreign systems can be located above the dedicated space if protection is installed to prevent damage to the electrical equipment from condensation, leaks, or breaks in the foreign systems, which can be as simple as a drip-pan. Figure 110–40

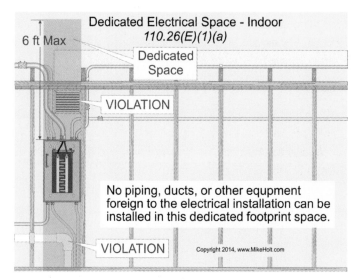

Figure 110–38

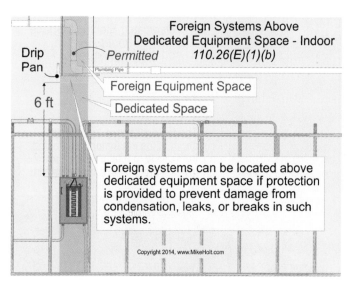

Figure 110–40

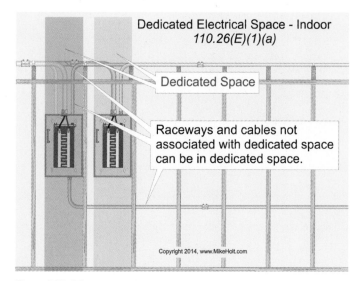

Figure 110–39

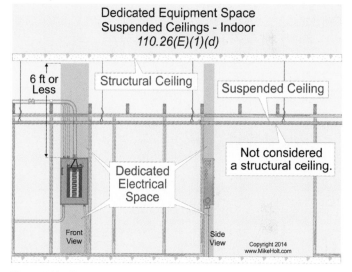

Figure 110–41

(c) Sprinkler Protection. Sprinkler protection piping isn't permitted in the dedicated space, but the *NEC* doesn't prohibit sprinklers from spraying water on electrical equipment.

(d) Suspended Ceilings. A dropped, suspended, or similar ceiling isn't considered a structural ceiling. Figure 110–41

(2) Outdoor. Outdoor installations must comply with 110.26(E)(2)(a) and (b).

(a) Installation Requirements. Outdoor electrical equipment must be installed in suitable enclosures and be protected from accidental contact by unauthorized personnel, or by vehicular traffic, or by accidental spillage or leakage from piping systems.

(b) Dedicated Electrical Space. The footprint space (width and depth of the equipment) extending from the floor to a height of 6 ft above the equipment must be dedicated for the electrical installation. No piping, ducts, or other equipment foreign to the electrical installation can be installed in this dedicated footprint space. Figure 110–42

Author's Comment:

■ See the definition of "Accessible as it applies to equipment" in Article 100.

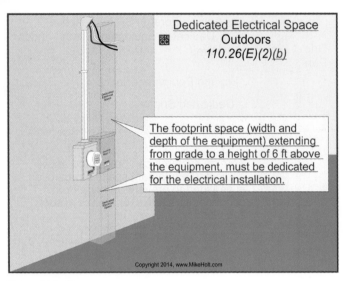

Figure 110–42

ARTICLE 210

BRANCH CIRCUITS

Introduction to Article 210—Branch Circuits

This article contains the requirements for branch circuits, such as conductor sizing and identification, GFCI protection, and receptacle and lighting outlet requirements. It consists of three parts:

- Part I. General Provisions
- Part II. Branch-Circuit Ratings
- Part III. Required Outlets

Table 210.2 of this article identifies specific-purpose branch circuits. The provisions for branch circuits that supply equipment listed in Table 210.2 amend or supplement the provisions given in Article 210 for branch circuits, so it's important to be aware of the contents of this table.

Mastering the branch-circuit requirements in Article 210 will give you a jump-start toward completing installations that are free of *Code* violations.

Part I. General Provisions

Essential Rule 12

210.4 Multiwire Branch Circuits

Author's Comment:

- A multiwire branch circuit consists of two or more ungrounded circuit conductors with a common neutral conductor. There must be a difference of potential (voltage) between the ungrounded conductors and an equal difference of potential (voltage) from each ungrounded conductor to the common neutral conductor. Figure 210–1

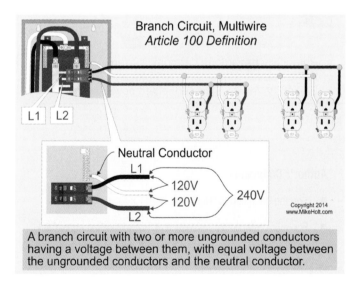

Figure 210–1

(A) General. A multiwire branch circuit can be considered a single circuit or a multiple circuit.

To prevent inductive heating and to reduce conductor impedance for fault currents, all conductors of a multiwire branch circuit must originate from the same panelboard.

Author's Comment:

- For more information on the inductive heating of metal parts, see 300.3(B), 300.5(I), and 300.20.

Note 1: Unwanted and potentially hazardous harmonic neutral currents can cause additional heating of the neutral conductor of a 4-wire, three-phase, 120/208V or 277/480V wye-connected system, which supplies nonlinear loads. To prevent fire or equipment damage from excessive harmonic neutral currents, the designer should consider: (1) increasing the size of the neutral conductor, or (2) installing a separate neutral for each phase. See 220.61(C)(2) and 310.15(B)(5)(c) in this textbook for additional information. Figure 210–2 and Figure 210–3

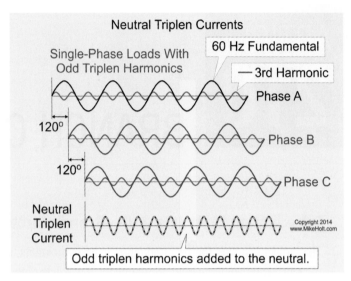

Figure 210–3

Note 2: See 300.13(B) for the requirements relating to the continuity of the neutral conductor on multiwire branch circuits. Figure 210–4

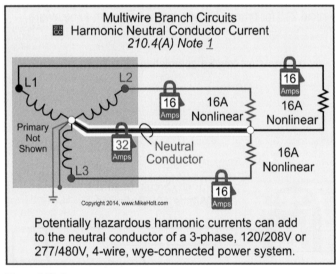

Figure 210–2

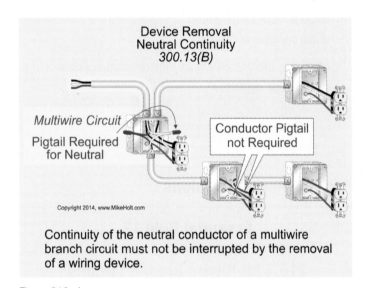

Figure 210–4

Author's Comment:

- See the definition of "Nonlinear Load" in Article 100.

- For more information, please visit www.MikeHolt.com. Click on "Technical Information" on the left side of the page, and then select "Power Quality."

⚠ **CAUTION:** *If the continuity of the neutral conductor of a multiwire circuit is interrupted (opened), the resultant over- or undervoltage can cause a fire and/or destruction of electrical equipment.* Figure 210–5 *and* Figure 210–6

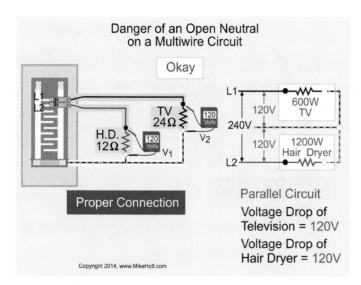

Figure 210–5

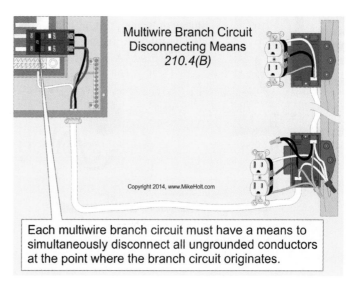

Figure 210–7

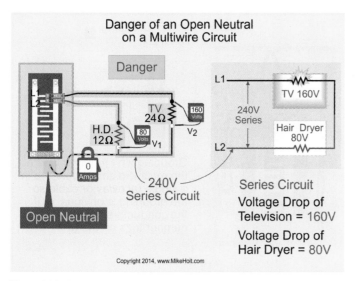

Figure 210–6

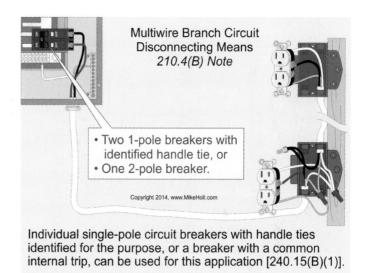

Figure 210–8

(B) Disconnecting Means. Each multiwire branch circuit must have a means to simultaneously disconnect all ungrounded conductors at the point where the branch circuit originates. Figure 210–7

> **Note:** Individual single-pole circuit breakers with handle ties identified for the purpose can be used for this application [240.15(B)(1)]. Figure 210–8

⚠ **CAUTION:** *This rule is intended to prevent people from working on energized circuits they thought were disconnected.*

(C) Line-to-Neutral Loads. Multiwire branch circuits must supply only line-to-neutral loads.

Ex 1: A multiwire branch circuit is permitted to supply an individual piece of line-to-line utilization equipment, such as a range or dryer. Figure 210–9

Ex 2: A multiwire branch circuit is permitted to supply both line-to-line and line-to-neutral loads if the circuit is protected by a device such as a multipole circuit breaker with a common internal trip that opens all ungrounded conductors of the multiwire branch circuit simultaneously under a fault condition. Figure 210–10

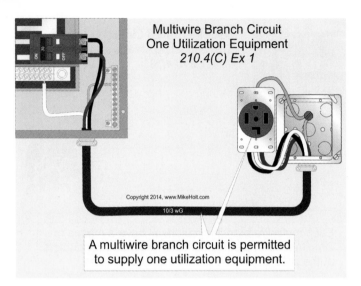

Multiwire Branch Circuit
One Utilization Equipment
210.4(C) Ex 1

A multiwire branch circuit is permitted
to supply one utilization equipment.

Figure 210–9

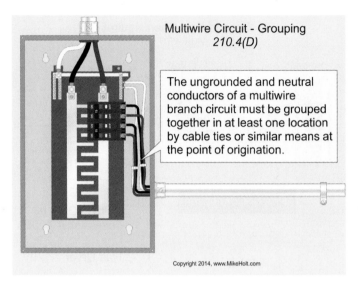

Multiwire Circuit - Grouping
210.4(D)

The ungrounded and neutral
conductors of a multiwire
branch circuit must be grouped
together in at least one location
by cable ties or similar means at
the point of origination.

Figure 210–11

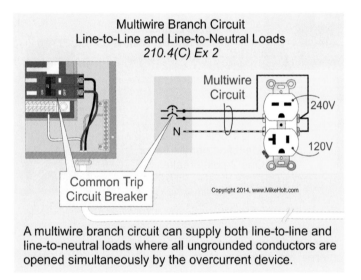

Multiwire Branch Circuit
Line-to-Line and Line-to-Neutral Loads
210.4(C) Ex 2

Multiwire
Circuit

240V

N

120V

Common Trip
Circuit Breaker

A multiwire branch circuit can supply both line-to-line and
line-to-neutral loads where all ungrounded conductors are
opened simultaneously by the overcurrent device.

Figure 210–10

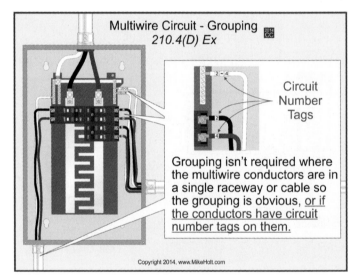

Multiwire Circuit - Grouping
210.4(D) Ex

Circuit
Number
Tags

Grouping isn't required where
the multiwire conductors are in
a single raceway or cable so
the grouping is obvious, <u>or if
the conductors have circuit
number tags on them.</u>

Figure 210–12

(D) Grouping. The ungrounded and neutral conductors of a multiwire branch circuit must be grouped together by cable ties or similar means at the point of origination. Figure 210–11

Ex: Grouping isn't required where the circuit conductors are contained in a single raceway or cable unique to that circuit that makes the grouping obvious, <u>or if the conductors have circuit number tags on them.</u> Figure 210–12

Author's Comment:

■ Grouping all associated conductors of a multiwire branch circuit together by cable ties or other means within the point of origination makes it easier to visually identify the conductors of the multiwire branch circuit. The grouping will assist in making sure that the correct neutral is used at junction points and in connecting multiwire branch-circuit conductors to circuit breakers correctly, particularly where twin breakers are used. If proper diligence isn't exercised when making these connections, two circuit conductors can be accidentally connected to the same phase or line.

CAUTION: *If the ungrounded conductors of a multiwire circuit aren't terminated to different phases or lines, the currents on the neutral conductor won't cancel, which can cause an overload on the neutral conductor.* Figure 210–13

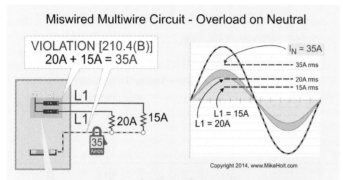

Caution: If the ungrounded conductors of a multiwire circuit aren't terminated to different phases or lines, the currents on the neutral conductor won't cancel, but will add, which can cause a dangerous overload on the neutral conductor.

Figure 210–13

Essential Rule 13

210.5 Identification for Branch Circuits

(A) Neutral Conductor. The neutral conductor of a branch circuit must be identified in accordance with 200.6.

(B) Equipment Grounding Conductor. Equipment grounding conductors can be bare, covered, or insulated. Insulated equipment grounding conductors size 6 AWG and smaller must have a continuous outer finish either green or green with one or more yellow stripes [250.119]. Figure 210–14

On equipment grounding conductors 4 AWG and larger, insulation can be permanently reidentified with green marking at the time of installation at every point where the conductor is accessible [250.119(A)].

(C) Identification of Ungrounded Conductors. Ungrounded conductors must be identified as follows:

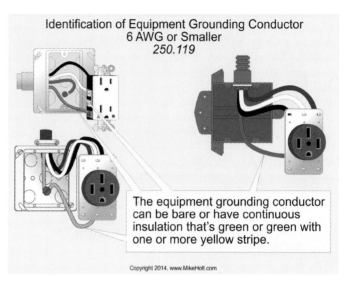

The equipment grounding conductor can be bare or have continuous insulation that's green or green with one or more yellow stripe.

Figure 210–14

(1) <u>More Than One Voltage System.</u> If the premises wiring system contains branch circuits supplied from more than one voltage system, each ungrounded conductor must be identified by phase and system at all termination, connection, and splice points <u>in accordance with 210.5(C)(1)(a) and (b).</u> Figure 210–15

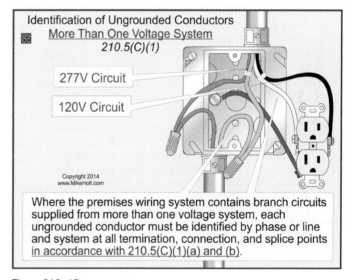

Where the premises wiring system contains branch circuits supplied from more than one voltage system, each ungrounded conductor must be identified by phase or line and system at all termination, connection, and splice points <u>in accordance with 210.5(C)(1)(a) and (b).</u>

Figure 210–15

<u>(a)</u> **Means of Identification.** Identification can be by color coding, marking tape, tagging, or other means approved by the authority having jurisdiction. Figure 210–16

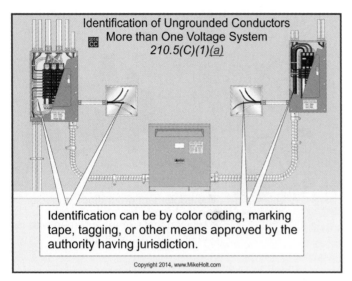

Figure 210–16

(b) Posting. The method of identification must be documented in a manner that's readily available or permanently posted at each branch-circuit panelboard. Figure 210–17

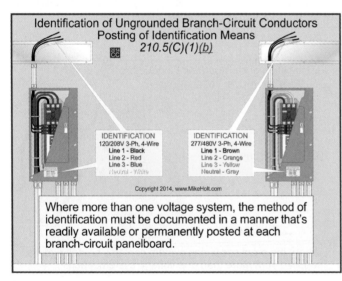

Figure 210–17

Author's Comment:

■ When a premises has more than one voltage system supplying branch circuits, the ungrounded conductors must be identified by phase and system. This can be done by permanently posting an identification legend that describes the method used, such as color-coded marking tape or color-coded insulation.

■ Conductors with insulation that's green or green with one or more yellow stripes can't be used for an ungrounded or neutral conductor [250.119].

■ Although the *NEC* doesn't require a specific color code for ungrounded conductors, electricians often use the following color system for power and lighting conductor identification:

☐ 120/240V, single-phase—black, red, and white

☐ 120/208V, three-phase—black, red, blue, and white

☐ 120/240V, three-phase—black, orange, blue, and white

☐ 277/480V, three-phase—brown, orange, yellow, and gray; or, brown, purple, yellow, and gray

Essential Rule 14

210.8 GFCI Protection

Ground-fault circuit interruption for personnel must be provided as required in 210.8(A) through (D). The ground-fault circuit-interrupter device must be installed at a readily accessible location. Figure 210–18

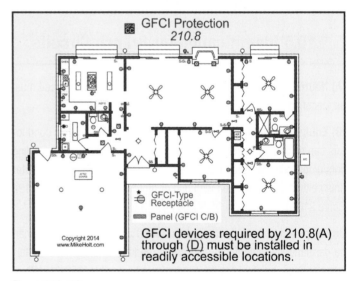

Figure 210–18

Author's Comment:

■ According to Article 100, "readily accessible" means capable of being reached quickly without having to climb over or remove obstacles, or resort to portable ladders.

(A) Dwelling Units. GFCI protection is required for all 15A and 20A, 125V receptacles installed in the following locations:

Author's Comment:

- See the definitions of "GFCI" and "Dwelling Unit" in Article 100.

(1) Bathroom Area. GFCI protection is required for all 15A and 20A, 125V receptacles in the bathroom area of a dwelling unit. Figure 210–19

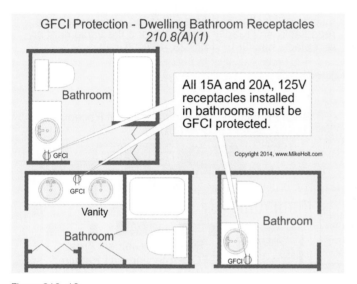

Figure 210–19

Author's Comment:

- See the definition of "Bathroom" in Article 100.

- In the continued interests of safety, proposals to allow receptacles for dedicated equipment in the bathroom area to be exempted from the GFCI protection requirements have been rejected.

(2) Garages and Accessory Buildings. GFCI protection is required for all 15A and 20A, 125V receptacles in garages, and in grade-level portions of accessory buildings used for storage or work areas of a dwelling unit. Figure 210–20

Author's Comment:

- See the definition of "Garage" in Article 100.

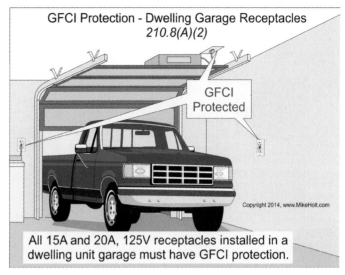

Figure 210–20

- A receptacle outlet is required in a dwelling unit attached garage [210.52(G)(1)], but a receptacle outlet isn't required in an accessory building or a detached garage without power. If a 15A or 20A, 125V receptacle is installed in an accessory building, it must be GFCI protected. Figure 210–21

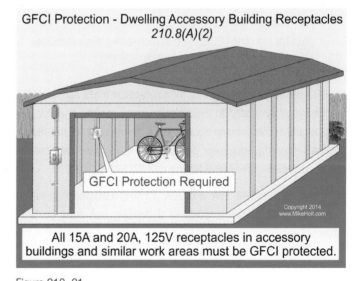

Figure 210–21

(3) Outdoors. All 15A and 20A, 125V receptacles located outdoors of dwelling units, including receptacles installed under the eaves of roofs, must be GFCI protected. Figure 210–22

GFCI Protection
Outdoor Dwelling Receptacles
210.8(A)(3)

All 15A and 20A, 125V receptacles installed
outside of a dwelling unit require GFCI protection.

Figure 210–22

Outdoor Receptacles - Dwelling
210.8(A)(3) Ex

GFCI protection isn't required for a receptacle supplied by
a branch circuit dedicated to fixed electric snow-melting or
deicing or pipeline and vessel heating equipment, if the
receptacle isn't readily accessible and the equipment or
receptacle has GFPE [426.28, 427.22].

Figure 210–23

Author's Comment:

- Each dwelling unit of a multifamily dwelling that has an individual entrance at grade level must have at least one GFCI-protected receptacle outlet accessible from grade level located not more than 6½ ft above grade [210.52(E)(2)].

- Balconies, decks, and porches that are attached to the dwelling unit and are accessible from inside the dwelling must have at least one GFCI-protected receptacle outlet accessible from the balcony, deck, or porch [210.52(E)(3)].

Ex: GFCI protection isn't required for a receptacle that's supplied by a branch circuit dedicated to fixed electric snow-melting or deicing or pipeline and vessel heating equipment, if the receptacle isn't readily accessible and the equipment or receptacle has ground-fault protection of equipment (GFPE) [426.28 and 427.22]. Figure 210–23

(4) Crawl Spaces. All 15A and 20A, 125V receptacles installed in crawl spaces at or below grade of a dwelling unit must be GFCI protected.

Author's Comment:

- The *Code* doesn't require a receptacle to be installed in a crawl space, except when heating, air-conditioning, and refrigeration equipment is installed there [210.63].

(5) Unfinished Basements. GFCI protection is required for all 15A and 20A, 125V receptacles located in the unfinished portion of a basement not intended as a habitable room and limited to storage and work areas. Figure 210–24

GFCI Protection - Dwelling Basement Receptacle
210.8(A)(5)

Finished Basement Area:
GFCI Protection isn't Required

All 15A and 20A, 125V receptacles in unfinished
areas of basements must be GFCI protected.

Figure 210–24

Ex: A receptacle supplying only a permanently installed fire alarm or burglar alarm system isn't required to be GFCI protected [760.41(B) and 760.121(B)].

Author's Comment:

- A receptacle outlet is required in each unfinished portion of a dwelling unit basement [210.52(G)(3)].

(6) Kitchen Countertop Surfaces. GFCI protection is required for all 15A and 20A, 125V receptacles that serve countertop surfaces in a dwelling unit. Figure 210–25

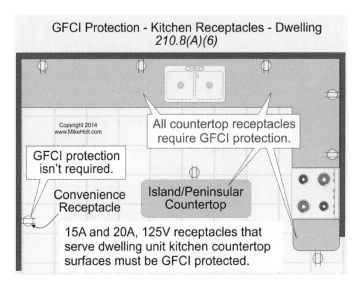

Figure 210–25

Author's Comment:

■ GFCI protection is required for all receptacles that serve countertop surfaces, but GFCI protection isn't required for receptacles that serve built-in appliances, such as dishwashers, trash compactors, exhaust fans, or kitchen waste disposals.

■ See 210.52(C) for the location requirements of countertop receptacles.

(7) Sinks. GFCI protection is required for all 15A and 20A, 125V receptacles located within an arc measurement of 6 ft from the outside edge of a sink. Figure 210–26 and Figure 210–27

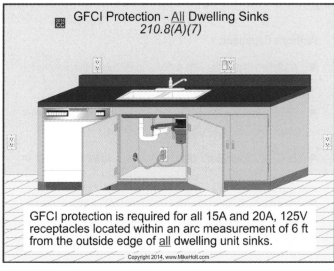

Figure 210–26

(8) Boathouses. GFCI protection is required for all 15A and 20A, 125V receptacles located in a dwelling unit boathouse. Figure 210–28

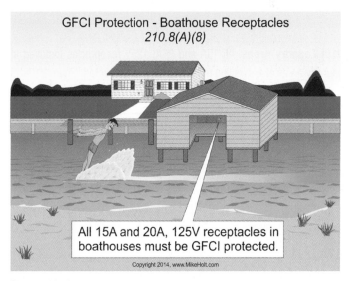

Figure 210–28

Author's Comment:

■ The *Code* doesn't require a 15A or 20A, 125V receptacle to be installed in a boathouse, but if one is installed, it must be GFCI protected.

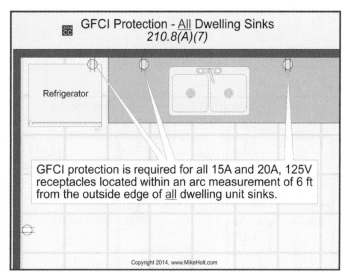

Figure 210–27

(9) Bathtubs or Shower Stalls. GFCI protection is required for all 15A and 20A, 125V receptacles located within 6 ft of the outside edge of a bathtub or shower stall. Figure 210–29

Figure 210–29

(10) Laundry Areas. All 15A and 20A, 125V receptacles installed in laundry areas of a dwelling unit must be GFCI protected. Figure 210–30

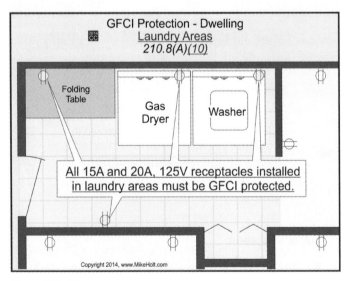

Figure 210–30

(B) Other than Dwelling Units. GFCI protection is required for all 15A and 20A, 125V receptacles installed in the following commercial/industrial locations:

(1) Bathrooms. All 15A and 20A, 125V receptacles installed in commercial or industrial bathrooms must be GFCI protected. Figure 210–31

Figure 210–31

Author's Comment:

- See the definition of "Bathroom" in Article 100.

- A 15A or 20A, 125V receptacle isn't required in a commercial or industrial bathroom, but if one is installed, it must be GFCI protected.

(2) Kitchens. All 15A and 20A, 125V receptacles installed in a kitchen, even those that don't supply the countertop surface, must be GFCI protected. Figure 210–32

Author's Comment:

- A kitchen is an area with a sink and permanent provisions for food preparation and cooking [Article 100]

- GFCI protection isn't required for receptacles rated other than 15A and 20A, 125V in these locations.

- GFCI protection isn't required for hard-wired equipment in these locations.

- An area such an employee break room with a sink and cord-and-plug-connected cooking appliance such as a microwave oven isn't considered a kitchen. Figure 210–33

Figure 210–32

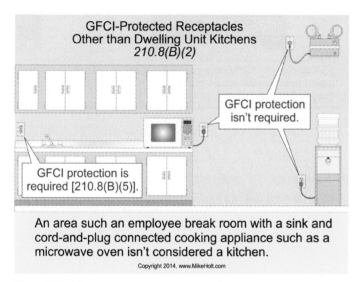

Figure 210–33

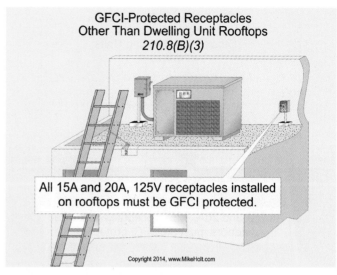

Figure 210–34

Figure 210–35

(3) Rooftops. All 15A and 20A, 125V receptacles installed on rooftops must be GFCI protected. Figure 210–34

Author's Comment:

- A 15A or 20A, 125V receptacle outlet must be installed within 25 ft of heating, air-conditioning, and refrigeration equipment [210.63].

Ex 1 to (3): Receptacles on rooftops aren't required to be readily accessible other than from the rooftop. Figure 210–35

(4) Outdoors. All 15A and 20A, 125V receptacles installed outdoors must be GFCI protected. Figure 210–36

Ex 2 to (3) and (4): GFCI protection isn't required for a receptacle that's supplied by a branch circuit dedicated to fixed electric snow-melting or deicing or pipeline and vessel heating equipment, if the receptacle isn't readily accessible and the equipment or receptacle has ground-fault protection of equipment (GFPE) [426.28 and 427.22].

(5) Sinks. All 15A and 20A, 125V receptacles installed within 6 ft of the outside edge of a sink must be GFCI protected. Figure 210–37

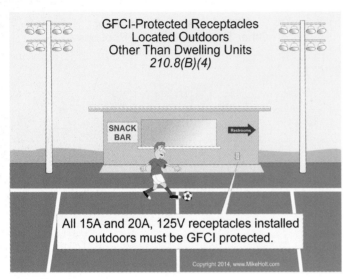

Figure 210–36

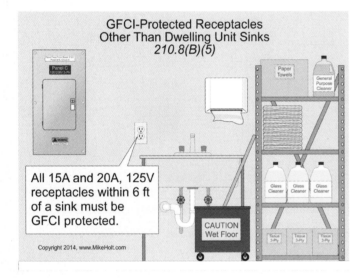

Figure 210–37

Ex 1: In industrial laboratories, receptacles used to supply equipment where removal of power would introduce a greater hazard aren't required to be GFCI protected.

Ex 2: Receptacles located in patient bed locations of general care or critical care areas of health care facilities aren't required to be GFCI protected.

(6) Indoor Wet Locations. All 15A and 20A, 125V receptacles installed indoors in wet locations must be GFCI protected.

(7) Locker Rooms. All 15A and 20A, 125V receptacles installed in locker rooms with associated showering facilities must be GFCI protected.

(8) Garages. All 15A and 20A, 125V receptacles installed in garages, service bays, and similar areas must be GFCI protected, unless they're in show rooms or exhibition halls. Figure 210–38

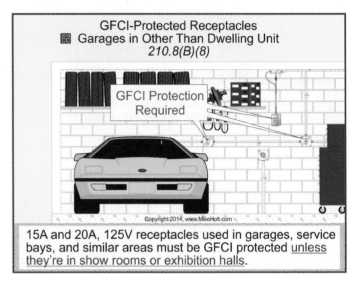

Figure 210–38

(C) Boat Hoists. GFCI protection is required for outlets supplying boat hoists in dwelling unit locations. Figure 210–39

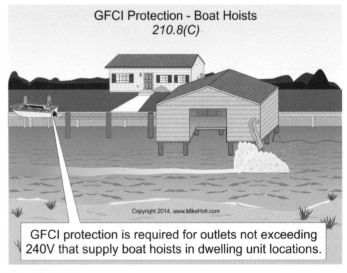

Figure 210–39

Author's Comment:

- See the definition of "Outlet" in Article 100.

- This ensures GFCI protection regardless of whether the boat hoist is cord-and-plug-connected or hard-wired.

(D) Dwelling Unit Dishwashers. Outlets supplying dishwashers in a dwelling unit must be GFCI protected. Figure 210–40

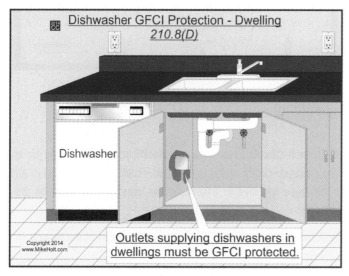

Figure 210–40

Essential Rule 15

210.12 Arc-Fault Circuit-Interrupter Protection

Arc-fault circuit-interrupter protection must be provided in accordance with 210.12(A), (B) and (C). AFCI devices must be installed in readily accessible locations.

(A) Where Required. All 15A or 20A, 120V branch circuits in dwelling units supplying outlets or devices in kitchens, family rooms, dining rooms, living rooms, parlors, libraries, dens, bedrooms, sunrooms, recreation rooms, closets, hallways, laundry areas, or similar rooms or areas must be protected by one of the following: Figure 210–41

(1) A listed combination type AFCI, installed to provide protection of the entire branch circuit.

Figure 210–41

(2) A listed branch/feeder type AFCI at the origin of the branch circuit, plus a listed outlet branch-circuit AFCI installed at the first outlet box of the branch circuit. The outlet box must be marked to indicate that it's the first outlet box of the circuit.

(3) A listed supplemental arc protection circuit breaker installed at the origin of the branch circuit, plus a listed outlet branch-circuit type AFCI installed at the first outlet box on the branch circuit. When using this option, the following must be met:

(a) The branch-circuit wiring must be continuous from the branch circuit overcurrent device to the AFCI device.

(b) The maximum length of the branch circuit to the AFCI is 50 ft for 14 AWG conductors or 70 ft for 12 AWG conductors.

(c) The first outlet box in the circuit must be marked.

(4) A regular fuse or circuit breaker, plus a listed outlet branch-circuit type AFCI installed at the first outlet of the branch circuit. When using this option, the following must be met:

(a) The branch-circuit wiring must be continuous from the branch-circuit overcurrent device to the AFCI device.

(b) The maximum length of the branch circuit to the AFCI is 50 ft for 14 AWG conductors or 70 ft for 12 AWG conductors.

(c) The first outlet box in the circuit must be marked.

(d) The combination of the branch-circuit overcurrent device and the AFCI must be listed and identified as meeting the requirements for a "System Combination" type AFCI.

(5) A listed outlet branch-circuit type AFCI at the first outlet can be used, if the wiring between the overcurrent device and the AFCI contains all metal boxes and is installed using any (or a combination) of the following: RMC, IMC, EMT, Type MC, Type AC cables meeting the requirements of 250.118, metal wireways, or metal auxiliary gutters.

(6) A listed outlet branch-circuit type AFCI at the first outlet of the circuit can be used, if the wiring between the overcurrent device and the AFCI is in a raceway with 2 in. of concrete encasement.

Author's Comment:

- The combination AFCI is a circuit breaker that protects downstream branch-circuit wiring as well as cord sets and power-supply cords; an outlet branch-circuit AFCI (receptacle) is installed as the first outlet in a branch circuit to protect downstream branch-circuit wiring, cord sets, and power-supply cords.

- The 120V circuit limitation means AFCI protection isn't required for equipment rated 230V, such as a baseboard heater or room air conditioner. For more information, visit www.MikeHolt.com, click on the "Search" link, and then search for "AFCI."

Ex: AFCI protection can be omitted for an individual branch circuit to a fire alarm system in accordance with 760.41(B) and 760.121(B), if the circuit conductors are installed in metal wireways, metal auxiliary gutters, RMC, IMC, EMT, or steel sheath Type AC or MC cable that qualifies as an equipment grounding conductor in accordance with 250.118, with metal outlet and junction boxes.

Note 3: See 760.41(B) and 760.121(B) for power-supply requirements for fire alarm systems.

Author's Comment:

- Smoke alarms connected to a 15A or 20A circuit in a dwelling unit must be AFCI protected if the smoke alarm is located in one of the areas specified in 210.12(A). The exemption from AFCI protection for the "fire alarm circuit" contained in 760.41(B) and 760.121(B) doesn't apply to the single- or multiple-station smoke alarm circuit typically installed in dwelling unit bedroom areas. This is because a smoke alarm circuit isn't a fire alarm circuit as defined in NFPA 72, *National Fire Alarm Code*. Unlike single- or multiple-station smoke alarms, fire alarm systems are managed by a fire alarm control panel. Figure 210–42

Figure 210–42

(B) Branch-Circuit Extensions or Modifications—Dwelling Units. Where branch-circuit wiring is modified, replaced, or extended in any of the areas specified in 210.12(A), the branch circuit must be protected by:

(1) A listed combination AFCI located at the origin of the branch circuit; or

(2) A listed outlet branch circuit AFCI located at the first receptacle outlet of the existing branch circuit.

Ex: AFCI protection isn't required for extensions less than 6 ft long, as long as there are no outlets or devices added.

(C) Dormitory Units. All 120V, single phase, 15A and 20A branch circuits supplying outlets installed in dormitory unit bedrooms, living rooms, hallways, closets, and similar rooms must be AFCI protected by one of the methods discussed in 210.12(A)(1) through (6).

Part II. Branch-Circuit Ratings

Essential Rule 16

210.19 Conductor Sizing

(A) Branch Circuits.

(1) General. Branch-circuit conductors must have an ampacity of not less than the maximum load to be served. The conductor must be the larger of (a) or (b).

(a) Conductors <u>must be sized</u> no less than 125 percent of the continuous loads, plus 100 percent of the noncontinuous loads, based on the terminal temperature rating ampacities as listed in Table 310.15(B)(16). Figure 210–43

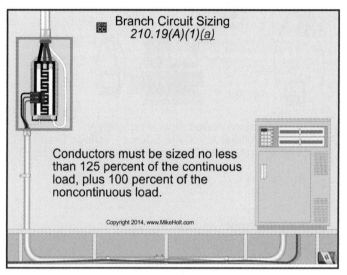

Branch Circuit Sizing
210.19(A)(1)(a)

Conductors must be sized no less than 125 percent of the continuous load, plus 100 percent of the noncontinuous load.

Copyright 2014, www.MikeHolt.com

Figure 210–43

(b) <u>Conductors must be sized to the maximum load to be served after the application of any adjustment or correction factors.</u> Figure 210–44

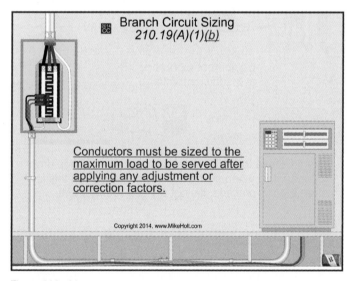

Branch Circuit Sizing
210.19(A)(1)(b)

<u>Conductors must be sized to the maximum load to be served after applying any adjustment or correction factors.</u>

Copyright 2014, www.MikeHolt.com

Figure 210–44

Ex 1: If the assembly and the overcurrent device are both listed for operation at 100 percent of its rating, the conductors can be sized at 100 percent of the continuous load.

Author's Comment:

- Equipment suitable for 100 percent continuous loading is rarely available in ratings under 400A.

- See the definition of "Continuous Load" in Article 100.

- See 210.20 for the sizing requirements for the branch-circuit overcurrent device for continuous and noncontinuous loads.

Question: What size branch-circuit conductors are required for a 4-wire circuit of a 45A nonlinear continuous load, if the equipment terminals are rated 75°C?

(a) 10 AWG   (b) 8 AWG   (c) 6 AWG   (d) 4 AWG

Answer: *(c) 6 AWG*

Since the load is 45A continuous, the conductors must be sized to have an ampacity of not less than 56A (45A x 1.25). According to the 75°C column of Table 310.15(B)(16), a 6 AWG conductor is suitable, because it has an ampere rating of 65A at 75°C. This satisfies the portion of the calculation discussed in 210.19(A)(1)(a).

For 210.19(A)(1)(b), we've to address ambient temperature and conductor bundling.

Because the neutral in this example is considered a current-carrying conductor [310.15(B)(5)(c)], there are four current-carrying conductors. Table 310.15(B)(3)(a) requires an adjustment factor of 80% for this example.

6 AWG rated 75A at 90°C x 0.80 = 60A after adjustment factors which is adequate for the 45A load. Figure 210–45

If we'd selected an 8 AWG rated 55A at 90°C, based on the 45A load, it would be too small for the load after applying the adjustment factor (55A x 0.80 = 44A).

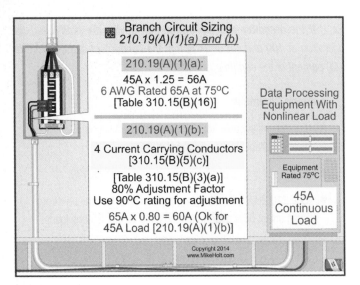

Figure 210–45

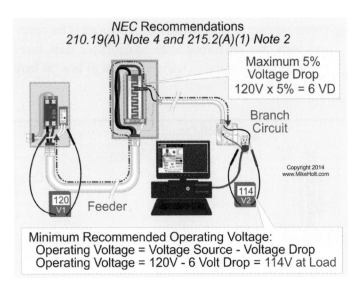

Figure 210–47

Note 4: To provide reasonable efficiency of operation of electrical equipment, branch-circuit conductors should be sized to prevent a voltage drop not to exceed 3 percent. In addition, the maximum total voltage drop on both feeders and branch circuits shouldn't exceed 5 percent. Figure 210–46 and Figure 210–47

Author's Comment:

■ Many believe the *NEC* requires conductor voltage drop, as per Note 4 to be applied when sizing conductors. Although this is often a good practice, it's not a *Code* requirement because Notes are only advisory statements [90.5(C)]. Figure 210–48

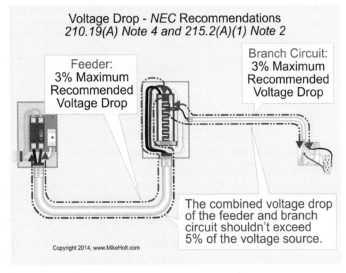

Figure 210–46

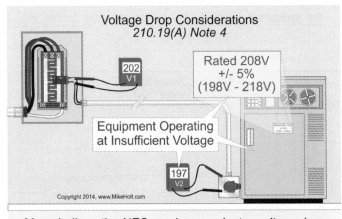

Figure 210–48

■ The *NEC* doesn't consider voltage drop to be a safety issue, except for sensitive electronic equipment [647.4(D)] and fire pumps [695.7].

(2) Branch Circuits Supplying More than One Receptacle. Branch circuits that supply more than one receptacle must have an ampacity not less than the rating of the circuit overcurrent device [210.3].

(3) Household Ranges and Cooking Appliances. Branch-circuit conductors that supply household ranges, wall-mounted ovens or counter-mounted cooking units must have an ampacity not less than the rating of the branch circuit, and not less than the maximum load to be served. For ranges of 8¾ kW or more rating, the minimum branch-circuit ampere rating is 40A.

Ex 1: Conductors tapped from a 50A branch circuit for electric ranges, wall-mounted electric ovens and counter-mounted electric cooking units must have an ampacity not less than 20A, and must have sufficient ampacity for the load to be served. The taps must not be longer than necessary for servicing the appliances. Figure 210–49

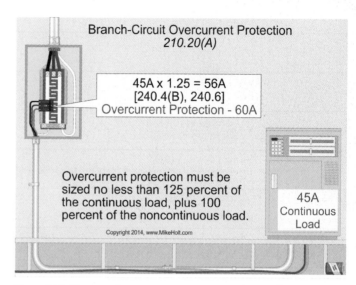

Figure 210–50

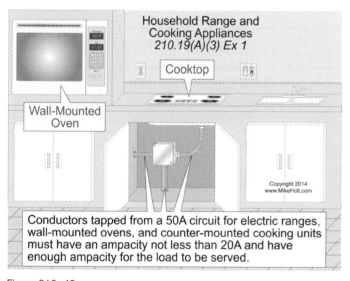

Figure 210–49

Essential Rule 17

210.20 Overcurrent Protection

(A) Continuous and Noncontinuous Loads. Branch-circuit overcurrent devices must have a rating of not less than 125 percent of the continuous loads, plus 100 percent of the noncontinuous loads. Figure 210–50

Author's Comment:

- See 210.19(A)(1) for branch-circuit conductor sizing requirements.

Ex: If the assembly and the overcurrent devices are both listed for operation at 100 percent of their rating, the branch-circuit overcurrent device can be sized at 100 percent of the continuous load.

Author's Comment:

- Equipment suitable for 100 percent continuous loading is rarely available in ratings under 400A.

(B) Conductor Protection. Branch-circuit conductors must be protected against overcurrent in accordance with 240.4.

(C) Equipment Protection. Branch-circuit equipment must be protected in accordance with 240.3.

ARTICLE
225

OUTSIDE BRANCH CIRCUITS AND FEEDERS

Introduction to Article 225—Outside Branch Circuits and Feeders

This article covers the installation requirements for equipment, including branch circuit and feeder conductors (overhead and underground), located outdoors on or between buildings, poles, and other structures on the premises. Conductors installed outdoors can serve many purposes such as area lighting, power for outdoor equipment, or providing power to a separate building or structure. It's important to remember that the power supply for buildings isn't always a service conductor, but in many cases may be feeders or branch-circuit conductors originating in another building. Be careful not to assume that the conductors supplying power to a building are service conductors until you've identified where the utility service point is and reviewed the Article 100 Definitions for feeders, branch circuits, and service conductors. If they're service conductors, use Article 230. For outside branch-circuit and feeder conductors, whatever they feed, use this article.

Table 225.3 shows other articles that may furnish additional requirements, then Part I of Article 225 goes on to address installation methods intended to provide a secure installation of outside conductors while providing sufficient conductor size, support, attachment means, and maintaining safe clearances.

Part II of this article limits the number of supplies (branch circuits or feeders) permitted to a building or structure and provides rules regarding disconnects for them. These rules include the disconnect rating, construction characteristics, labeling, and where to locate the disconnecting means and the grouping of multiple disconnects.

Outside branch circuits and feeders over 1,000V are the focus of Part III of Article 225.

Part II. Buildings or Other Structures Supplied by a Feeder(s) or Branch Circuit(s)

Essential Rule 18

225.32 Disconnect Location

The disconnecting means for a building must be installed at a readily accessible location either outside or inside nearest the point of entrance of the conductors. Figure 225–1

Supply conductors are considered outside of a building or other structure where they're encased or installed under not less than 2 in. of concrete or brick [230.6]. Figure 225–2

Ex 1: If documented safe switching procedures are established and maintained, the building disconnecting means can be located elsewhere on the premises, if monitored by qualified persons.

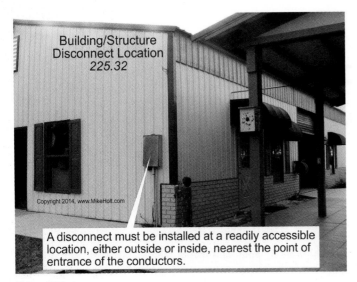

Figure 225–1

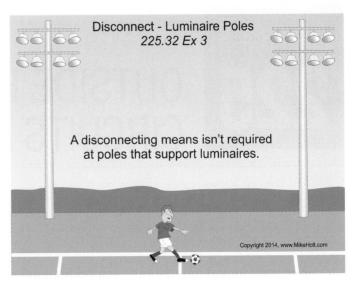

Figure 225–3

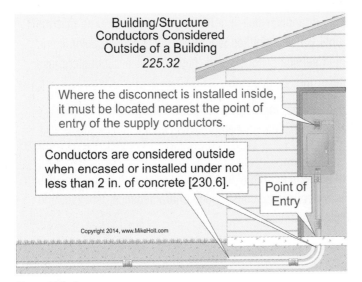

Figure 225–2

Author's Comment:

- A "Qualified Person" is one who has skills and knowledge related to the construction and operation of the electrical equipment and installation, and has received safety training to recognize and avoid the hazards involved with electrical systems [Article 100].

Ex 3: A disconnecting means isn't required within sight of poles that support luminaires. Figure 225–3

Author's Comment:

- According to Article 100, within sight means that it's visible and not more than 50 ft from one to the other.

Ex 4: The disconnecting means for a sign must be controlled by an externally operable switch or circuit breaker that opens all ungrounded conductors to the sign. The sign disconnecting means must be within sight of the sign, or the disconnecting means must be capable of being locked in the open position [600.6(A)]. Figure 225–4

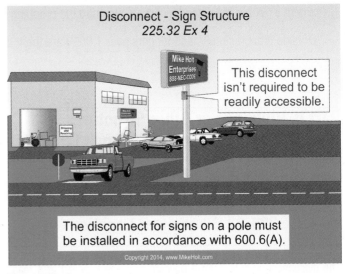

Figure 225–4

ARTICLE 230

SERVICES

Introduction to Article 230—Services

This article covers the installation requirements for service conductors and service equipment. The requirements for service conductors differ from those for other conductors. For one thing, service conductors for one building can't pass through the interior of another building or structure [230.3], and you apply different rules depending on whether a service conductor is inside or outside a building. When are they "outside" as opposed to "inside?" The answer may seem obvious, but 230.6 should be consulted before making this decision.

Let's review the following definitions in Article 100 to understand when the requirements of Article 230 apply:

- **Service Point.** The point of connection between the serving utility and the premises wiring.

- **Service Conductors.** The conductors from the service point to the service disconnecting means. Service-entrance conductors can either be overhead or underground.

- **Service Equipment.** The necessary equipment, usually consisting of circuit breakers or switches and fuses and their accessories, connected to the load end of service conductors at a building or other structure, and intended to constitute the main control and cutoff of the electrical supply. Service equipment doesn't include individual meter socket enclosures [230.66].

After reviewing these definitions, you should understand that service conductors originate at the serving utility (service point) and terminate on the line side of the service disconnecting means. Conductors and equipment on the load side of service equipment are considered feeder conductors or branch circuits, and must be installed in accordance with Articles 210 and 215. They must also comply with Article 225 if they're outside branch circuits and feeders, such as the supply to a building. Feeder conductors include: Figure 230–1 and Figure 230–2

- – Secondary conductors from customer-owned transformers,
- – Conductors from generators, UPS systems, or PV systems, and
- – Conductors to remote buildings

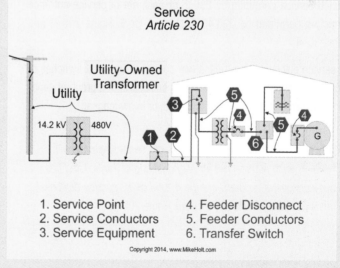

1. Service Point
2. Service Conductors
3. Service Equipment
4. Feeder Disconnect
5. Feeder Conductors
6. Transfer Switch

Copyright 2014, www.MikeHolt.com

Figure 230–1

Article 230 consists of seven parts:

- Part I. General
- Part II. Overhead Service Conductors
- Part III. Underground Service Conductors
- Part IV. Service-Entrance Conductors
- Part V. Service Equipment
- Part VI. Disconnecting Means
- Part VIII. Overcurrent Protection

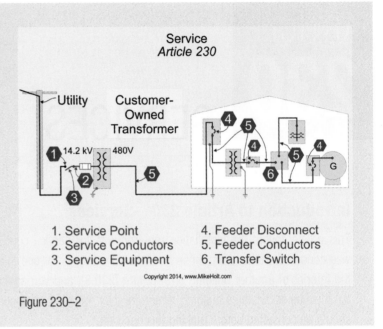

Figure 230–2

Part VI. Service Equipment—Disconnecting Means

Essential Rule 19

230.71 Number of Disconnects

(A) Maximum. There must be no more than six service disconnects for each service permitted by 230.2, or each set of service-entrance conductors permitted by 230.40 Ex 1, 3, 4, or 5. Figure 230–3 and Figure 230–4

The service disconnecting means can consist of up to six switches or six circuit breakers mounted in a single enclosure, in a group of separate enclosures, or in or on a switchboard, or in switchgear.

⚠ **CAUTION:** *The rule is six disconnecting means for each service, not for each building. If the building has two services, then there can be a total of 12 service disconnects (six disconnects per service).* Figure 230–5

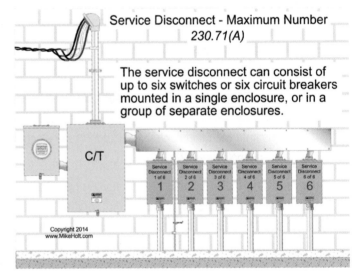

Figure 230–3

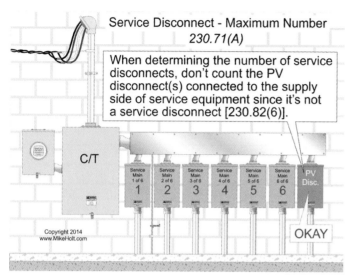

Service Disconnect - Maximum Number
230.71(A)

When determining the number of service disconnects, don't count the PV disconnect(s) connected to the supply side of service equipment since it's not a service disconnect [230.82(6)].

OKAY

Figure 230–4

Service Disconnect - Maximum Number
230.71(A)

Service 1   Service 2

There must be no more than six disconnects for each service permitted by 230.2.

Figure 230–5

Essential Rule 20

230.72 Grouping of Disconnects

(A) Two to Six Disconnects. The service disconnecting means for each service must be grouped.

(B) Additional Service Disconnecting Means. To minimize the possibility of simultaneous interruption of power, the disconnecting means for fire pumps [Article 695], emergency [Article 700], legally required standby [Article 701], or optional standby [Article 702] systems must be located remote from the one to six service disconnects for normal service.

Author's Comment:

■ Because emergency systems are just as important as fire pumps and standby systems, they need to have the same safety precautions to prevent unintended interruption of the supply of electricity.

(C) Access to Occupants. In a multiple-occupancy building, each occupant must have access to their service disconnecting means.

Ex: In multiple-occupancy buildings where electrical maintenance is provided by continuous building management, the service disconnecting means can be accessible only to building management personnel.

Notes

Mike Holt's Illustrated Guide to Essential Rules of the 2014 National Electrical Code

ARTICLE 240

OVERCURRENT PROTECTION

Introduction to Article 240—Overcurrent Protection

This article provides the requirements for selecting and installing overcurrent devices. Overcurrent exists when current exceeds the rating of equipment or the ampacity of a conductor, due to an overload, short circuit, or ground fault [Article 100].

- **Overload.** An overload is a condition where equipment or conductors carry current exceeding their current rating [Article 100]. A fault, such as a short circuit or ground fault, isn't an overload. An example of an overload is plugging two 12.50A (1,500W) hair dryers into a 20A branch circuit.

- **Short Circuit.** A short circuit is the unintentional electrical connection between any two normally current-carrying conductors of an electrical circuit, either line-to-line or line-to-neutral.

- **Ground Fault.** A ground fault is an unintentional, electrically conducting connection between an ungrounded conductor of an electrical circuit and the normally noncurrent-carrying conductors, metallic enclosures, metallic raceways, metallic equipment, or the earth [Article 100]. During the period of a ground fault, dangerous voltages will be present on metal parts until the circuit overcurrent device opens.

Overcurrent devices protect conductors and equipment. Selecting the proper overcurrent protection for a specific circuit can become more complicated than it sounds. The general rule for overcurrent protection is that conductors must be protected in accordance with their ampacities at the point where they receive their supply [240.4 and 240.21]. There are many special cases that deviate from this basic rule, such as the overcurrent protection limitations for small conductors [240.4(D)] and the rules for specific conductor applications found in other articles, as listed in Table 240.4(G). There are also a number of rules allowing tap conductors in specific situations [240.21(B)]. Article 240 even has limits on where overcurrent devices are allowed to be located [240.24].

An overcurrent protection device must be capable of opening a circuit when an overcurrent situation occurs, and must also have an interrupting rating sufficient to avoid damage in fault conditions [110.9]. Carefully study the provisions of this article to be sure you provide sufficient overcurrent protection in the correct location.

Part II. Location

Essential Rule 21

240.21 Overcurrent Protection Location in Circuit

Except as permitted by (A) through (H), overcurrent devices must be placed at the point where the branch-circuit or feeder conductors receive their power. Taps and transformer secondary conductors aren't permitted to supply another conductor (tapping a tap isn't permitted). Figure 240–1

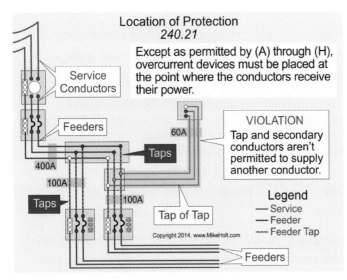

Figure 240–1

(A) Branch-Circuit Taps. Branch-circuit taps are permitted in accordance with 210.19.

(B) Feeder Taps. Conductors can be tapped to a feeder as specified in 240.21(B)(1) through (B)(5). The "next size up protection rule" of 240.4(B) isn't permitted for tap conductors. Figure 240–2

(1) 10-Foot Feeder Tap. Feeder tap conductors up to 10 ft long are permitted without overcurrent protection at the tap location if the tap conductors comply with the following:

(1) The ampacity of the tap conductor must not be less than: Figure 240–3

    a. The calculated load in accordance with Article 220, and

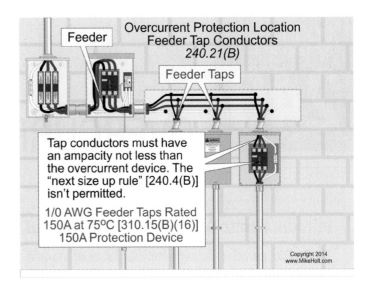

Figure 240–2

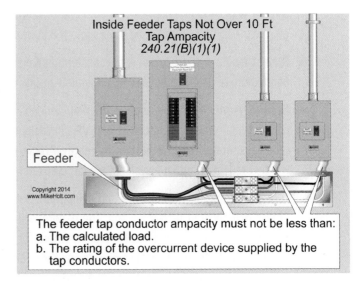

Figure 240–3

    b. The rating of the overcurrent device supplied by the tap conductors.

Ex: Listed equipment, such as a surge protection device, can have their conductors sized in accordance with the manufacturer's instructions.

(2) The tap conductors must not extend beyond the equipment they supply.

(3) The tap conductors are installed in a raceway when they leave the enclosure.

(4) The tap conductors must have an ampacity not less than 10 percent of the rating of the overcurrent device that protects the feeder. Figure 240–4

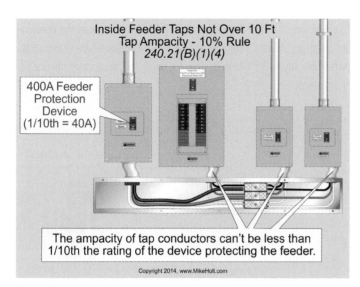

Figure 240–4

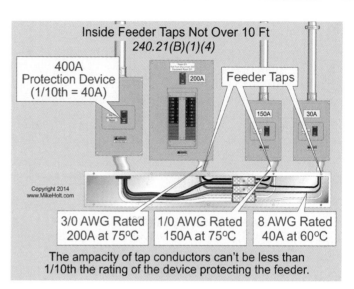

Figure 240–5

Note: See 408.36 for the overcurrent protection requirements for panelboards.

Ten-Foot Tap Rule

Example: *A 400A breaker protects a set of 500 kcmil feeder conductors. There are three taps fed from the 500 kcmil feeder that supply disconnects with 200A, 150A, and 30A overcurrent devices. What are the minimum size conductors for these taps?* Figure 240–5

- *200A: 3/0 AWG is rated 200A at 75°C, and is greater than 10 percent of the rating of the overcurrent device (400A).*

- *150A: 1/0 AWG is rated 150A at 75°C, and is greater than 10 percent of the rating of the overcurrent device (400A).*

- *30A: 8 AWG rated 40A at 60°C. The tap conductors from the 400A feeder to the 30A overcurrent device can't be less than 40A (10 percent of the rating of the 400A feeder overcurrent device.*

---

(2) 25-Foot Feeder Tap. Feeder tap conductors up to 25 ft long are permitted without overcurrent protection at the tap location if the tap conductors comply with the following: Figure 240–6 and Figure 240–7

(1) The ampacity of the tap conductors must not be less than one-third the rating of the overcurrent device that protects the feeder.

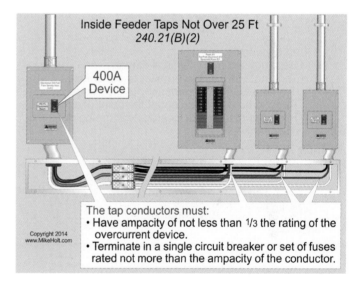

Figure 240–6

(2) The tap conductors terminate in an overcurrent device rated no more than the tap conductor ampacity in accordance with 310.15.

(5) Outside Feeder Taps of Unlimited Length. Outside feeder tap conductors can be of unlimited length, without overcurrent protection at the point they receive their supply, if they comply with the following: Figure 240–8

(1) The tap conductors are suitably protected from physical damage in a raceway or manner approved by the authority having jurisdiction.

(2) The tap conductors must terminate at a single circuit breaker or a single set of fuses that limits the load to the ampacity of the conductors.

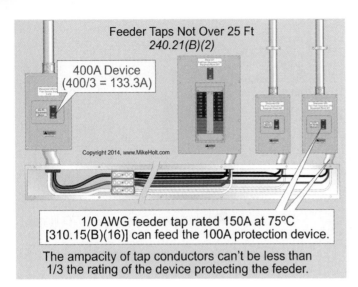

Figure 240–7

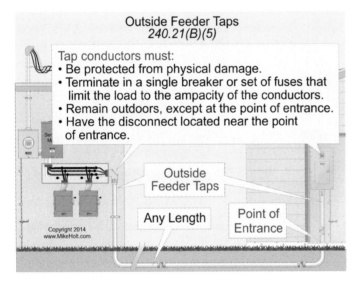

Figure 240–8

(3) The overcurrent device for the tap conductors is an integral part of the disconnecting means, or it's located immediately adjacent to it.

(4) The disconnecting means is located at a readily accessible location, either outside the building, or nearest the point of entry of the conductors.

(C) Transformer Secondary Conductors. A set of conductors supplying single or separate loads is permitted to be connected to a transformer secondary without overcurrent protection in accordance with (1) through (6).

The permission of the "next size up" protection rule when the conductor ampacity doesn't correspond with the standard size overcurrent protection device of 240.4(B) doesn't apply to transformer secondary conductors. Figure 240–9

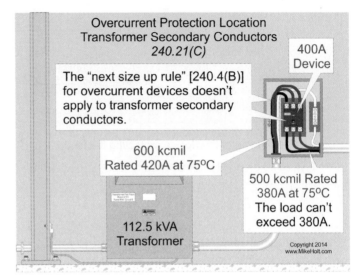

Figure 240–9

(1) Protection by Primary Overcurrent Device. The primary overcurrent device sized in accordance with 450.3(B) is considered suitable to protect the secondary conductors of a 2-wire (single-voltage) system, provided the primary overcurrent device doesn't exceed the value determined by multiplying the secondary conductor ampacity by the secondary-to-primary transformer voltage ratio.

Question: *What's the minimum size secondary conductor required for a 2-wire, 480V to 120V transformer rated 1.50 kVA with 60°C terminals?* Figure 240–10

(a) 16 AWG *(b) 14 AWG*   *(c) 12 AWG*   *(d) 10 AWG*

Answer: *(c) 12 AWG*

Primary Current = VA/E

VA = 1,500 VA

E = 480V

Primary Current = 1,500 VA/480V

Primary Current = 3.13A

Primary Protection [450.3(B)] = 3.13A x 1.67

Primary Protection [450.3(B)] = 5.22A or 5A Fuse

Secondary Current = 1,500 VA/120V

Secondary Current = 12.50A

Secondary Conductor = 12 AWG, rated 20A at 60°C,
[Table 310.15(B)(16)]

The 5A primary overcurrent device can be used to protect 12 AWG secondary conductors because it doesn't exceed the value determined by multiplying the secondary conductor ampacity by the secondary-to-primary transformer voltage ratio.

Overcurrent Device = 20A x (120V/480V)

Overcurrent Device = 20A x 0.25

Overcurrent Device = 5A fuse

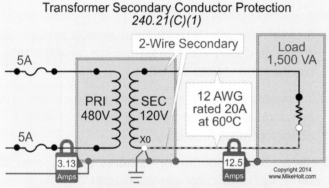

Figure 240–10

(2) 10 Ft Secondary Conductors. Secondary conductors can be run up to 10 ft without overcurrent protection if installed as follows:

(1) The ampacity of the secondary conductor must not be less than: Figure 240–11

  a. The calculated load in accordance with Article 220, and

  b. The rating of the overcurrent device at the termination of the secondary conductors

Ex: Listed equipment, such as a surge protection device, can have their conductors sized in accordance with the manufacturer's instructions.

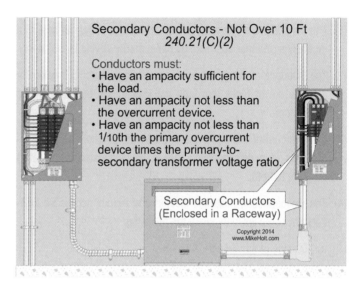

Figure 240–11

(2) The secondary conductors must not extend beyond the switchboard, switchgear, panelboard, disconnecting means, or control devices they supply.

(3) The secondary conductors are enclosed in a raceway.

(4) Not less than 10 percent of the rating of the overcurrent device protecting the primary of the transformer, multiplied by the primary-to-secondary transformer voltage ratio.

(4) Outside Secondary Conductors of Unlimited Length. Outside secondary conductors can be of unlimited length, without overcurrent protection at the point they receive their supply, if they're installed as follows: Figure 240–12

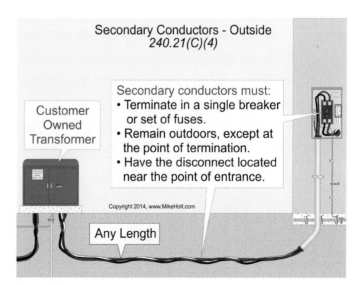

Figure 240–12

(1) The conductors are suitably protected from physical damage in a raceway or manner approved by the authority having jurisdiction.

(2) The conductors must terminate at a single circuit breaker or a single set of fuses that limit the load to the ampacity of the conductors.

(3) The overcurrent device for the ungrounded conductors is an integral part of a disconnecting means or it's located immediately adjacent thereto.

(4) The disconnecting means is located at a readily accessible location that complies with one of the following:

    a. Outside of a building.

    b. Inside, nearest the point of entrance of the conductors.

    c. If installed in accordance with 230.6, nearest the point of entrance of the conductors.

(5) Secondary Conductors from a Feeder Tapped Transformer. Transformer secondary conductors must be installed in accordance with 240.21(B)(3).

(6) 25-Foot Secondary Conductor. Secondary conductors can be run up to 25 ft without overcurrent protection if they comply with all of the following: Figure 240–13

(1) The secondary conductors have an ampacity not less than the value of the primary-to-secondary voltage ratio multiplied by one-third of the rating of the overcurrent device that protects the primary of the transformer.

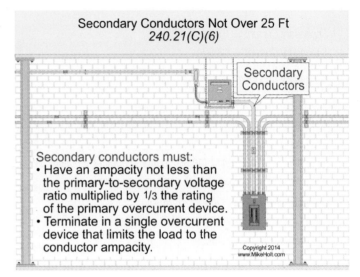

Figure 240–13

(2) Secondary conductors terminate in a single circuit breaker or set of fuses rated no more than the tap conductor ampacity in accordance with 310.15 [Table 310.15(B)(16)].

(3) The secondary conductors are protected from physical damage by being enclosed in a manner approved by the authority having jurisdiction, such as within a raceway.

(D) Service Conductors. Service conductors must be protected against overload in accordance with 230.90 and 91.

(H) Battery Conductors. Overcurrent protection is installed as close as practicable to the storage battery terminals.

ARTICLE 250
GROUNDING AND BONDING

Introduction to Article 250—Grounding and Bonding

No other article can match Article 250 for misapplication, violation, and misinterpretation. Terminology used in this article has been a source for much confusion, but that has improved during the last few *NEC* revisions. It's very important to understand the difference between grounding and bonding in order to correctly apply the provisions of Article 250. Pay careful attention to the definitions that apply to grounding and bonding both here and in Article 100 as you begin the study of this important article. Article 250 covers the grounding requirements for providing a path to the earth to reduce overvoltage from lightning, and the bonding requirements for a low-impedance fault current path back to the source of the electrical supply to facilitate the operation of overcurrent devices in the event of a ground fault.

Over the past several *Code* cycles, this article was extensively revised to organize it better and make it easier to understand and implement. It's arranged in a logical manner, so it's a good idea to just read through Article 250 to get a big picture view—after you review the definitions. Next, study the article closely so you understand the details. The illustrations will help you understand the key points.

Part I. General

Essential Rule 22

250.2 Definition

Bonding Jumper, Supply-Side. The conductor on the supply side of the service or separately derived system overcurrent protection device that ensures electrical conductivity between metal parts and the grounded conductor. Figure 250–1 and Figure 250–2

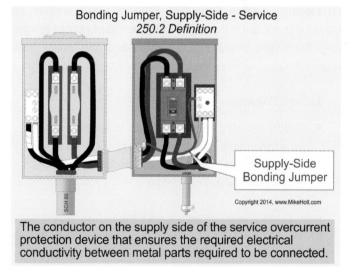

Bonding Jumper, Supply-Side - Service
250.2 Definition

Supply-Side Bonding Jumper

Copyright 2014, www.MikeHolt.com

The conductor on the supply side of the service overcurrent protection device that ensures the required electrical conductivity between metal parts required to be connected.

Figure 250–1

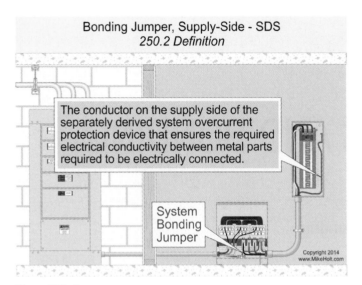

Bonding Jumper, Supply-Side - SDS
250.2 Definition

The conductor on the supply side of the separately derived system overcurrent protection device that ensures the required electrical conductivity between metal parts required to be electrically connected.

System Bonding Jumper

Figure 250–2

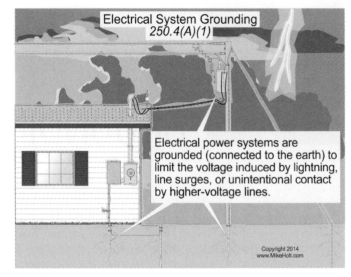

Electrical System Grounding
250.4(A)(1)

Electrical power systems are grounded (connected to the earth) to limit the voltage induced by lightning, line surges, or unintentional contact by higher-voltage lines.

Figure 250–3

Essential Rule 23

250.4 General Requirements for Grounding and Bonding

 Scan the QR code for a video clip of this *Code* rule. See page x for additional products to help you learn.

(A) Solidly Grounded Systems.

(1) Electrical System Grounding. Electrical power systems are grounded (connected to the earth) to limit the voltage induced by lightning, line surges, or unintentional contact by higher-voltage lines. Figure 250–3

Author's Comment:

■ System grounding helps reduce fires in buildings as well as voltage stress on electrical insulation, thereby ensuring longer insulation life for motors, transformers, and other system components. Figure 250–4

Note: To limit imposed voltage, the grounding electrode conductors shouldn't be any longer than necessary and unnecessary bends and loops should be avoided. Figure 250–5

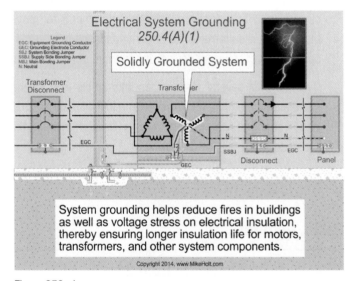

Electrical System Grounding
250.4(A)(1)

Legend
EGC: Equipment Grounding Conductor
GEC: Grounding Electrode Conductor
SBJ: System Bonding Jumper
SSBJ: Supply Side Bonding Jumper
MBJ: Main Bonding Jumper
N: Neutral

Solidly Grounded System

Transformer Disconnect

Transformer

System grounding helps reduce fires in buildings as well as voltage stress on electrical insulation, thereby ensuring longer insulation life for motors, transformers, and other system components.

Figure 250–4

(2) Equipment Grounding. Metal parts of electrical equipment are grounded to reduce arcing within the buildings/structures from induced voltage from indirect lightning strikes. Figure 250–6

DANGER: *Failure to ground metal parts to earth can result in induced voltage on metal parts from an indirect lightning strike seeking a path to the earth within the building—possibly resulting in a fire and/or electric shock from a sideflash.* Figure 250–7

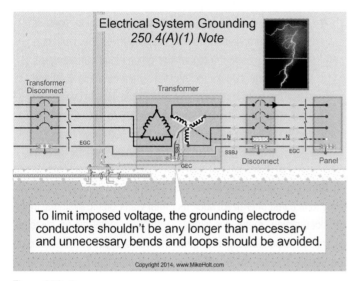

Figure 250–5

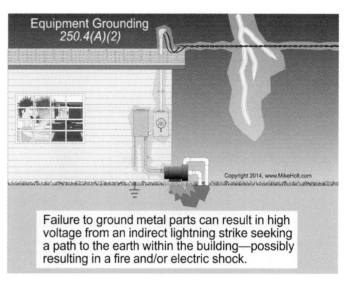

Figure 250–7

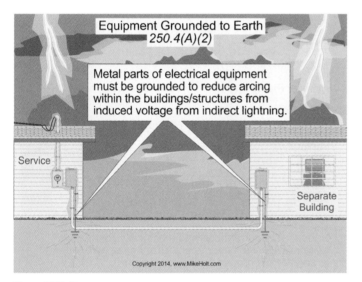

Figure 250–6

Author's Comment:

■ Grounding metal parts helps drain off static electricity charges before flashover potential is reached. Static grounding is often used in areas where the discharge (arcing) of the voltage buildup (static) can cause dangerous or undesirable conditions [500.4 Note 3].

DANGER: *Because the contact resistance of an electrode to the earth is so high, very little fault current returns to the power supply if the earth is the only fault current return path. Result—the circuit overcurrent device won't open and clear the ground fault, and all metal parts associated with the electrical installation, metal piping, and structural building steel will become and remain energized.* Figure 250–8

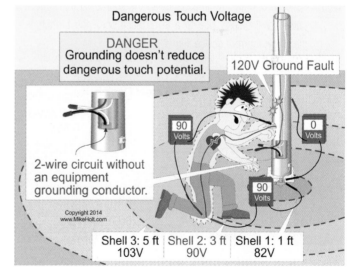

Figure 250–8

(3) Equipment Bonding. Metal parts of electrical raceways, cables, enclosures, and equipment must be connected to the supply source via an effective ground-fault current path. Figure 250–9

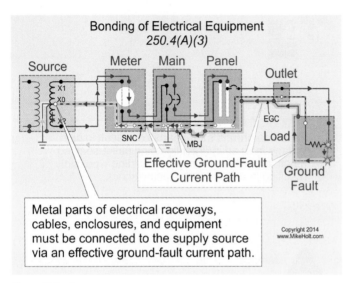

Figure 250–9

Author's Comment:

■ To quickly remove dangerous voltage on metal parts from a ground fault, the effective ground-fault current path must have sufficiently low impedance to the source so that fault current will quickly rise to a level that'll open the branch-circuit overcurrent device. Figure 250–10

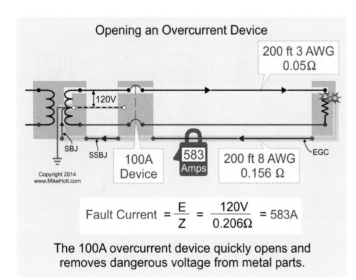

Figure 250–10

■ The time it takes for an overcurrent device to open is inversely proportional to the magnitude of the fault current. This means the higher the ground-fault current value, the less time it'll take for the overcurrent device to open and clear the fault. For example, a 20A circuit with an overload of 40A (two times the 20A rating) takes 25 to 150 seconds to open the circuit overcurrent device. At 100A (five times the 20A rating) the 20A breaker trips in 5 to 20 seconds.

(4) Bonding Conductive Materials. Electrically conductive materials likely to become energized, such as metal water piping systems, metal sprinkler piping, metal gas piping, and other metal-piping systems, as well as exposed structural steel members, must be connected to the supply source via an effective ground-fault current path. Figure 250–11

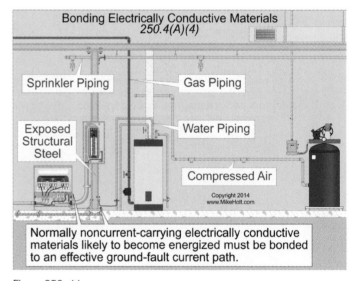

Figure 250–11

Author's Comment:

■ The phrase "likely to become energized" is subject to interpretation by the authority having jurisdiction.

(5) Effective Ground-Fault Current Path. Metal parts of electrical raceways, cables, enclosures, or equipment must be bonded together and to the supply source in a manner that creates a low-impedance path for ground-fault current that facilitates the operation of the circuit overcurrent device. Figure 250–12

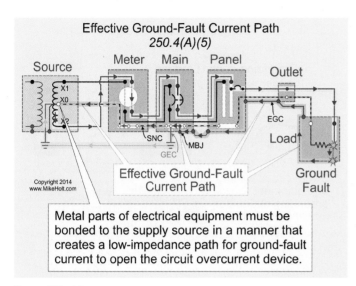

Effective Ground-Fault Current Path
250.4(A)(5)

Metal parts of electrical equipment must be bonded to the supply source in a manner that creates a low-impedance path for ground-fault current to open the circuit overcurrent device.

Figure 250–12

Author's Comment:

■ To ensure a low-impedance ground-fault current path, all circuit conductors must be grouped together in the same raceway, cable, or trench [300.3(B), 300.5(I), and 300.20(A)]. Figure 250–13

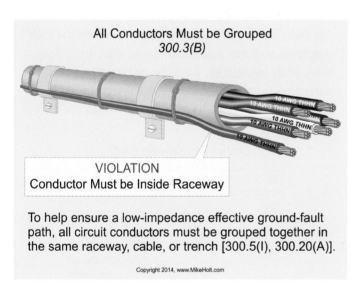

All Conductors Must be Grouped
300.3(B)

VIOLATION
Conductor Must be Inside Raceway

To help ensure a low-impedance effective ground-fault path, all circuit conductors must be grouped together in the same raceway, cable, or trench [300.5(I), 300.20(A)].

Copyright 2014, www.MikeHolt.com

Figure 250–13

Because the earth isn't suitable to serve as the required effective ground-fault current path, an equipment grounding conductor is required to be installed with all circuits. Figure 250–14

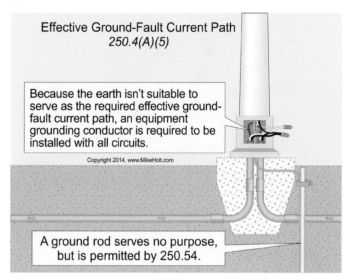

Effective Ground-Fault Current Path
250.4(A)(5)

Because the earth isn't suitable to serve as the required effective ground-fault current path, an equipment grounding conductor is required to be installed with all circuits.

Copyright 2014, www.MikeHolt.com

A ground rod serves no purpose, but is permitted by 250.54.

Figure 250–14

Question: What's the maximum fault current that can flow through the earth to the power supply from a 120V ground fault to metal parts of a light pole without an equipment grounding conductor that's grounded (connected to the earth) via a rod having a contact resistance to the earth of 25 ohms? Figure 250–15

(a) 4.80A   (b) 20A   (c) 40A   (d) 100A

Answer: (a) 4.80A

$$I = E/R$$

I = 120V/25 ohms
I = 4.80A

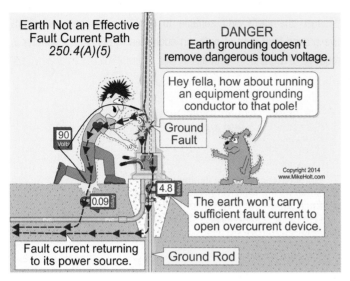

Figure 250–15

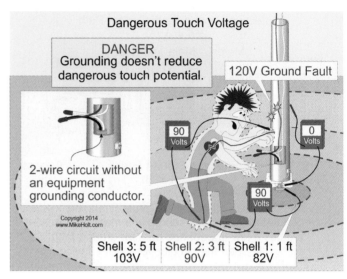

Figure 250–17

DANGER: *Because the contact resistance of an electrode to the earth is so high, very little fault current returns to the power supply if the earth is the only fault current return path.* Figure 250–16

Result—the circuit overcurrent device won't open and all metal parts associated with the electrical installation, metal piping, and structural building steel will become and remain energized. Figure 250–17

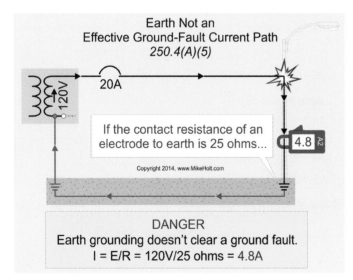

Figure 250–16

Earth Shells

According to ANSI/IEEE 142, *Recommended Practice for Grounding of Industrial and Commercial Power Systems* (Green Book) [4.1.1], the resistance of the soil outward from a rod is equal to the sum of the series resistances of the earth shells. The shell nearest the rod has the highest resistance and each successive shell has progressively larger areas and progressively lower resistances. Don't be concerned if you don't understand this statement; just review the table below. Figure 250–18

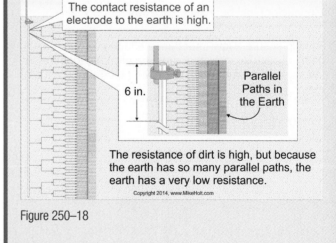

Figure 250–18

Distance from Rod	Soil Contact Resistance
1 ft (Shell 1)	68% of total contact resistance
3 ft (Shells 1 and 2)	75% of total contact resistance
5 ft (Shells 1, 2, and 3)	86% of total contact resistance

Since voltage is directly proportional to resistance, the voltage gradient of the earth around an energized rod will be as follows, assuming a 120V ground fault:

Distance from Rod	Soil Contact Resistance	Voltage Gradient
1 ft (Shell 1)	68%	82V
3 ft (Shells 1 and 2)	75%	90V
5 ft (Shells 1, 2, and 3)	86%	103V

(B) Ungrounded Systems.

Author's Comment:

- Ungrounded systems are those systems with no connection to the ground or to a conductive body that extends the ground connection [Article 100]. Figure 250–19

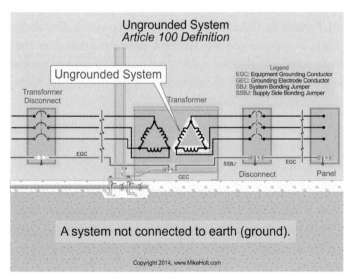

Figure 250–19

(1) Equipment Grounding. Metal parts of electrical equipment are grounded (connected to the earth) to reduce induced voltage on metal parts from lightning so as to prevent fires from an arc within the buildings. Figure 250–20

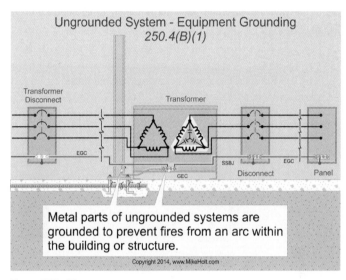

Figure 250–20

Author's Comment:

- Grounding metal parts helps drain off static electricity charges before an electric arc takes place (flashover potential). Static grounding is often used in areas where the discharge (arcing) of the voltage buildup (static) can cause dangerous or undesirable conditions [500.4 Note 3].

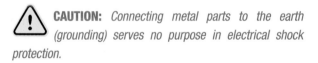 **CAUTION:** *Connecting metal parts to the earth (grounding) serves no purpose in electrical shock protection.*

(2) Equipment Bonding. Metal parts of electrical raceways, cables, enclosures, or equipment must be bonded together in a manner that creates a low-impedance path for ground-fault current to facilitate the operation of the circuit overcurrent device.

The fault current path must be capable of safely carrying the maximum ground-fault current likely to be imposed on it from any point on the wiring system where a ground fault may occur to the electrical supply source.

(3) Bonding Conductive Materials. Conductive materials such as metal water piping systems, metal sprinkler piping, metal gas piping, and other metal-piping systems, as well as exposed structural steel members likely to become energized must be bonded together in a manner that creates a low-impedance fault current path that's capable of carrying the maximum fault current likely to be imposed on it. Figure 250–21

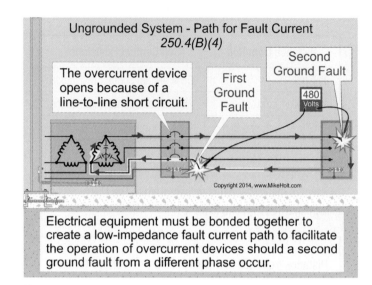

Figure 250–22

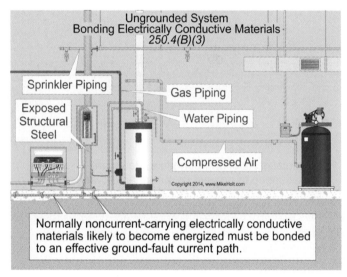

Figure 250–21

Author's Comment:

■ The phrase "likely to become energized" is subject to interpretation by the authority having jurisdiction.

(4) Fault Current Path. Electrical equipment, wiring, and other electrically conductive material likely to become energized must be installed in a manner that creates a low-impedance fault current path to facilitate the operation of overcurrent devices should a second ground fault from a different phase occur. Figure 250–22

Author's Comment:

■ A single ground fault can't be cleared on an ungrounded system because there's no low-impedance fault current path to the power source. The first ground fault simply grounds the system and initiates the ground detector. However, a second ground fault on a different phase results in a line-to-line short circuit between the two ground faults. The

conductive path, between the ground faults, provides the low-impedance fault current path necessary so the overcurrent device will open.

Essential Rule 24

250.6 Objectionable Current

 Scan the QR code for a video clip of this *Code* rule. See page x for additional products to help you learn.

(A) Preventing Objectionable Current. To prevent a fire, electric shock, or improper operation of circuit overcurrent devices or electronic equipment, electrical systems and equipment must be installed in a manner that prevents objectionable neutral current from flowing on metal parts. Figure 250–23

(C) Temporary Currents Not Classified as Objectionable Currents. Temporary currents from abnormal conditions, such as ground faults, aren't to be classified as objectionable current. Figure 250–24

(D) Limitations to Permissible Alterations. Currents that introduce noise or data errors in electronic equipment aren't considered objectionable currents for the purposes of this section. Circuits that supply electronic equipment must be connected to an equipment grounding conductor.

Objectionable Current
250.6(A)

To prevent a fire, electric shock, or improper operation of circuit overcurrent devices or electronic equipment, electrical systems and equipment must be installed in a manner that prevents objectionable neutral current from flowing on metal parts.

Copyright 2014, www.MikeHolt.com

Figure 250–23

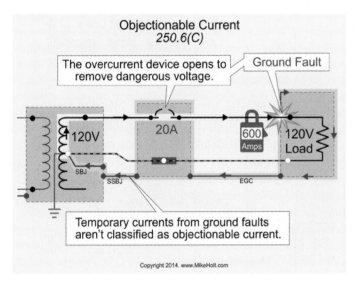

Objectionable Current
250.6(C)

The overcurrent device opens to remove dangerous voltage.

Ground Fault

120V   20A   600 Amps   120V Load

SBJ   SSBJ   EGC

Temporary currents from ground faults aren't classified as objectionable current.

Copyright 2014, www.MikeHolt.com

Figure 250–24

Objectionable Current

Objectionable neutral current occurs because of improper neutral-to-case connections or wiring errors that violate 250.142(B).

Improper Neutral-to-Case Connection [250.142]

Panelboards. Objectionable neutral current will flow on metal parts and the equipment grounding conductor when the neutral conductor is connected to the metal case of a panelboard on the load side of service equipment. Figure 250–25

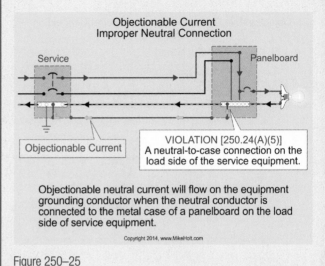

Objectionable Current
Improper Neutral Connection

Service   Panelboard

Objectionable Current

VIOLATION [250.24(A)(5)]
A neutral-to-case connection on the load side of the service equipment.

Objectionable neutral current will flow on the equipment grounding conductor when the neutral conductor is connected to the metal case of a panelboard on the load side of service equipment.

Copyright 2014, www.MikeHolt.com

Figure 250–25

Separately Derived Systems. Objectionable neutral current will flow on metal parts if the neutral conductor is connected to the circuit equipment grounding conductor on the load side of the system bonding jumper for a separately derived system. Figure 250–26

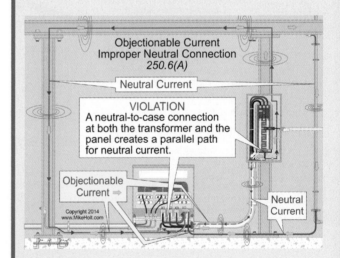

Objectionable Current
Improper Neutral Connection
250.6(A)

Neutral Current

VIOLATION
A neutral-to-case connection at both the transformer and the panel creates a parallel path for neutral current.

Objectionable Current →

Neutral Current

Copyright 2014
www.MikeHolt.com

Figure 250–26

Generator. Objectionable neutral current will flow on metal parts and the equipment grounding conductor if a generator is connected to a transfer switch with a solidly connected neutral and a neutral-to-case connection is made at the generator. Figure 250–27

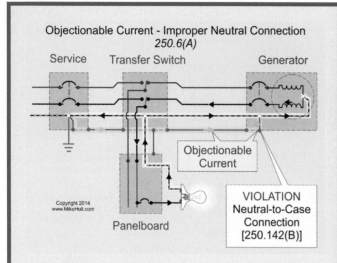

Objectionable Current - Improper Neutral Connection
250.6(A)

Service   Transfer Switch   Generator

Objectionable
Current

VIOLATION
Neutral-to-Case
Connection
[250.142(B)]

Panelboard

Figure 250–27

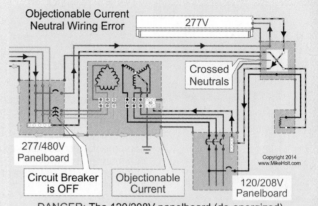

Objectionable Current
Neutral Wiring Error

277V

Crossed
Neutrals

277/480V
Panelboard

Circuit Breaker
is OFF

Objectionable
Current

120/208V
Panelboard

DANGER: The 120/208V panelboard (de-energized)
can have dangerous voltage from the 277V lighting
circuit because of the crossed neutrals.

Figure 250–29

Disconnects. Objectionable neutral current will flow on metal parts and the equipment grounding conductor when the neutral conductor is connected to the metal case of a disconnecting means that's not part of the service equipment. Figure 250–28

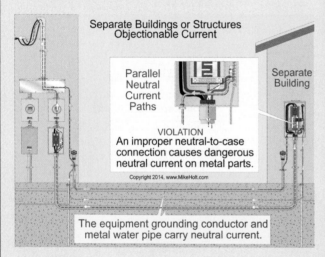

Separate Buildings or Structures
Objectionable Current

Parallel
Neutral
Current
Paths

Separate
Building

VIOLATION
An improper neutral-to-case
connection causes dangerous
neutral current on metal parts.

The equipment grounding conductor and
metal water pipe carry neutral current.

Figure 250–28

Wiring Errors. Objectionable neutral current will flow on metal parts and equipment grounding conductors when the neutral conductor from one system is used as the neutral conductor for a different system. Figure 250–29

Objectionable neutral current will flow on the equipment grounding conductor when the circuit equipment grounding conductor is used as a neutral conductor such as where:

- A 230V time-clock motor is replaced with a 115V time-clock motor, and the circuit equipment grounding conductor is used for neutral return current.

- A 115V water filter is wired to a 240V well-pump motor circuit, and the circuit equipment grounding conductor is used for neutral return current. Figure 250–30

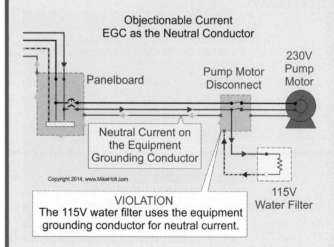

Objectionable Current
EGC as the Neutral Conductor

230V
Pump
Motor

Pump Motor
Disconnect

Panelboard

Neutral Current on
the Equipment
Grounding Conductor

115V
Water Filter

VIOLATION
The 115V water filter uses the equipment
grounding conductor for neutral current.

Figure 250–30

- The circuit equipment grounding conductor is used for neutral return current. Figure 250–31

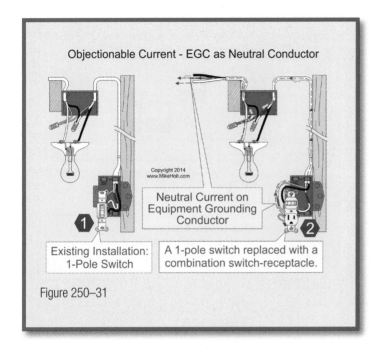

Objectionable Current - EGC as Neutral Conductor

Copyright 2014
www.MikeHolt.com

Neutral Current on Equipment Grounding Conductor

1 Existing Installation: 1-Pole Switch

2 A 1-pole switch replaced with a combination switch-receptacle.

Figure 250–31

Dangers of Objectionable Current

Objectionable neutral current on metal parts can cause electric shock, fires, and improper operation of electronic equipment and overcurrent devices such as GFPs, GFCIs, and AFCIs.

Shock Hazard. When objectionable neutral current flows on metal parts or the equipment grounding conductor, electric shock and even death can occur from the elevated voltage on those metal parts. Figure 250–32 and Figure 250–33

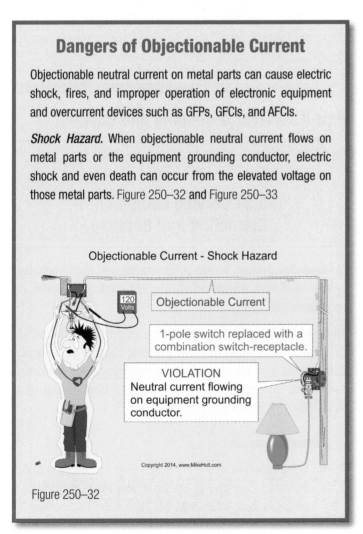

Objectionable Current - Shock Hazard

120 Volts

Objectionable Current

1-pole switch replaced with a combination switch-receptacle.

VIOLATION
Neutral current flowing on equipment grounding conductor.

Copyright 2014, www.MikeHolt.com

Figure 250–32

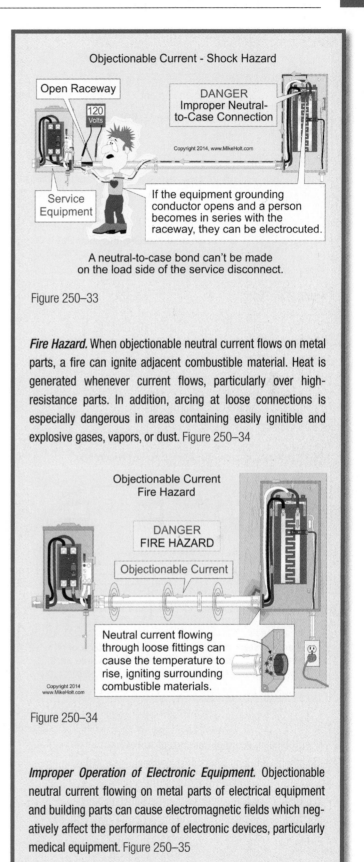

Objectionable Current - Shock Hazard

Open Raceway

120 Volts

DANGER
Improper Neutral-to-Case Connection

Copyright 2014, www.MikeHolt.com

Service Equipment

If the equipment grounding conductor opens and a person becomes in series with the raceway, they can be electrocuted.

A neutral-to-case bond can't be made on the load side of the service disconnect.

Figure 250–33

Fire Hazard. When objectionable neutral current flows on metal parts, a fire can ignite adjacent combustible material. Heat is generated whenever current flows, particularly over high-resistance parts. In addition, arcing at loose connections is especially dangerous in areas containing easily ignitible and explosive gases, vapors, or dust. Figure 250–34

Objectionable Current
Fire Hazard

DANGER
FIRE HAZARD

Objectionable Current

Copyright 2014
www.MikeHolt.com

Neutral current flowing through loose fittings can cause the temperature to rise, igniting surrounding combustible materials.

Figure 250–34

Improper Operation of Electronic Equipment. Objectionable neutral current flowing on metal parts of electrical equipment and building parts can cause electromagnetic fields which negatively affect the performance of electronic devices, particularly medical equipment. Figure 250–35

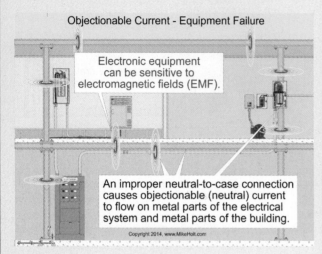

Figure 250–35

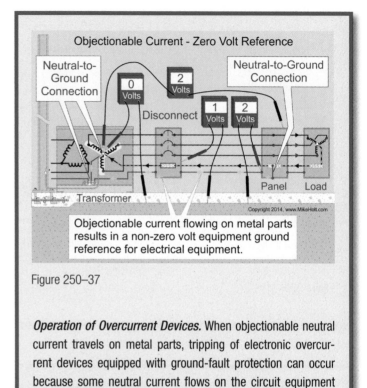

Figure 250–37

For more information, visit www.MikeHolt.com, click on the "Technical Link," and then on "Power Quality."

When a solidly grounded system is properly bonded, the voltage of all metal parts to the earth and to each other will be zero. Figure 250–36

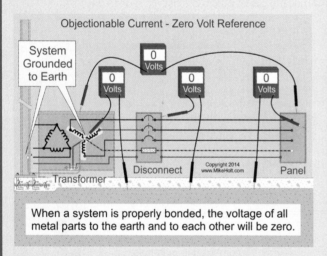

Figure 250–36

When objectionable neutral current travels on metal parts and equipment grounding conductors because of the improper bonding of the neutral to metal parts, a difference of potential will exist between all metal parts. This situation can cause some electronic equipment to operate improperly. Figure 250–37

Operation of Overcurrent Devices. When objectionable neutral current travels on metal parts, tripping of electronic overcurrent devices equipped with ground-fault protection can occur because some neutral current flows on the circuit equipment grounding conductor instead of the neutral conductor.

Part II. System Grounding and Bonding

Essential Rule 25

250.24 Service Equipment— Grounding and Bonding

(A) Grounded System. Service equipment supplied from a grounded system must have the grounding electrode conductor terminate in accordance with (1) through (5).

(1) Grounding Location. A grounding electrode conductor must connect the service neutral conductor to the grounding electrode at any accessible location, from the load end of the overhead service conductors, service drop, underground service conductors, or service lateral, up to and including the service disconnecting means. Figure 250–38

Author's Comment:

■ Some inspectors require the service neutral conductor to be grounded (connected to the earth) from the meter socket enclosure, while other inspectors insist that it be grounded

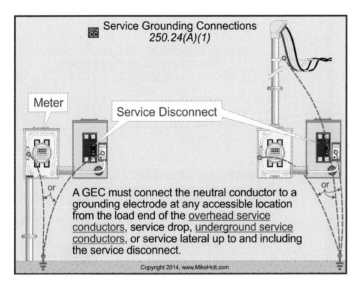

Figure 250–38

(connected to the earth) only from the service disconnect. Grounding at either location complies with this rule.

(4) Grounding Termination. When the service neutral conductor is connected to the service disconnecting means [250.24(B)] by a wire or busbar [250.28], the grounding electrode conductor is permitted to terminate to either the neutral terminal or the equipment grounding terminal within the service disconnect.

(5) Neutral-to-Case Connection. A neutral-to-case connection isn't permitted on the load side of service equipment, except as permitted by 250.142(B). Figure 250–39

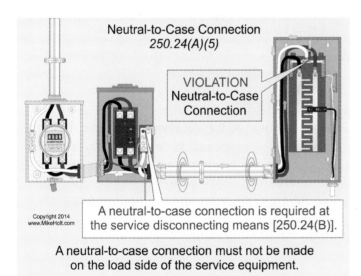

Figure 250–39

Author's Comment:

■ If a neutral-to-case connection is made on the load side of service equipment, dangerous objectionable neutral current will flow on conductive metal parts of electrical equipment [250.6(A)]. Objectionable neutral current on metal parts of electrical equipment can cause electric shock and even death from ventricular fibrillation, as well as a fire. Figure 250–40 and Figure 250–41

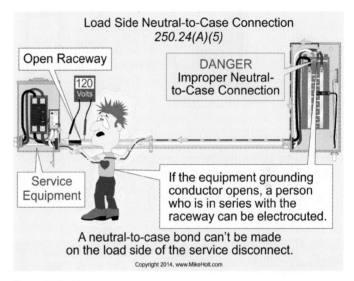

Figure 250–40

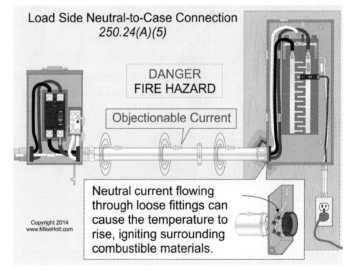

Figure 250–41

(B) Main Bonding Jumper. A main bonding jumper [250.28] is required to connect the neutral conductor to the equipment grounding conductor within the service disconnecting means. Figure 250–42 and Figure 250–43

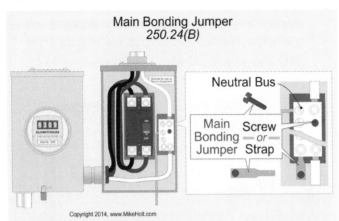

Main Bonding Jumper
250.24(B)

Neutral Bus

Main Bonding Jumper — Screw *or* Strap

Copyright 2014, www.MikeHolt.com

A main bonding jumper is required to connect the neutral conductor to the equipment grounding conductor within the service disconnecting means.

Figure 250–42

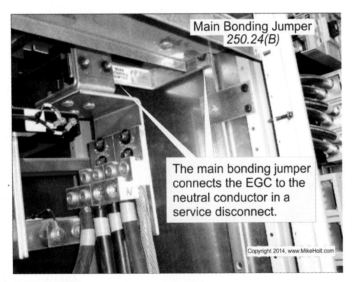

Main Bonding Jumper
250.24(B)

The main bonding jumper connects the EGC to the neutral conductor in a service disconnect.

Copyright 2014, www.MikeHolt.com

Figure 250–43

(C) Neutral Conductor Brought to Service Equipment. A service neutral conductor must be run from the electric utility supply with the ungrounded conductors and terminate to the service disconnect neutral terminal. A main bonding jumper [250.24(B)] must be installed between the service neutral terminal and the service disconnecting means enclosure [250.28]. Figure 250–44 and Figure 250–45

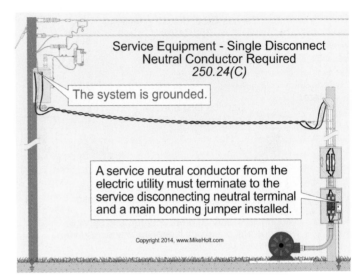

Service Equipment - Single Disconnect
Neutral Conductor Required
250.24(C)

The system is grounded.

A service neutral conductor from the electric utility must terminate to the service disconnecting neutral terminal and a main bonding jumper installed.

Copyright 2014, www.MikeHolt.com

Figure 250–44

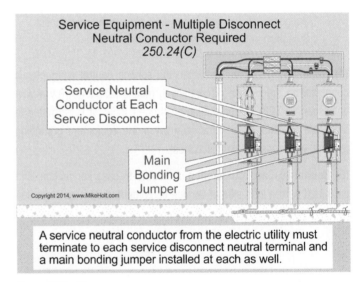

Service Equipment - Multiple Disconnect
Neutral Conductor Required
250.24(C)

Service Neutral Conductor at Each Service Disconnect

Main Bonding Jumper

Copyright 2014, www.MikeHolt.com

A service neutral conductor from the electric utility must terminate to each service disconnect neutral terminal and a main bonding jumper installed at each as well.

Figure 250–45

Author's Comment:

- The service neutral conductor provides the effective ground-fault current path to the power supply to ensure that dangerous voltage from a ground fault will be quickly removed by opening the overcurrent device [250.4(A)(3) and 250.4(A)(5)]. Figure 250–46

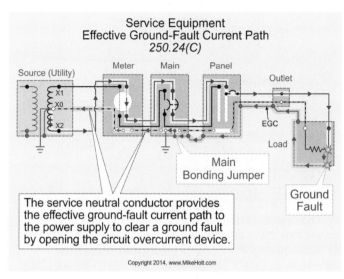

Figure 250–46

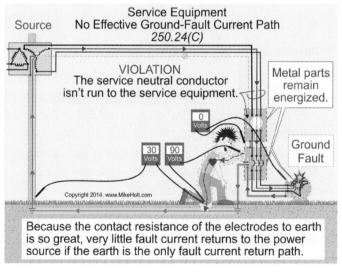

Figure 250–47

DANGER: *Dangerous voltage from a ground fault won't be removed from metal parts, metal piping, and structural steel if the service disconnecting means enclosure isn't connected to the service neutral conductor. This is because the contact resistance of a grounding electrode to the earth is so great that insufficient fault current returns to the power supply if the earth is the only fault current return path to open the circuit overcurrent device.* Figure 250–47

Author's Comment:

■ If the neutral conductor is opened, dangerous voltage will be present on metal parts under normal conditions, providing the potential for electric shock. If the earth's ground resistance is 25 ohms and the load's resistance is 25 ohms, the voltage drop across each of these resistors will be half of the voltage source. Since the neutral is connected to the service disconnect, all metal parts will be elevated to 60V above the earth's potential for a 120/240V system. Figure 250–48

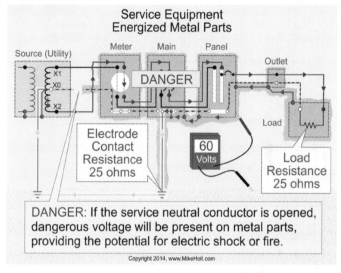

Figure 250–48

■ To determine the actual voltage on the metal parts from an open service neutral conductor, you need to do some complex calculations. Visit www.MikeHolt.com and go to the "Free Resources" link to download a spreadsheet for this purpose.

(1) Single Raceway. Because the service neutral conductor serves as the effective ground-fault current path to the source for ground faults, the neutral conductor must be sized so it can safely carry the maximum fault current likely to be imposed on it [110.10 and 250.4(A)(5)]. This is accomplished by sizing the neutral conductor not smaller than specified in Table 250.102(C)(1), based on the cross-sectional area of the largest ungrounded service conductor. Figure 250–49

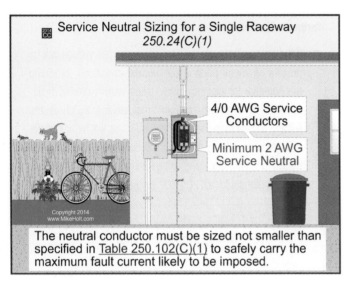

Figure 250–49

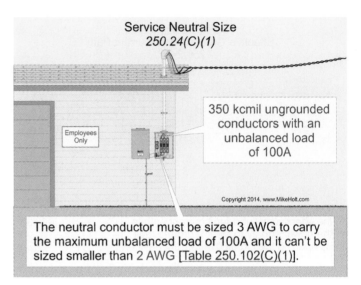

Figure 250–50

Author's Comment:

- In addition, the neutral conductors must have the capacity to carry the maximum unbalanced neutral current in accordance with 220.61.

Question: What's the minimum size service neutral conductor required where the ungrounded service conductors are 350 kcmil and the maximum unbalanced load is 100A? Figure 250–50

(a) 3 AWG   (b) 2 AWG   (c) 1 AWG   (d) 1/0 AWG

Answer: (b) 2 AWG [Table 250.102(C)(1)]

The unbalanced load of 100A requires a 3 AWG service neutral conductor, which is rated 100A at 75°C in accordance with Table 310.15(B)(16) [220.61], but the neutral conductor can be smaller than 2 AWG to carry fault current, based on the 350 kcmil ungrounded conductors [Table 250.102(C)(1)].

(2) Parallel Conductors in Two or More Raceways. If service conductors are paralleled in two or more raceways, a neutral conductor must be installed in each of the parallel raceways. The size of the neutral conductor in each raceway must not be smaller than specified in Table 250.102(C)(1), based on the cross-sectional area of the largest ungrounded service conductor in each raceway. In no case can the neutral conductor in each parallel set be sized smaller than 1/0 AWG [310.10(H)(1)].

Author's Comment:

- In addition, the neutral conductors must have the capacity to carry the maximum unbalanced neutral current in accordance with 220.61.

Question: What's the minimum size service neutral conductor required for each of two raceways, where the ungrounded service conductors in each of the raceways are 350 kcmil and the maximum unbalanced load is 100A? Figure 250–51

(a) 3 AWG   (b) 2 AWG   (c) 1 AWG   (d) 1/0 AWG

Answer: (d) 1/0 AWG per raceway [Table 250.102(C)(1) and 310.10(H)]

The unbalanced load of 50A in each raceway requires an 8 AWG service neutral conductor, which is rated 50A at 75°C in accordance with Table 310.15(B)(16) [220.61]. Also, Table 250.102(C)(1) requires a minimum of 2 AWG in each raceway, however, 1/0 AWG is the smallest conductor permitted to be parallel [310.10(H) and Table 310.15(B)(16)].

(D) Grounding Electrode Conductor. A grounding electrode conductor, sized in accordance with 250.66 based on the area of the ungrounded service conductor, must connect the neutral conductor and metal parts of service equipment enclosures to a grounding electrode in accordance with Part III of Article 250.

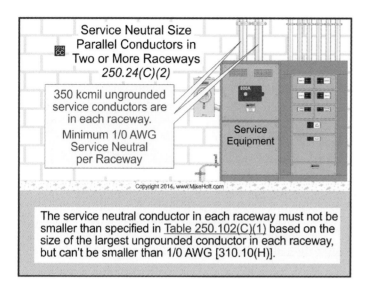

Figure 250–51

Question: What's the minimum size grounding electrode conductor for a 400A service where the ungrounded service conductors are sized at 500 kcmil? Figure 250–52

(a) 3 AWG   (b) 2 AWG   (c) 1 AWG   (d) 1/0 AWG

Answer: (d) 1/0 AWG [Table 250.66]

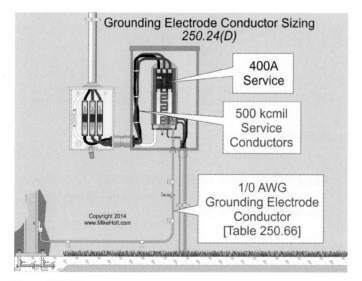

Figure 250–52

Author's Comment:

■ If the grounding electrode conductor is connected to a rod(s), the portion of the conductor that's the sole connection to the rod(s) isn't required to be larger than 6 AWG copper [250.66(A)]. Figure 250–53

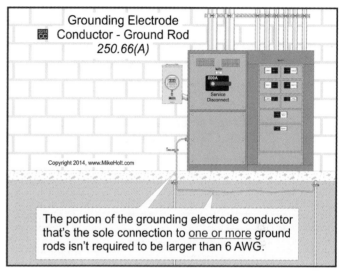

Figure 250–53

■ If the grounding electrode conductor is connected to a concrete-encased electrode(s), the portion of the conductor that's the sole connection to the concrete-encased electrode(s) isn't required to be larger than 4 AWG copper [250.66(B)]. Figure 250–54

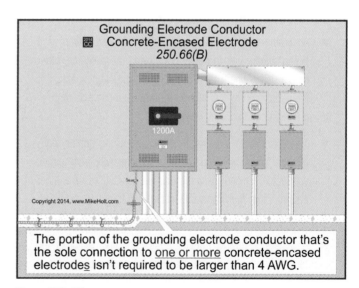

Figure 250–54

Essential Rule 26

250.30 Separately Derived Systems— Grounding and Bonding

Note 1: An alternate alternating-current power source such as an on-site generator isn't a separately derived system if the neutral conductor is solidly interconnected to a service-supplied system neutral conductor. An example is a generator provided with a transfer switch that includes a neutral conductor that's not switched. Figure 250–55

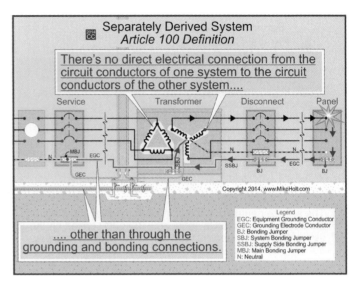

Figure 250–56

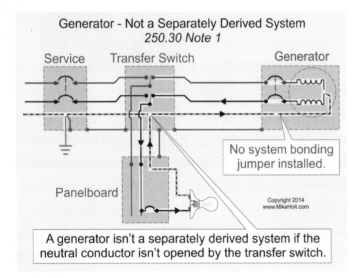

Figure 250–55

Author's Comment:

- According to Article 100, a separately derived system is a wiring system whose power is derived from a source, other than a utility, where there's no direct electrical connection to the supply conductors of another system, other than through grounding and bonding connections.

- Transformers are separately derived when the primary conductors have no direct electrical connection from circuit conductors of one system to circuit conductors of another system, other than connections through grounding and bonding connections. Figure 250–56

- A generator having transfer equipment that switches the neutral conductor, or one that has no neutral conductor at all, is a separately derived system and must be grounded and bonded in accordance with 250.30(A). Figure 250–57

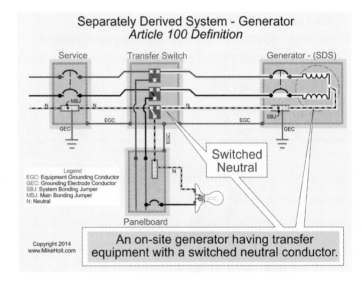

Figure 250–57

Note 2: For nonseparately derived systems, see 445.13 for the minimum size neutral conductors necessary to carry fault current. Figure 250–58 and Figure 250–59

(A) Grounded Systems. Separately derived systems must be grounded and bonded in accordance with (A)(1) through (A)(8).

A neutral-to-case connection must not be made on the load side of the system bonding jumper, except as permitted by 250.142(B).

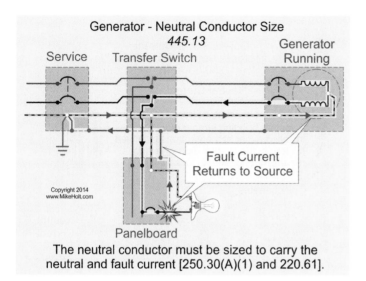

Figure 250–58

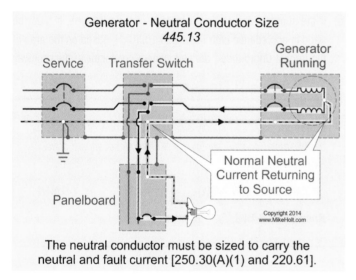

Figure 250–59

(1) System Bonding Jumper. A system bonding jumper must be installed at the same location where the grounding electrode conductor terminates to the neutral terminal of the separately derived system; either at the separately derived system or the system disconnecting means, but not at both locations [250.30(A)(5)].

(a) System Bonding Jumper at Source. Where the system bonding jumper is installed at the source of the separately derived system, the system bonding jumper must connect the neutral conductor of the derived system to the metal enclosure of the derived system. Figure 250–60

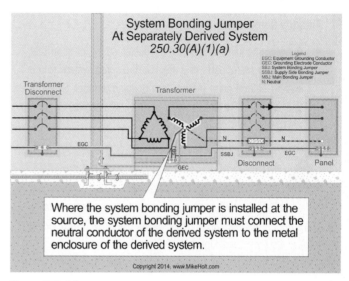

Figure 250–60

(b) System Bonding Jumper at Disconnecting Means. Where the system bonding jumper is installed at the first disconnecting means of a separately derived system, the system bonding jumper must connect the neutral conductor of the derived system to the metal disconnecting means enclosure. Figure 250–61

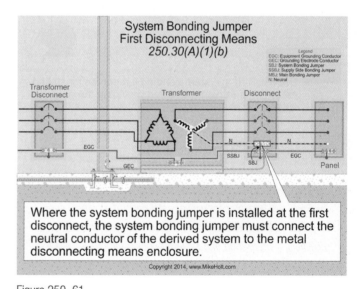

Figure 250–61

Author's Comment:

■ A system bonding jumper is a conductor, screw, or strap that bonds the metal parts of a separately derived system to the system neutral point [Article 100 Bonding Jumper, System], and it's sized to Table 250.102(C)(1) in accordance with 250.28(D).

⚠ **DANGER:** *During a ground fault, metal parts of electrical equipment, as well as metal piping and structural steel, will become and remain energized providing the potential for electric shock and fire if the system bonding jumper isn't installed.* Figure 250–62

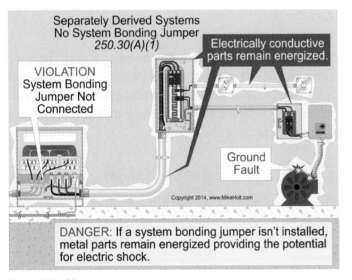

Figure 250–62

⚠ **CAUTION:** *Dangerous objectionable neutral current will flow on conductive metal parts of electrical equipment as well as metal piping and structural steel, in violation of 250.6(A), if more than one system bonding jumper is installed, or if it's not located where the grounding electrode conductor terminates to the neutral conductor.* Figure 250–63

(2) Supply-Side Bonding Jumper to Disconnect. A supply-side bonding jumper (nonflexible metal raceway or wire) must be run from the derived system to the derived system disconnecting means.

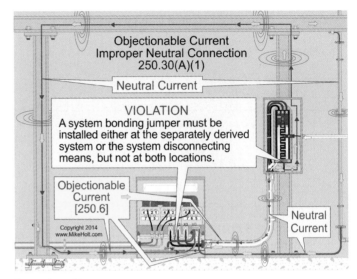

Figure 250–63

(a) If the supply-side bonding jumper is of the wire type, it must be sized in accordance with Table 250.102(C)(1), based on the area of the largest ungrounded derived system conductor in the raceway or cable.

> **Question:** *What size supply-side bonding jumper is required for flexible metal conduit containing 300 kcmil secondary conductors?* Figure 250–64
>
> *(a) 3 AWG*   *(b) 2 AWG*   *(c) 1 AWG*   *(d) 1/0 AWG*
>
> **Answer:** *(b) 2 AWG [Table 250.102(C)(1)]*

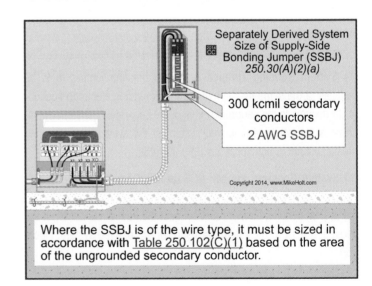

Figure 250–64

(3) System Bonding Jumper at Disconnect—Neutral Conductor Size. If the system bonding jumper is installed at the disconnecting means instead of at the source, the following requirements apply:

(a) Sizing for Single Raceway. The neutral conductor must be routed with the ungrounded conductors of the derived system to the disconnecting means and be sized not smaller than specified in Table 250.102(C)(1), based on the area of the ungrounded conductor of the derived system. Figure 250–65

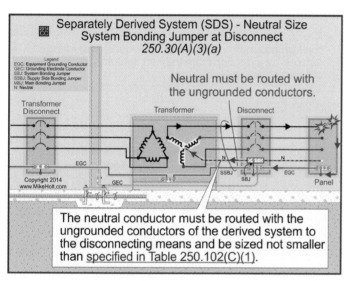

Figure 250–65

(b) Parallel Conductors in Two or More Raceways. If the conductors from the derived system are installed in parallel in two or more raceways, the neutral conductor of the derived system in each raceway or cable must be sized not smaller than specified in Table 250.102(C)(1), based on the area of the largest ungrounded conductor of the derived system in the raceway or cable. In no case is the neutral conductor of the derived system permitted to be smaller than 1/0 AWG [310.10(H)].

Author's Comment:

■ If the system bonding jumper is installed at the disconnecting means instead of at the source, a supply side bonding jumper must connect the metal parts of the separately derived system to the neutral conductor at the disconnecting means [250.30(A)(2)].

(4) Grounding Electrode. The grounding electrode for a separately derived system must be as near as practicable, and preferably in the same area where the system bonding jumper is installed and be one of the following: Figure 250–66

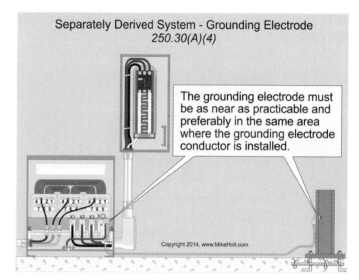

Figure 250–66

(1) Metal water pipe electrode, within 5 ft of the entry to the building [250.52(A)(1)].

(2) Metal building frame electrode [250.52(A)(2)].

Ex 1: If the water pipe or structural metal electrode aren't available, one of the following electrodes can be used:

- *A concrete-encased electrode encased by not less than 2 in. of concrete, located horizontally or vertically, and within that portion of concrete foundation or footing that's in direct contact with the earth [250.52(A)(3)].*

- *A ground ring electrode encircling the building, buried not less than 30 in. below grade, consisting of at least 20 ft of bare copper conductor not smaller than 2 AWG [250.52(A)(4) and 250.53(F)].*

- *A rod electrode having not less than 8 ft of contact with the soil meeting the requirements of 250.52(A)(5) and 250.53(G).*

- *Other metal underground systems, piping systems, or underground tanks [250.52(A)(8)].*

Note 1: Interior metal water piping in the area served by separately derived systems must be bonded to the separately derived system in accordance with 250.104(D).

(5) Grounding Electrode Conductor, Single Separately Derived System. The grounding electrode conductor must be sized in accordance with 250.66, based on the area of the largest ungrounded conductor of the derived system. A grounding electrode conductor must terminate to the neutral at the same point on the separately derived system where the system bonding jumper is connected. Figure 250–67

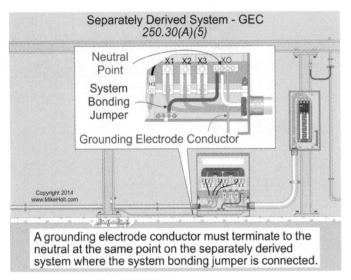

Figure 250–67

Author's Comment:

- System grounding helps reduce fires in buildings as well as voltage stress on electrical insulation, thereby ensuring longer insulation life for motors, transformers, and other system components. Figure 250–68

- To prevent objectionable neutral current from flowing [250.6] onto metal parts, the grounding electrode conductor must originate at the same point on the separately derived system where the system bonding jumper is connected [250.30(A)(1)].

Ex 1: The grounding electrode conductor is permitted to terminate to the equipment grounding terminal at the derived system or first system disconnecting means in accordance with 250.30(A)(1). Figure 250–69

Ex 3: Separately derived systems rated 1 kVA or less aren't required to be grounded (connected to the earth).

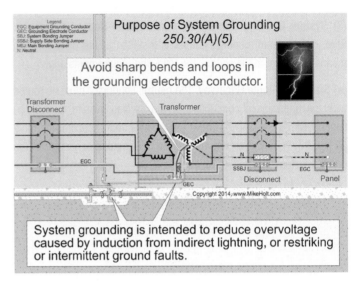

Figure 250–68

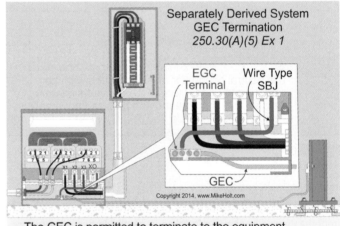

Figure 250–69

(6) Grounding Electrode Conductor, Multiple Separately Derived Systems. Where there are multiple separately derived systems, a grounding electrode conductor tap from each separately derived system to a common grounding electrode conductor is permitted. This connection is to be made at the same point on the separately derived system where the system bonding jumper is connected [250.30(A)(1)]. Figure 250–70

Ex 1: If the system bonding jumper is a wire or busbar, the grounding electrode conductor tap can terminate to either the neutral terminal or the equipment grounding terminal, bar, or bus in accordance with 250.30(A)(1).

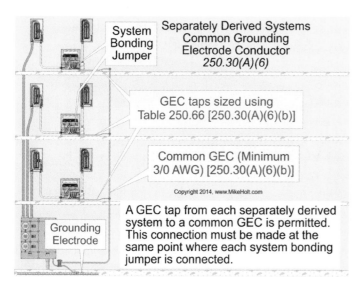

Figure 250–70

Ex 2: Separately derived systems rated 1 kVA or less aren't required to be grounded (connected to the earth).

(a) Common Grounding Electrode Conductor. The common grounding electrode conductor can be one of the following:

(1) A conductor not smaller than 3/0 AWG copper or 250 kcmil aluminum.

(2) The metal frame of the buildings that complies with 250.52(A)(2) or is connected to the grounding electrode system by a conductor not smaller than 3/0 AWG copper or 250 kcmil aluminum.

(b) Tap Conductor Size. Grounding electrode conductor taps must be sized in accordance with Table 250.66, based on the area of the largest ungrounded conductor of the given derived system.

(c) Connections. All tap connections to the common grounding electrode conductor must be made at an accessible location by one of the following methods:

(1) A connector listed as grounding and bonding equipment.

(2) Listed connections to aluminum or copper busbars not less than ¼ in. in depth x 2 in. in width

(3) Exothermic welding.

Grounding electrode conductor taps must be connected to the common grounding electrode conductor so the common grounding electrode conductor isn't spliced.

(7) Installation. The grounding electrode conductor must comply with the following:

- Be of copper where within 18 in. of the earth [250.64(A)].

- Be securely fastened to the surface on which it's carried [250.64(B)].

- Be adequately protected if exposed to physical damage [250.64(B)].

- Metal enclosures enclosing a grounding electrode conductor must be made electrically continuous from the point of attachment to cabinets or equipment to the grounding electrode [250.64(E)].

(8) Structural Steel and Metal Piping. To ensure dangerous voltage from a ground fault is removed quickly, structural steel and metal piping in the area served by a separately derived system must be connected to the neutral conductor at the separately derived system in accordance with 250.104(D).

(C) Outdoor Source. Separately derived systems located outside the building must have the grounding electrode connection made at the separately derived system location. Figure 250–71

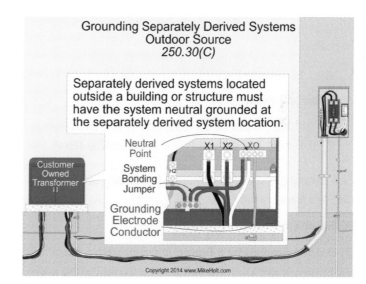

Figure 250–71

Essential Rule 27

250.32 Buildings Supplied by a Feeder

(A) Equipment Grounding Electrode. Building feeder disconnects must be connected to a grounding electrode to reduce induced voltages on the metal parts from nearby lightning strikes. Figure 250–72

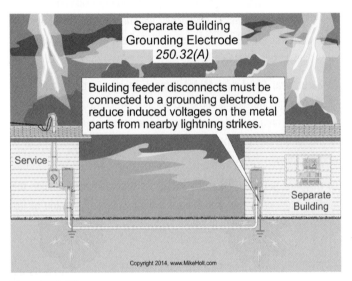

Figure 250–72

Author's Comment:

- The *Code* prohibits the use of the earth to serve as an effective ground-fault current path [250.4(A)(5) and 250.4(B)(4)].

Ex: A grounding electrode is not required for a building disconnect supplied by a branch circuit. Figure 250–73

(B) Equipment Grounding Conductor.

(1) Building Supplied by a Feeder. To quickly clear a ground fault and remove dangerous voltage from metal parts, the building disconnecting means must be connected to the circuit equipment grounding conductor, of the type(s) described in 250.118. If the supply circuit equipment grounding conductor is of the wire type, it must be sized in accordance with 250.122, based on the rating of the overcurrent device. Figure 250–74

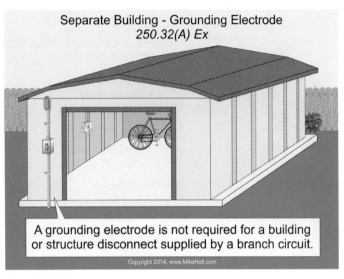

Figure 250–73

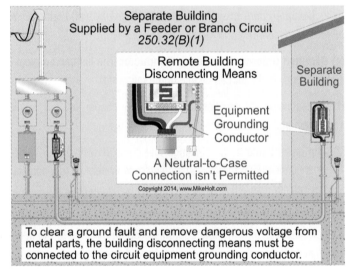

Figure 250–74

⚠ **CAUTION:** *To prevent dangerous objectionable neutral current from flowing on metal parts [250.6(A)], the supply circuit neutral conductor isn't permitted to be connected to the remote building disconnecting means [250.142(B)].* Figure 250–75

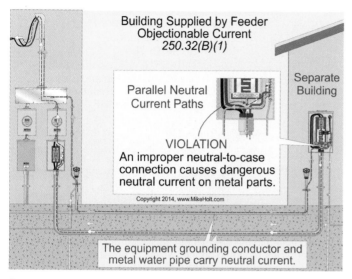

Figure 250–75

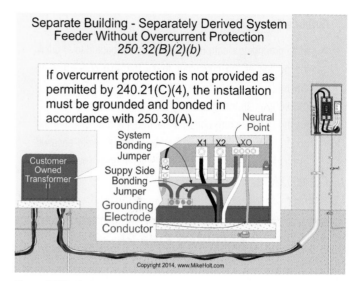

Figure 250–76

Ex 1: The neutral conductor can serve as the ground-fault return path for the building disconnecting means for existing installations in compliance with previous editions of the Code where there are no continuous metallic paths between buildings and structures, ground-fault protection of equipment isn't installed on the supply side of the circuit, and the neutral conductor is sized no smaller than the larger of:

(1) The maximum unbalanced neutral load in accordance with 220.61.

(2) The minimum equipment grounding conductor size in accordance with 250.122.

(2) Building Supplied by Separately Derived System.

(a) With Feeder Overcurrent Protection. If overcurrent protection is provided for the feeders from the separately derived system to the building, the supply conductors must contain an equipment grounding conductor in accordance with 250.32(B)(1).

(b) Without Feeder Overcurrent Protection. If overcurrent protection isn't provided for the feeder conductors supplying the building as permitted by 240.21(C)(4), grounding and bonded must be in accordance with 250.30(A). Figure 250–76

(E) Grounding Electrode Conductor Size. The grounding electrode conductor must terminate to the equipment grounding terminal of the disconnecting means (not neutral terminal), and it must be sized in accordance with 250.66, based on the conductor area of the ungrounded feeder conductor.

Question: *What size grounding electrode conductor is required for a building disconnect supplied with a 3/0 AWG feeder? Figure 250–77*

(a) 4 AWG 　 *(b) 3 AWG* 　 *(c) 2 AWG* 　 *(d) 1 AWG*

Answer: *(a) 4 AWG [Table 250.66]*

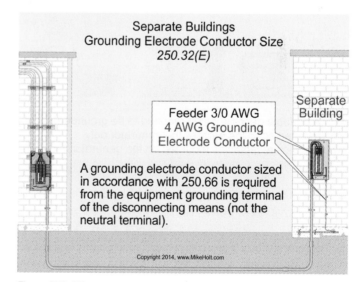

Figure 250–77

Author's Comment:

- If the grounding electrode conductor is connected to a rod(s), the portion of the conductor that's the sole connection to the rod(s) isn't required to be larger than 6 AWG copper [250.66(A)]. If the grounding electrode conductor is connected to a concrete-encased electrode(s), the portion of the conductor that's the sole connection to the concrete-encased electrode(s) isn't required to be larger than 4 AWG copper [250.66(B)].

Essential Rule 28

250.34 Generators—Portable and Vehicle-Mounted

(A) Portable Generators. A portable generator isn't required to be grounded (connected to the earth) if: Figure 250–78

Portable Generator
Grounding Not Required
250.34(A)

Portable Generator

A portable generator isn't required to be grounded (connected to the earth) if the generator only supplies receptacles mounted on the generator.

Copyright 2014, www.MikeHolt.com

Figure 250–78

(1) The generator only supplies equipment or receptacles mounted on the generator, and

(2) The metal parts of the generator and the receptacle grounding terminal are connected to the generator frame.

(B) Vehicle-Mounted Generators. A vehicle-mounted generator isn't required to be grounded (connected to the earth) if: Figure 250–79

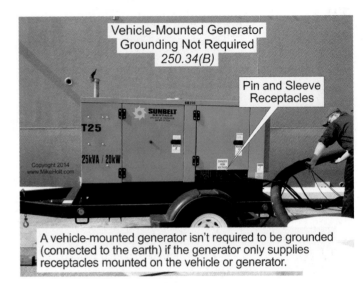

Vehicle-Mounted Generator
Grounding Not Required
250.34(B)

Pin and Sleeve Receptacles

A vehicle-mounted generator isn't required to be grounded (connected to the earth) if the generator only supplies receptacles mounted on the vehicle or generator.

Figure 250–79

(1) The generator frame is bonded to the vehicle frame,

(2) The generator only supplies equipment or receptacles mounted on the vehicle or generator, and

(3) The metal parts of the generator and the receptacle grounding terminal are connected to the generator frame.

Part III. Grounding Electrode System and Grounding Electrode Conductor

Essential Rule 29

250.50 Grounding Electrode System

Any grounding electrode described in 250.52(A)(1) through (A)(7) that's present at a building must be bonded together to form the grounding electrode system. Figure 250–80

- Underground metal water pipe [250.52(A)(1)]
- Metal frame of the buildings [250.52(A)(2)]
- Concrete-encased electrode [250.52(A)(3)]
- Ground ring [250.52(A)(4)]
- Rod [250.52(A)(5)]
- Other listed electrodes [250.52(A)(6)]
- Grounding plate [250.52(A)(7)]

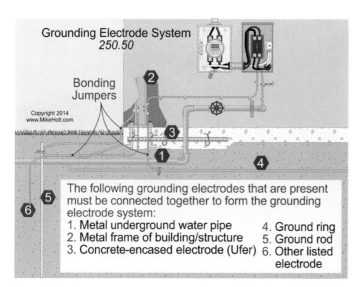

Figure 250–80

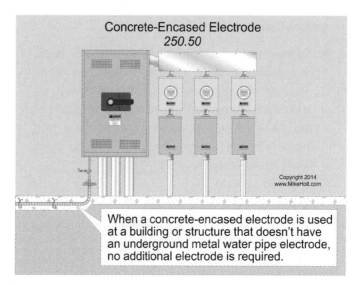

Figure 250–82

Ex: Concrete-encased electrodes aren't required for existing buildings where the conductive steel reinforcing bars aren't accessible without chipping up the concrete. Figure 250–81

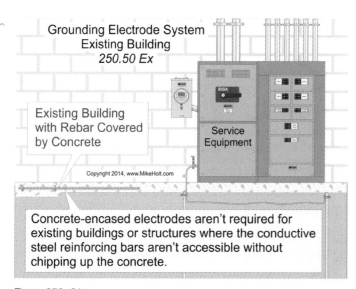

Figure 250–81

Author's Comment:

- When a concrete-encased electrode is used at a building that doesn't have an underground metal water pipe electrode, no additional electrode is required. Figure 250–82

Essential Rule 30

250.52 Grounding Electrode Types

(A) Electrodes Permitted for Grounding.

(1) Underground Metal Water Pipe Electrode. Underground metal water pipe in direct contact with the earth for 10 ft or more can serve as a grounding electrode. Figure 250–83

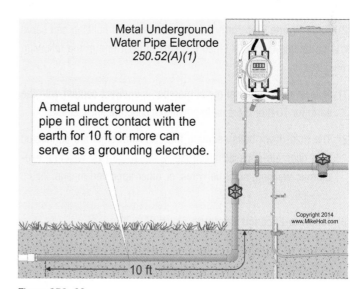

Figure 250–83

Author's Comment:

- Controversy about using metal underground water piping as a grounding electrode has existed since the early 1900s. The water industry believes that neutral current flowing on water piping corrodes the metal. For more information, contact the American Water Works Association about their report—*Effects of Electrical Grounding on Pipe Integrity and Shock Hazard*, Catalog No. 90702, 1.800.926.7337. Figure 250–84

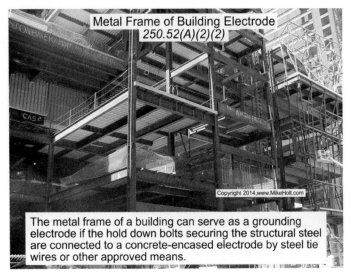

The metal frame of a building can serve as a grounding electrode if the hold down bolts securing the structural steel are connected to a concrete-encased electrode by steel tie wires or other approved means.

Figure 250–85

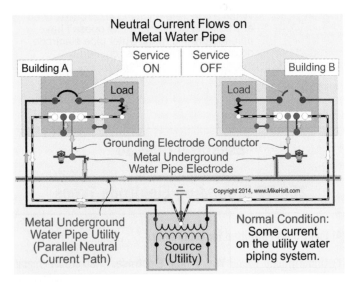

Figure 250–84

(2) Metal Frame Electrode. The metal frame of a building can serve as a grounding electrode when it meets at least one of the following conditions:

(1) At least one structural metal member is in direct contact with the earth for 10 ft or more, with or without concrete encasement.

(2) The hold-down bolts securing the structural steel are connected to a concrete-encased electrode [250.52(A)(3)] by welding, exothermic welding, steel tie wires, or other approved means. Figure 250–85

(3) Concrete-Encased Electrode. Figure 250–86

(1) One or more electrically conductive steel reinforcing bars of not less than ½ in. diameter, mechanically connected together by steel tie wires, or other effective means to create a 20 ft or greater length can serve as a grounding electrode.

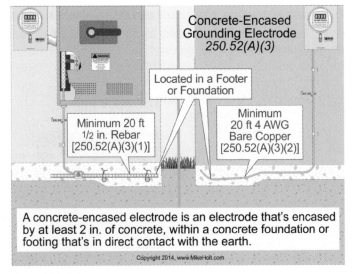

A concrete-encased electrode is an electrode that's encased by at least 2 in. of concrete, within a concrete foundation or footing that's in direct contact with the earth.

Figure 250–86

(2) Bare copper conductor not smaller than 4 AWG of 20 ft or greater length.

The reinforcing bars or bare copper conductor must be encased by at least 2 in. of concrete located horizontally of a concrete footing or vertically within a concrete foundation that's in direct contact with the earth can serve as a grounding electrode.

Where multiple concrete-encased electrodes are present at a building, only one is required to serve as a grounding electrode. Figure 250–87

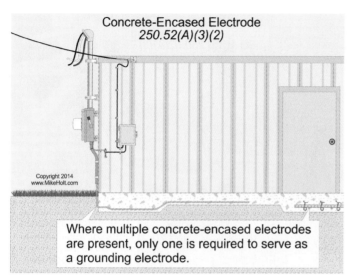

Figure 250–87

Note: Concrete separated from the earth because of insulation, vapor barriers, or similar items isn't considered to be in direct contract with the earth. Figure 250–88

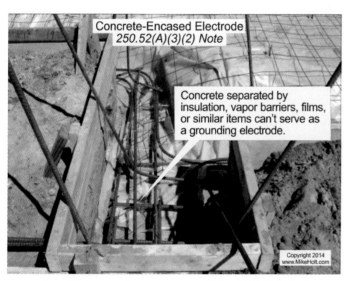

Figure 250–88

Author's Comment:

■ The grounding electrode conductor to a concrete-encased grounding electrode isn't required to be larger than 4 AWG copper [250.66(B)].

■ The concrete-encased grounding electrode is also called a "Ufer Ground," named after a consultant working for the U.S. Army during World War II. The technique Mr. Ufer came up with was necessary because the site needing grounding had no underground water table and little rainfall. The desert site was a series of bomb storage vaults in the area of Flagstaff, Arizona. This type of grounding electrode generally offers the lowest ground resistance for the cost.

(4) Ground Ring Electrode. A ground ring consisting of at least 20 ft of bare copper conductor not smaller than 2 AWG buried in the earth encircling a building, can serve as a grounding electrode. Figure 250–89

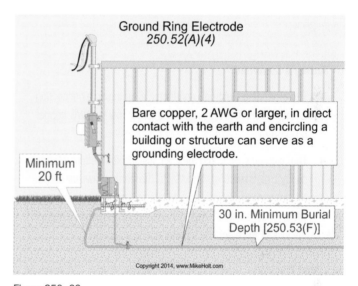

Figure 250–89

Author's Comment:

■ The ground ring must be buried not less than 30 in. [250.53(F)], and the grounding electrode conductor to a ground ring isn't required to be larger than the ground ring conductor size [250.66(C)].

(5) Rod Electrode. Rod electrodes must have at less 8 ft in length in contact with the earth [250.53(G)].

(b) Rod-type electrodes must have a diameter of at least ⅝ in., unless listed. Figure 250–90

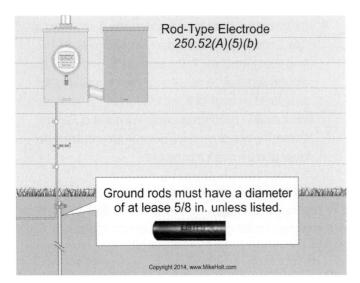

Rod-Type Electrode
250.52(A)(5)(b)

Ground rods must have a diameter of at lease 5/8 in. unless listed.

Copyright 2014, www.MikeHolt.com

Figure 250–90

Underground Metal Piping Electrode
250.52(A)(8)

Metal underground piping systems such as underground tanks or metal well casings can serve as a grounding electrode.

Copyright 2014 www.MikeHolt.com

Figure 250–91

Author's Comment:

■ The grounding electrode conductor, if it's the sole connection to the rod(s), isn't required to be larger than 6 AWG copper [250.66(A)].

■ The diameter of a rod has an insignificant effect on the contact resistance of a rod(s) to the earth. However, larger diameter rods (¾ in. and 1 in.) are sometimes installed where mechanical strength is desired, or to compensate for the loss of the electrode's metal due to corrosion.

(6) Listed Electrode. Other listed grounding electrodes can serve as a grounding electrode.

(7) Ground Plate Electrode. A bare or conductively coated iron or steel plate with not less than ¼ in. of thickness, or a solid uncoated copper metal plate not less than 0.06 in. of thickness, with an exposed surface area of not less than 2 sq ft can serve as a grounding electrode.

(8) Metal Underground Piping Electrode. Metal underground piping and well casings can serve as a grounding electrode. Figure 250–91

Author's Comment:

■ The grounding electrode conductor to the metal underground system must be sized in accordance with Table 250.66.

(B) Not Permitted for Use as a Grounding Electrode.

(1) Underground metal gas-piping systems aren't permitted to be used as a grounding electrode. Figure 250–92

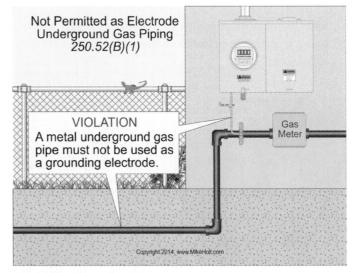

Not Permitted as Electrode
Underground Gas Piping
250.52(B)(1)

VIOLATION
A metal underground gas pipe must not be used as a grounding electrode.

Gas Meter

Copyright 2014, www.MikeHolt.com

Figure 250–92

Essential Rule 31

250.53 Grounding Electrode Installation Requirements

(A) Rod Electrodes.

(1) Below Permanent Moisture Level. If practicable, pipe electrodes must be embedded below the permanent moisture level and be free from nonconductive coatings such as paint or enamel.

(2) Supplemental Electrode. A rod electrode must be supplemented by an additional electrode that's bonded to: Figure 250–93

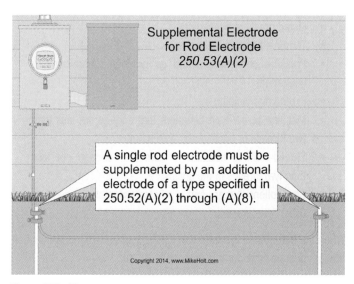

Figure 250–93

(1) Another rod electrode

(2) The grounding electrode conductor

(3) The service neutral conductor

(4) Nonflexible metal service raceway

(5) The service disconnect

Ex: A single rod electrode having a contact resistance to the earth of 25 ohms or less, isn't required to have a supplemental electrode. Figure 250–94

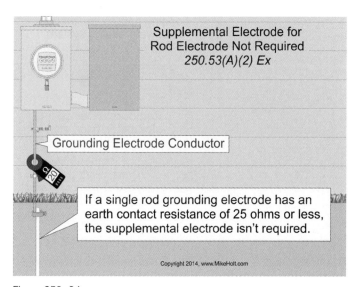

Figure 250–94

(3) Spacing. The supplemental electrode for a rod electrode must be installed not less than 6 ft from the rod electrode. Figure 250–95

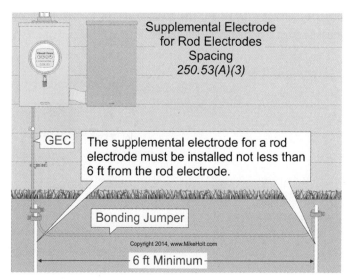

Figure 250–95

(B) Electrode Spacing. Electrodes for premises systems must be located no closer than 6 ft from lightning protection system grounding electrodes. Two or more grounding electrodes that are bonded together are considered a single grounding electrode system. Figure 250–96

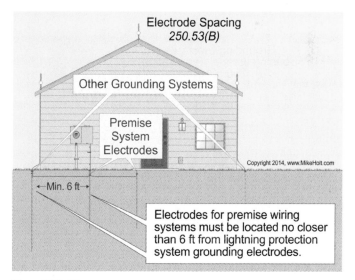

Figure 250–96

(C) Grounding Electrode Bonding Jumper. Grounding electrode bonding jumpers must be copper when within 18 in. of the earth [250.64(A)], be securely fastened to the surface, and be protected from physical damage [250.64(B)]. The bonding jumper to each electrode must be sized in accordance with 250.66. Figure 250–97

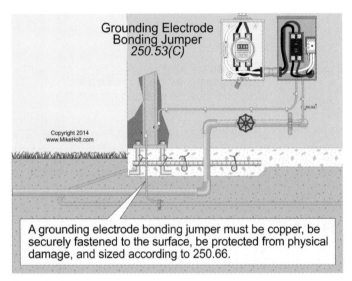

A grounding electrode bonding jumper must be copper, be securely fastened to the surface, be protected from physical damage, and sized according to 250.66.

Figure 250–97

The grounding electrode bonding jumpers must terminate by one of the following means in accordance with 250.8(A): Figure 250–98

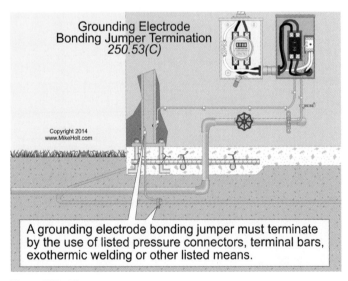

A grounding electrode bonding jumper must terminate by the use of listed pressure connectors, terminal bars, exothermic welding or other listed means.

Figure 250–98

- Listed pressure connectors
- Terminal bars
- Pressure connectors listed as grounding and bonding equipment
- Exothermic welding
- Machine screw-type fasteners that engage not less than two threads or are secured with a nut
- Thread-forming machine screws that engage not less than two threads in the enclosure
- Connections that are part of a listed assembly
- Other listed means

When the termination is encased in concrete or buried, the termination fittings must be listed for this purpose [250.70].

(D) Underground Metal Water Pipe Electrode.

(1) Interior Metal Water Piping. The bonding connection for the interior metal water piping system, as required by 250.104(A), must not be dependent on water meters, filtering devices, or similar equipment likely to be disconnected for repairs or replacement. When necessary, a bonding jumper must be installed around insulated joints and equipment likely to be disconnected for repairs or replacement. Figure 250–99

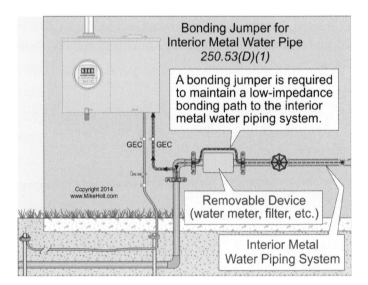

A bonding jumper is required to maintain a low-impedance bonding path to the interior metal water piping system.

Figure 250–99

(2) Underground Metal Water Pipe Supplemental Electrode. When an underground metal water pipe grounding electrode is present, it must be used as part of the grounding electrode system [250.52(A)(1)], and it must be supplemented by one of the following electrodes:

- Metal frame of the building electrode [250.52(A)(2)]
- Concrete-encased electrode [250.52(A)(3)] Figure 250–100
- Ground ring electrode [250.52(A)(4)]
- Rod electrode [250.52(A)(5)]
- Other listed electrode [250.52(A)(6)]
- Metal underground piping electrode [250.52(A)(8)]

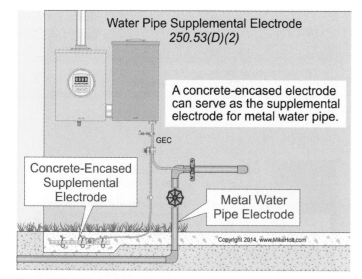

Figure 250–100

The supplemental grounding electrode conductor must terminate to one of the following: Figure 250–101

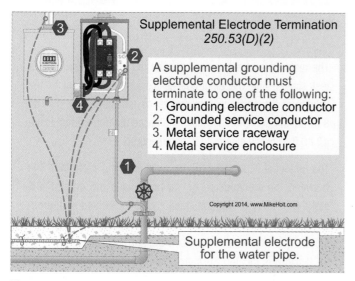

Figure 250–101

(1) Grounding electrode conductor

(2) Service neutral conductor

(3) Metal service raceway

(4) Service equipment enclosure

Ex: The supplemental electrode is permitted to be bonded to interior metal water piping located not more than 5 ft from the point of entrance to the building [250.68(C)(1)].

(E) Supplemental Rod Electrode. The grounding electrode conductor to a rod(s) that serves as a supplemental electrode, isn't required to be larger than 6 AWG copper.

(F) Ground Ring. A ground ring electrode (conductor) that encircling the building, consisting of at least 20 ft of bare copper conductor not smaller than 2 AWG, must be buried not less than 30 in. [250.52(A)(4)]. Figure 250–102

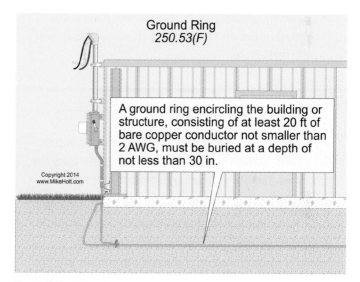

Figure 250–102

(G) Rod Electrodes. Rod electrodes must be installed so that not less than 8 ft of length is in contact with the soil. If rock bottom is encountered, the rod must be driven at an angle not to exceed 45 degrees from vertical. If rock bottom is encountered at an angle up to 45 degrees from vertical, the rod can be buried in a minimum 30 in. deep trench. Figure 250–103

The upper end of the rod must be flush with or underground unless the grounding electrode conductor attachment is protected against physical damage as specified in 250.10.

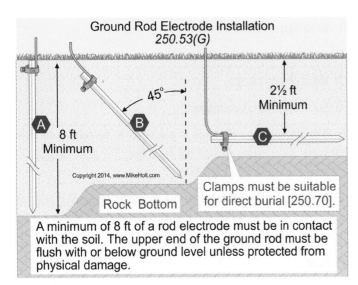

Figure 250–103

Author's Comment:

- When the grounding electrode attachment fitting is located underground, it must be listed for direct soil burial [250.68(A) Ex 1 and 250.70].

Measuring the Ground Resistance

A ground resistance clamp meter, or a three-point fall of potential ground resistance meter, can be used to measure the contact resistance of a grounding electrode to the earth.

Ground Clamp Meter. The ground resistance clamp meter measures the contact resistance of the grounding electrode system to the earth by injecting a high-frequency signal via the service neutral conductor to the utility grounding connection, and then measuring the strength of the return signal through the earth to the grounding electrode being measured. Figure 250–104

Fall of Potential Ground Resistance Meter. The three-point fall of potential ground resistance meter determines the contact resistance of a single grounding electrode to the earth by using Ohm's Law: $R = E/I$. Figure 250–105

This meter divides the voltage difference between the electrode to be measured and a driven potential test stake (P) by the current flowing between the electrode to be measured and a driven current test stake (C). The test stakes are typically made of ¼ in. diameter steel rods, 24 in. long, driven two-thirds of their length into the earth.

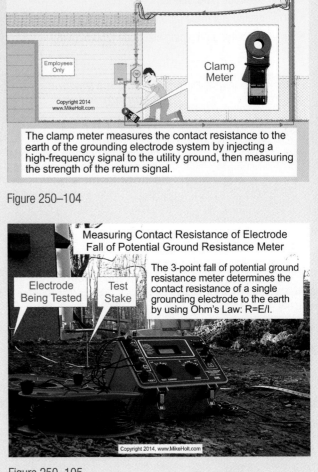

Figure 250–104

Figure 250–105

The distance and alignment between the potential and current test stakes, and the electrode, is extremely important to the validity of the earth contact resistance measurements. For an 8 ft rod, the accepted practice is to space the current test stake (C) 80 ft from the electrode to be measured.

The potential test stake (P) is positioned in a straight line between the electrode to be measured and the current test stake (C). The potential test stake should be located at approximately 62 percent of the distance the current test stake is located from the electrode. Since the current test stake (C) for an 8 ft rod is located 80 ft from the grounding electrode, the potential test stake (P) will be about 50 ft from the electrode to be measured.

Question: *If the voltage between the rod and the potential test stake (P) is 3V and the current between the rod and the current test stake (C) is 0.20A, then the earth contact resistance of the electrode to the earth will be _____. Figure 250–106*

(a) 5 ohms   (b) 10 ohms   (c) 15 ohms   (d) 25 ohms

Answer: *(c) 15 ohms*

> **Resistance = Voltage/Current**

E (Voltage) = 3V
I (Current) = 0.20A

> **R = E/I**

Resistance = 3V/0.20A
Resistance = 15 ohms

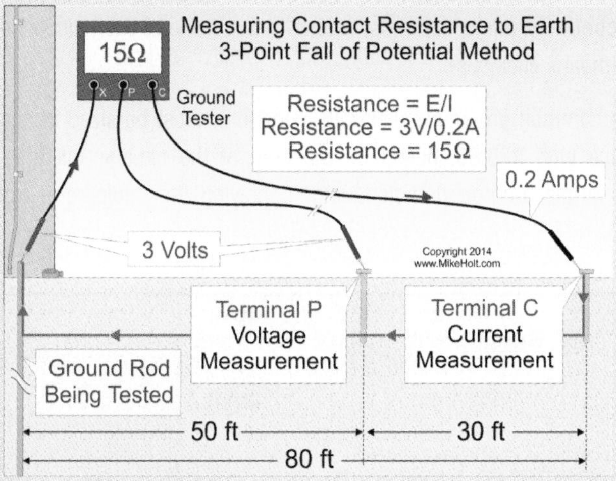

Measuring Contact Resistance to Earth
3-Point Fall of Potential Method

15Ω

Ground Tester

Resistance = E/I
Resistance = 3V/0.2A
Resistance = 15Ω

0.2 Amps

3 Volts

Copyright 2014
www.MikeHolt.com

Terminal P
Voltage
Measurement

Terminal C
Current
Measurement

Ground Rod
Being Tested

50 ft   30 ft
80 ft

Figure 250–106

Author's Comment:

■ The three-point fall of potential meter should only be used to measure the contact resistance of one electrode to the earth at a time, and this electrode must be independent and not connected to any part of the electrical system. The contact resistance of two electrodes bonded together must not be measured until they've been separated. The contact resistance of two separate electrodes to the earth can be thought of as two resistors in parallel, if they're outside each other's sphere of influence.

Soil Resistivity

The earth's ground resistance is directly impacted by soil resistivity, which varies throughout the world. Soil resistivity is influenced by electrolytes, which consist of moisture, minerals, and dissolved salts. Because soil resistivity changes with moisture content, the resistance of any grounding system varies with the seasons of the year. Since moisture is stable at greater distances below the surface of the earth, grounding systems are generally more effective if the grounding electrode can reach the water table. In addition, placing the grounding electrode below the frost line helps to ensure less deviation in the system's contact resistance to the earth year round.

The contact resistance to the earth can be lowered by chemically treating the earth around the grounding electrodes with electrolytes designed for this purpose.

Essential Rule 32

250.64 Grounding Electrode Conductor Installation

Grounding electrode conductors must be installed as specified in (A) through (F).

(A) Aluminum Conductors. Aluminum grounding electrode conductors must not be in contact with masonry, subject to corrosive conditions, or within 18 in. of the earth.

(B) Conductor Protection. Where installed exposed, grounding electrode conductors must be protected where subject to physical damage and are permitted to be installed on or through framing members. Grounding electrode conductors 6 AWG and larger can be installed exposed along the surface of the building if securely fastened and not subject to physical damage. Figure 250–107

Grounding electrode conductors sized 8 AWG must be protected by installing them in rigid metal conduit, intermediate metal conduit, PVC conduit, electrical metallic tubing, or reinforced thermosetting resin conduit.

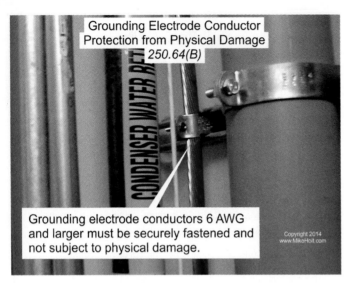

Figure 250–107

Author's Comment:

- A ferrous metal raceway containing a grounding electrode conductor must be made electrically continuous by bonding each end of the raceway to the grounding electrode conductor [250.64(E)], so it's best to use nonmetallic conduit.

Grounding electrode conductors and bonding jumpers located underground, aren't required to comply with the cover requirements of 300.5. Figure 250–108

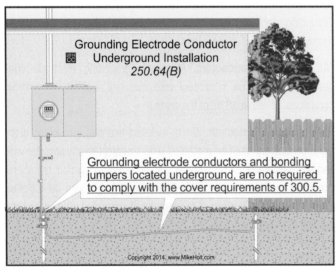

Figure 250–108

(C) Continuous. Grounding electrode conductor(s) must be installed without a splice or joint except by:

(1) Irreversible compression-type connectors or exothermic welding.

(2) Busbars connected together.

(3) Bolted, riveted, or welded connections of structural metal frames of buildings.

(4) Threaded, welded, brazed, soldered or bolted-flange connections of metal water piping.

(D) Grounding Electrode Conductor for Multiple Building or Structure Disconnects. If a service or building disconnect consists of more than a single enclosure, grounding electrode connections must be made in one of the following methods:

(1) Common Grounding Electrode Conductor and Taps. A grounding electrode conductor tap must extend to the inside of each disconnecting means enclosure.

The common grounding electrode conductor must be sized in accordance with 250.66, based on the sum of the circular mil area of the largest ungrounded conductor supplying the equipment. Figure 250–109

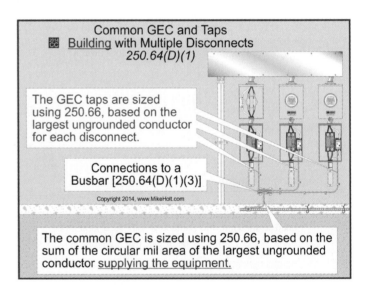

Figure 250–109

A grounding electrode conductor must extend from each disconnecting means, sized no smaller than specified in Table 250.66, based on the area of the largest ungrounded conductor for each disconnecting means.

The grounding electrode tap conductors must be connected to the common grounding electrode conductor, without splicing the common grounding electrode conductor, by one of the following methods:

(1) Exothermic welding.

(2) Connectors listed as grounding and bonding equipment.

(3) Connections to a busbar of sufficient length and not less than ¼ in. thick × 2 in. wide that's securely fastened and installed in an accessible location.

(2) Individual Grounding Electrode Conductors. A grounding electrode conductor, sized in accordance with 250.66 based on the ungrounded conductor(s) supplying the individual disconnecting means, must be connected between the grounding electrode system and one or more of the following:

(1) The service neutral conductor, Figure 250–110

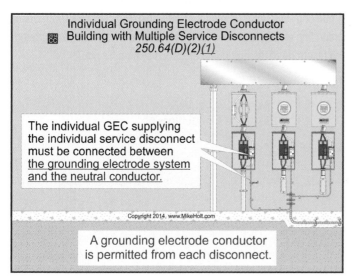

Figure 250–110

(2) The equipment grounding conductor of the feeder circuit,

(3) The supply-side bonding jumper.

(3) Common Grounding Electrode Conductor Location. A single grounding electrode conductor, sized not smaller than specified in Table 250.66, based on the area of the ungrounded conductor at the location, must connect the grounding electrode system to one or more of the following locations:

(1) The service neutral conductor, Figure 250–111

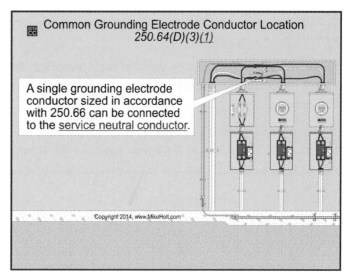

Figure 250–111

(2) The equipment grounding conductor of the feeder circuit,

(3) The supply-side bonding jumper.

(E) Ferrous Enclosures and Raceways Containing Grounding Electrode Conductor.

(1) General. To prevent inductive choking of grounding electrode conductors, ferrous raceways and enclosures containing grounding electrode conductors must have each end of the raceway or enclosure bonded to the grounding electrode or grounding electrode conductor. Figure 250–112

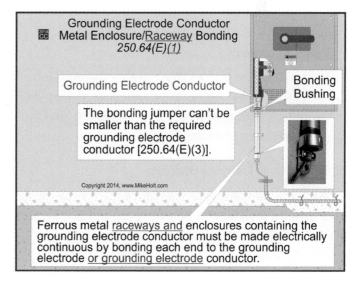

Figure 250–112

(2) Methods. Bonding must be done by one of the methods discussed in 250.92(B)(2) through (B)(4).

(3) Size. Bonding jumpers must be the same size or larger than the required size of the grounding electrode conductor in the raceway or other enclosure.

(4) Wiring Methods. When a raceway is used for a grounding electrode conductor, it must meet all of the requirements for the raceway, such as securing and supporting, number of bends, conductor fill, and so forth.

Author's Comment:

- Nonferrous metal raceways, such as aluminum rigid metal conduit, enclosing the grounding electrode conductor aren't required to meet the "bonding each end of the raceway to the grounding electrode conductor" provisions of this section.

⚠ **CAUTION:** *The effectiveness of a grounding electrode is significantly reduced if a ferrous metal raceway containing a grounding electrode conductor isn't bonded to the ferrous metal raceway at both ends. This is because a single conductor carrying high-frequency induced lightning current in a ferrous raceway causes the raceway to act as an inductor, which severely limits (chokes) the current flow through the grounding electrode conductor. ANSI/IEEE 142— Recommended Practice for Grounding of Industrial and Commercial Power Systems (Green Book) states: "An inductive choke can reduce the current flow by 97 percent."*

Author's Comment:

- To save a lot of time and effort, install the grounding electrode conductor exposed if it's not subject to physical damage [250.64(B)], or enclose it in nonmetallic conduit suitable for the application [352.10(F)].

(F) Termination to Grounding Electrode.

(1) Single Grounding Electrode Conductor. A single grounding electrode conductor is permitted to terminate to any grounding electrode of the grounding electrode system. Figure 250–113

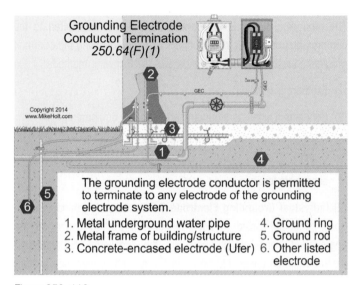

The grounding electrode conductor is permitted to terminate to any electrode of the grounding electrode system.
1. Metal underground water pipe
2. Metal frame of building/structure
3. Concrete-encased electrode (Ufer)
4. Ground ring
5. Ground rod
6. Other listed electrode

Figure 250–113

(2) Multiple Grounding Electrode Conductors. When multiple grounding electrode conductors are installed [250.64(D)(2)], each grounding electrode conductor is permitted to terminate to any grounding electrode of the grounding electrode system. Figure 250–114

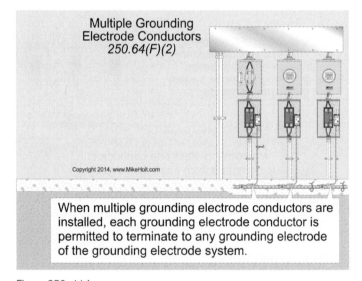

When multiple grounding electrode conductors are installed, each grounding electrode conductor is permitted to terminate to any grounding electrode of the grounding electrode system.

Figure 250–114

(3) Termination to Busbar. Grounding electrode conductors and grounding electrode bonding jumpers are permitted to terminate to a busbar sized not less than ¼ in. × 2 in. that's securely fastened at an accessible location. The terminations to the busbar must be made by a listed connector or by exothermic welding. Figure 250–115

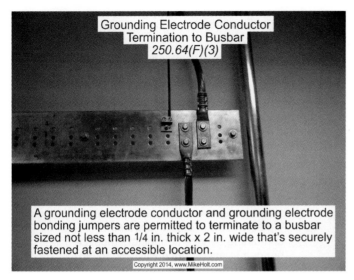

Figure 250–115

Essential Rule 33

250.66 Sizing Grounding Electrode Conductor

Except as permitted in (A) through (C), the grounding electrode conductor must be sized in accordance with Table 250.66.

(A) Rod. If the grounding electrode conductor is connected to one or more rods, as permitted in 250.52(A)(5), that portion of the grounding electrode conductor that's the sole connection to the rod(s) isn't required to be larger than 6 AWG copper. Figure 250–116

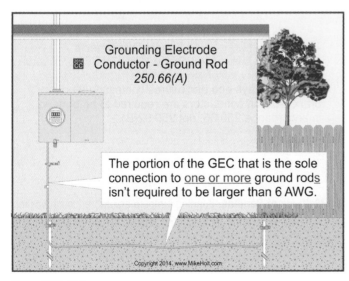

Figure 250–116

(B) Concrete-Encased Grounding Electrode. If the grounding electrode conductor is connected to one or more concrete-encased electrodes, as permitted in 250.52(A)(3), that portion of the grounding electrode conductor that's the sole connection to the concrete-encased electrode(s) isn't required to be larger than 4 AWG copper. Figure 250–117

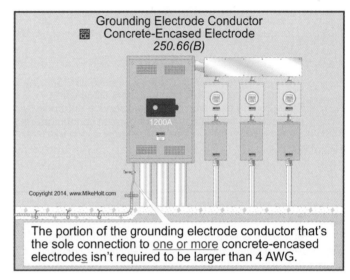

Figure 250–117

(C) Ground Ring. If the grounding electrode conductor is connected to a ground ring, the portion of the conductor that's the sole connection to the ground ring isn't required to be larger than the conductor used for the ground ring.

Author's Comment:

- A ground ring encircling the buildings in direct contact with the earth must consist of at least 20 ft of bare copper conductor not smaller than 2 AWG [250.52(A)(4)]. See 250.53(F) for the installation requirements for a ground ring.

- Table 250.66 is used to size the grounding electrode conductor when the conditions of 250.66(A), (B), or (C) don't apply. Figure 250–118

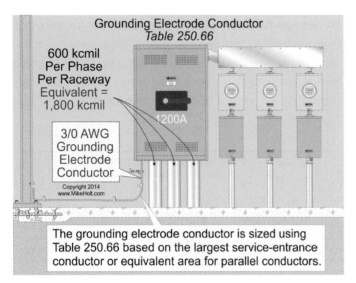

The grounding electrode conductor is sized using Table 250.66 based on the largest service-entrance conductor or equivalent area for parallel conductors.

Figure 250–118

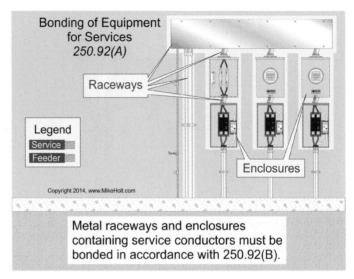

Metal raceways and enclosures containing service conductors must be bonded in accordance with 250.92(B).

Figure 250–119

Table 250.66 Sizing Grounding Electrode Conductor

Conductor or Area of Parallel Conductors	Copper Grounding Electrode Conductor
12 through 2 AWG	8 AWG
1 or 1/0 AWG	6 AWG
2/0 or 3/0 AWG	4 AWG
Over 3/0 through 350 kcmil	2 AWG
Over 350 through 600 kcmil	1/0 AWG
Over 600 through 1,100 kcmil	2/0 AWG
Over 1,100 kcmil	3/0 AWG

Part V. Bonding

Essential Rule 34

250.92 Bonding Equipment for Services

(A) Bonding Requirements for Equipment for Services. The metal parts of equipment indicated below must be bonded together in accordance with 250.92(B). Figure 250–119

(1) Metal raceways containing service conductors.

(2) Metal enclosures containing service conductors.

Author's Comment:

■ Metal raceways or metal enclosures containing feeder and branch-circuit conductors are required to be connected to the circuit equipment grounding conductor in accordance with 250.86. Figure 250–120

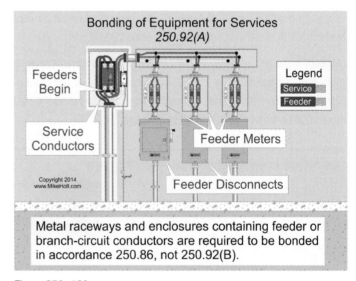

Metal raceways and enclosures containing feeder or branch-circuit conductors are required to be bonded in accordance 250.86, not 250.92(B).

Figure 250–120

(B) Methods of Bonding. Bonding jumpers around reducing washers or oversized, concentric, or eccentric knockouts are required. Figure 250–121

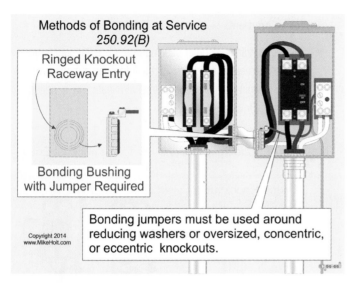

Methods of Bonding at Service
250.92(B)

Ringed Knockout Raceway Entry

Bonding Bushing with Jumper Required

Bonding jumpers must be used around reducing washers or oversized, concentric, or eccentric knockouts.

Copyright 2014
www.MikeHolt.com

Figure 250–121

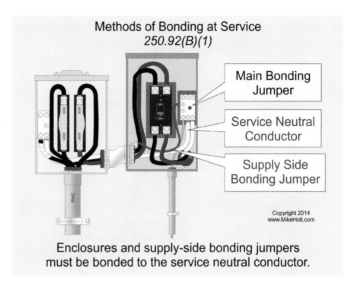

Methods of Bonding at Service
250.92(B)(1)

Main Bonding Jumper

Service Neutral Conductor

Supply Side Bonding Jumper

Copyright 2014
www.MikeHolt.com

Enclosures and supply-side bonding jumpers must be bonded to the service neutral conductor.

Figure 250–123

Standard locknuts are permitted to make a mechanical connection of the raceway(s), but they can't serve as the bonding means required by this section. Figure 250–122

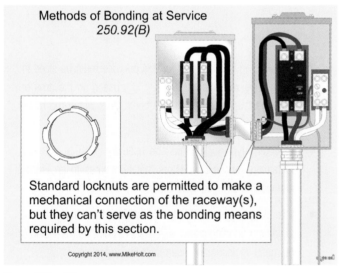

Methods of Bonding at Service
250.92(B)

Standard locknuts are permitted to make a mechanical connection of the raceway(s), but they can't serve as the bonding means required by this section.

Copyright 2014, www.MikeHolt.com

Figure 250–122

Electrical continuity at service equipment, service raceways, and service conductor enclosures must be ensured by one of the following methods:

(1) Bonding the metal parts to the service neutral conductor. Figure 250–123

Author's Comment:

■ A main bonding jumper is required to bond the service disconnect to the service neutral conductor [250.24(B) and 250.28].

■ At service equipment, the service neutral conductor provides the effective ground-fault current path to the power supply [250.24(C)]; therefore, an equipment grounding conductor isn't required to be installed within PVC conduit containing service-entrance conductors [250.142(A)(1) and 352.60 Ex 2]. Figure 250–124

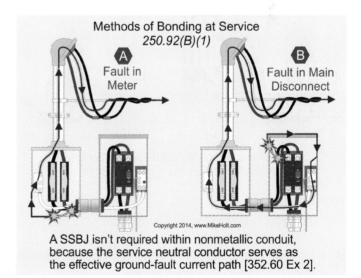

Methods of Bonding at Service
250.92(B)(1)

A — Fault in Meter

B — Fault in Main Disconnect

Copyright 2014, www.MikeHolt.com

A SSBJ isn't required within nonmetallic conduit, because the service neutral conductor serves as the effective ground-fault current path [352.60 Ex 2].

Figure 250–124

(2) Terminating metal raceways to metal enclosures by threaded hubs on enclosures if made up wrenchtight. Figure 250–125

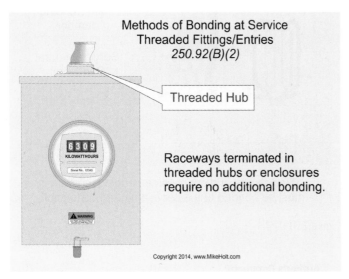

Figure 250–125

(3) Terminating metal raceways to metal enclosures by threadless fittings if made up tight. Figure 250–126

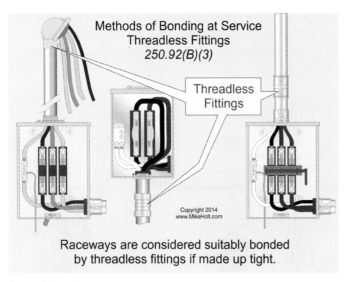

Figure 250–126

(4) Other listed devices, such as bonding-type locknuts, bushings, wedges, or bushings with bonding jumpers.

Author's Comment:

■ A listed bonding wedge or bushing with a bonding jumper to the service neutral conductor is required when a metal raceway containing service conductors terminates to a ringed knockout. Figure 250–127

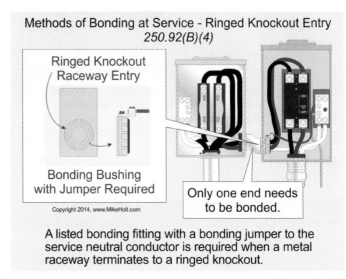

Figure 250–127

■ The bonding jumper used for this purpose must be sized in accordance with Table 250.102(C)(1), based on the area of the largest ungrounded service conductors within the raceway [250.102(C)].

■ A bonding-type locknut can be used for a metal raceway containing service conductors that terminates to an enclosure without a ringed knockout. Figure 250–128

■ A bonding locknut differs from a standard locknut in that it contains a bonding screw with a sharp point that drives into the metal enclosure to ensure a solid connection.

■ Bonding one end of a service raceway to the service neutral provides the low-impedance fault current path to the source. Figure 250–129

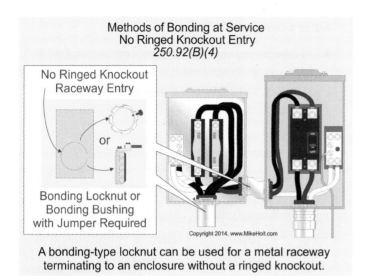

Methods of Bonding at Service
No Ringed Knockout Entry
250.92(B)(4)

No Ringed Knockout
Raceway Entry

or

Bonding Locknut or
Bonding Bushing
with Jumper Required

A bonding-type locknut can be used for a metal raceway
terminating to an enclosure without a ringed knockout.

Figure 250–128

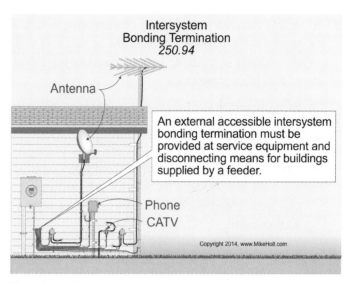

Intersystem
Bonding Termination
250.94

Antenna

An external accessible intersystem
bonding termination must be
provided at service equipment and
disconnecting means for buildings
supplied by a feeder.

Phone
CATV

Figure 250–130

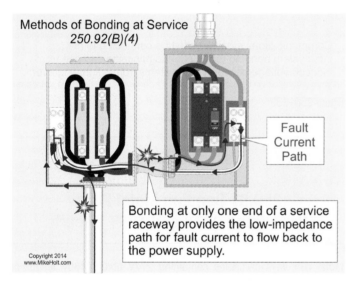

Methods of Bonding at Service
250.92(B)(4)

Fault
Current
Path

Bonding at only one end of a service
raceway provides the low-impedance
path for fault current to flow back to
the power supply.

Figure 250–129

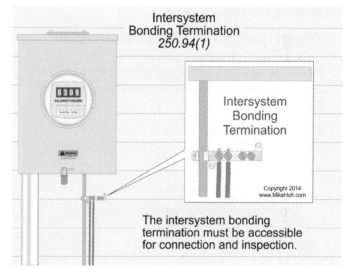

Intersystem
Bonding Termination
250.94(1)

Intersystem
Bonding
Termination

The intersystem bonding
termination must be accessible
for connection and inspection.

Figure 250–131

Essential Rule 35

250.94 Intersystem Bonding Termination

An external accessible intersystem bonding termination for the connection of communications systems bonding conductors must be
provided at service equipment and disconnecting means for buildings
supplied by a feeder. Figure 250–130

The intersystem bonding termination must:

(1) Be accessible for connection and inspection. Figure 250–131

(2) Consist of a set of terminals with the capacity for connection of not
less than three intersystem bonding conductors.

(3) Not interfere with opening the enclosure for a service, building disconnecting means, or metering equipment.

(4) Be securely mounted and electrically connected to service equipment, the meter enclosure, or exposed nonflexible metallic service
raceway, or be mounted at one of these enclosures and be connected to the enclosure or grounding electrode conductor with a
minimum 6 AWG copper conductor.

(5) Be securely mounted to the building's disconnecting means, or be mounted at the disconnecting means and be connected to the metallic enclosure or grounding electrode conductor with a minimum 6 AWG copper conductor.

(6) The terminals must be listed as grounding and bonding equipment.

Author's Comment:

- According to Article 100, an intersystem bonding termination is a device that provides a means to connect communications systems bonding conductors to the building grounding electrode system.

Ex: At existing buildings, an external accessible means for bonding communications systems together can be by the use of a:

(1) Nonflexible metallic raceway,

(2) Grounding electrode conductor, or

(3) Connection approved by the authority having jurisdiction.

Note 2: Communications systems must be bonded to the intersystem bonding termination in accordance with the following requirements: Figure 250–132

- Antennas/Satellite Dishes, 810.15 and 810.21
- CATV, 820.100
- Telephone Circuits, 800.100

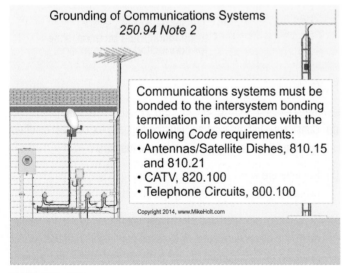

Figure 250–132

Author's Comment:

- All external communications systems must be connected to the intersystem bonding termination to minimize the damage to them from induced potential (voltage) differences between the systems from a lightning event. Figure 250–133

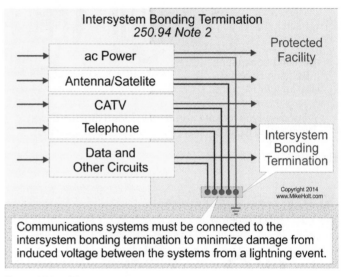

Figure 250–133

Essential Rule 36

250.97 Bonding Metal Parts Containing 277V and 480V Circuits

Metal raceways or cables containing 277V and/or 480V feeder or branch circuits terminating at ringed knockouts must be bonded to the metal enclosure with a bonding jumper sized in accordance with 250.122, based on the rating of the circuit overcurrent device [250.102(D)]. Figure 250–134

Author's Comment:

- Bonding jumpers for raceways and cables containing 277V or 480V circuits are required at ringed knockout terminations to ensure the ground-fault current path has the capacity to safely conduct the maximum ground-fault current likely to be imposed [110.10, 250.4(A)(5), and 250.96(A)].

- Ringed knockouts aren't listed to withstand the heat generated by a 277V ground fault, which generates five times as much heat as a 120V ground fault. Figure 250–135

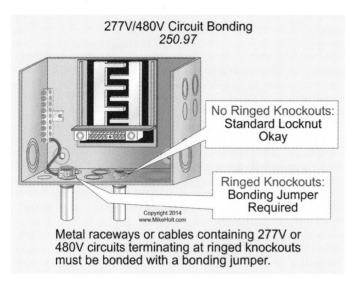

Figure 250–134

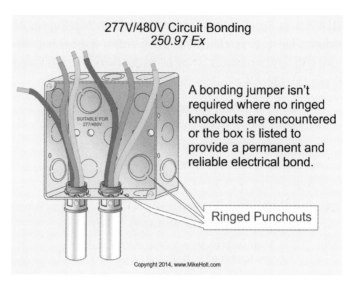

Figure 250–136

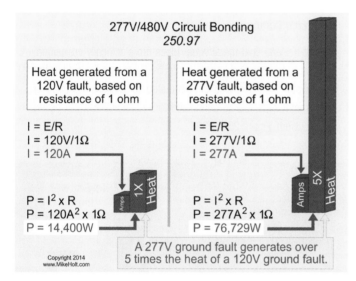

Figure 250–135

Ex: A bonding jumper isn't required where ringed knockouts aren't encountered, knockouts are totally punched out, or where the box is listed to provide a reliable bonding connection. Figure 250–136

Essential Rule 37

250.104 Bonding of Piping Systems and Exposed Structural Metal

Author's Comment:

- To remove dangerous voltage on metal parts from a ground fault, electrically conductive metal water piping systems, metal sprinkler piping, metal gas piping, as well as exposed structural metal members likely to become energized, must be connected to an effective ground-fault current path [250.4(A)(4)].

(A) Metal Water Piping System. Metal water piping systems that are interconnected to form a mechanically and electrically continuous system must be bonded in accordance with 250.104(A)(1), (A)(2), or (A)(3). The bonding jumper must be copper where within 18 in. of the earth [250.64(A)], securely fastened to the surface on which it's mounted [250.64(B)], and adequately protected if exposed to physical damage [250.64(B)]. In addition, all points of attachment must be accessible, except as permitted in 250.68(A) Ex.

(1) Buildings Supplied by a Service. The metal water piping system, including the metal sprinkler water piping system of a building, supplied with service conductors must be bonded to one of the following: Figure 250–137

- Service equipment enclosure,
- Service neutral conductor,
- Grounding electrode conductor of sufficient size, or
- Grounding electrode system.

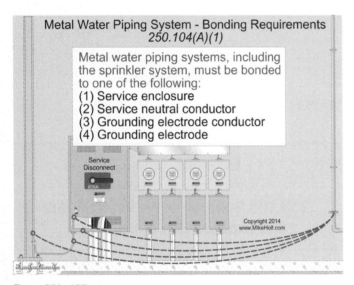

Figure 250–137

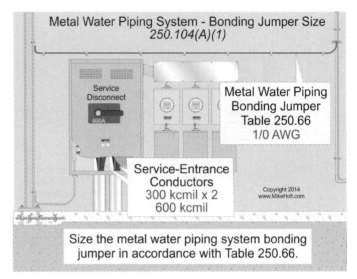

Figure 250–138

The metal water piping system bonding jumper must be sized in accordance with Table 250.66, based on the cross-sectional area of the ungrounded service conductors.

> **Question:** What size bonding jumper is required for a metal water piping system, if the 300 kcmil service conductors are paralleled in two raceways? Figure 250–138
>
> (a) 6 AWG (b) 4 AWG (c) 2 AWG (d) 1/0 AWG
>
> **Answer:** (d) 1/0 AWG, based on 600 kcmil conductors, in accordance with Table 250.66.

Author's Comment:

- If hot and cold metal water pipes are electrically connected, only one bonding jumper is required, either to the cold or hot water pipe. Bonding isn't required for isolated sections of metal water piping connected to a nonmetallic water piping system. Figure 250–139

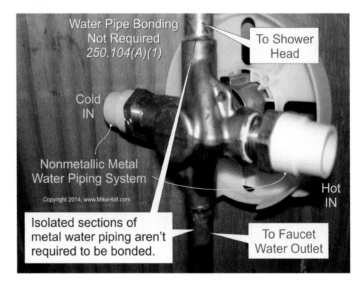

Figure 250–139

(2) Multiple Occupancy Building. When a metal water piping system in an individual occupancy is metallically isolated from other occupancies, the metal water piping system for that occupancy can be bonded to the equipment grounding terminal of the occupancy's <u>switchgear,</u> switchboard, <u>or panelboard</u>. The bonding jumper must be sized in accordance with Table 250.122, based on the ampere rating of the occupancy's feeder overcurrent device. Figure 250–140

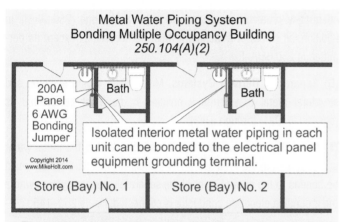

**Metal Water Piping System
Bonding Multiple Occupancy Building
250.104(A)(2)**

200A Panel 6 AWG Bonding Jumper

Bath

Bath

Isolated interior metal water piping in each unit can be bonded to the electrical panel equipment grounding terminal.

Copyright 2014 www.MikeHolt.com

Store (Bay) No. 1

Store (Bay) No. 2

The metal water piping system bonding jumper is sized using Table 250.122 based on the ampere rating of the occupancy's feeder overcurrent device.

Figure 250–140

(3) Buildings Supplied by a Feeder. The metal water piping system of a building supplied by a feeder must be bonded to one of the following:

- The equipment grounding terminal of the building disconnect enclosure,
- The feeder equipment grounding conductor, or
- The grounding electrode system.

The bonding jumper is sized to Table 250.66, based on the cross-sectional area of the ungrounded feeder conductor.

(B) Other Metal-Piping Systems. Metal-piping systems such as gas or air that are likely to become energized are permitted to be bonded to the equipment grounding conductor for the circuit that's likely to energize the piping. Figure 250–141

Note 1: Bonding all piping and metal air ducts within the premises will provide additional safety. Figure 250–142

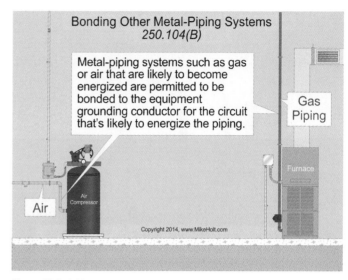

**Bonding Other Metal-Piping Systems
250.104(B)**

Metal-piping systems such as gas or air that are likely to become energized are permitted to be bonded to the equipment grounding conductor for the circuit that's likely to energize the piping.

Gas Piping

Furnace

Air

Air Compressor

Copyright 2014, www.MikeHolt.com

Figure 250–141

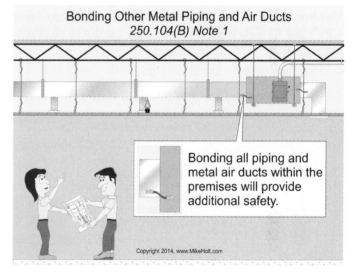

**Bonding Other Metal Piping and Air Ducts
250.104(B) Note 1**

Bonding all piping and metal air ducts within the premises will provide additional safety.

Copyright 2014, www.MikeHolt.com

Figure 250–142

Note 2: The *National Fuel Gas Code*, NFPA 54, Section 7.13 contains further information about bonding gas piping. Figure 250–143

Author's Comment

- Informational Notes in the *NEC* are for information purposes only and aren't enforceable as a requirement of the *Code* [90.5(C)].

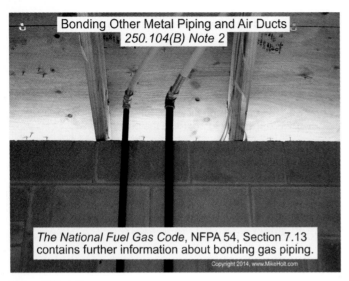

Figure 250–143

(C) Structural Metal. An exposed metal structural building frame that's likely to become energized must be bonded to the: Figure 250–144

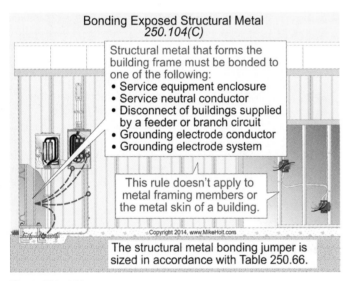

Figure 250–144

- Service equipment enclosure,
- Service neutral conductor,
- Building disconnecting means for buildings supplied by a feeder,
- Grounding electrode conductor if of sufficient size, or
- Grounding electrode system.

Author's Comment:

- This rule doesn't require the bonding of sheet metal framing members (studs) or the metal skin of a wood-frame building.

The bonding jumper must be sized in accordance with Table 250.66, based on the area of the ungrounded supply conductors. The bonding jumper must be copper where within 18 in. of the earth [250.64(A)], securely fastened to the surface on which it's carried [250.64(B)], and adequately protected if exposed to physical damage [250.64(B)]. In addition, all points of attachment must be accessible, except as permitted in 250.68(A) Ex.

(D) Separately Derived Systems. Metal water piping systems and structural metal that forms a building frame must be bonded as required in (D)(1) through (D)(3).

(1) Metal Water Pipe. The nearest available point of the metal water piping system in the area served by a separately derived system must be bonded to the neutral point of the separately derived system where the grounding electrode conductor is connected. Figure 250–145

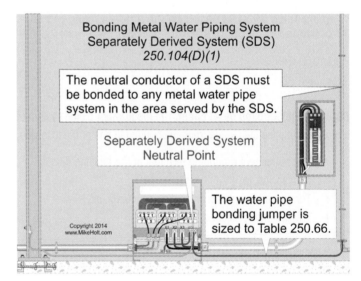

Figure 250–145

The bonding jumper must be sized in accordance with Table 250.66, based on the area of the ungrounded conductor of the derived system.

Ex 2: The metal water piping system is permitted to be bonded to the structural metal building frame if it serves as the grounding electrode [250.52(A)(1)] for the separately derived system. Figure 250–146

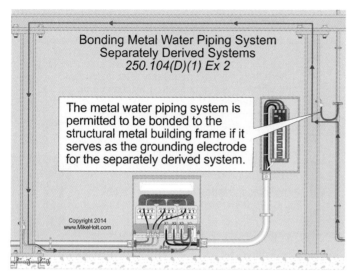

Figure 250–146

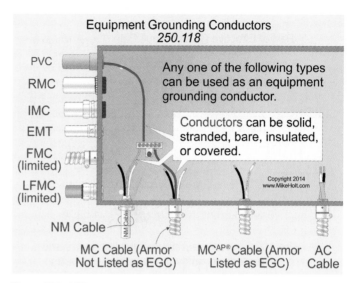

Figure 250–147

(2) Structural Metal. Exposed structural metal interconnected to form the building frame must be bonded to the neutral point of each separately derived system where the grounding electrode conductor is connected.

The bonding jumper must be sized in accordance with Table 250.66, based on the area of the ungrounded conductors of the derived system.

Ex 1: Bonding to the separately derived system isn't required if the metal structural frame serves as the grounding electrode [250.52(A)(2)] for the separately derived system.

Part VI. Equipment Grounding and Equipment Grounding Conductors

Essential Rule 38

250.118 Types of Equipment Grounding Conductors

An equipment grounding conductor can be any one or a combination of the following: Figure 250–147

Note: The equipment grounding conductor is intended to serve as part of the effective ground-fault current path. See 250.2. Figure 250–148

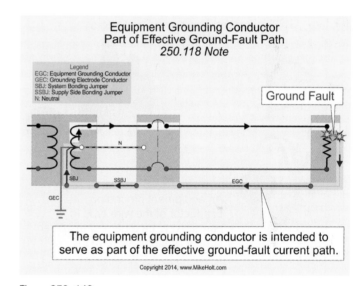

Figure 250–148

Author's Comment:

■ The effective ground-fault path is an intentionally constructed low-impedance conductive path designed to carry fault current from the point of a ground fault on a wiring system to the electrical supply source. Its purpose is to quickly remove dangerous voltage from a ground fault by opening the circuit overcurrent device [250.2]. Figure 250–149

(1) An equipment grounding conductor of the wire type is permitted to be bare or insulated copper or aluminum conductor. Figure 250–150

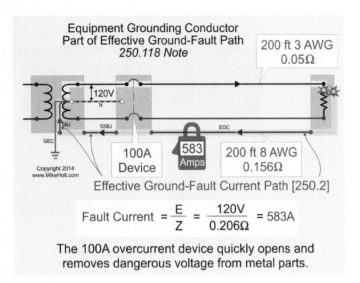

Figure 250–149

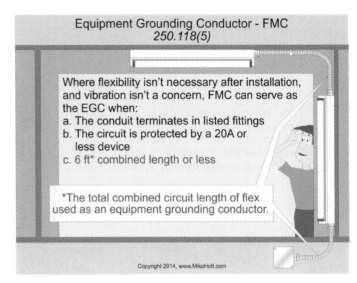

Figure 250–151

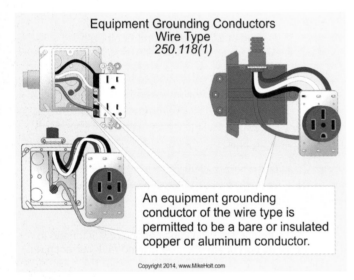

Figure 250–150

(2) Rigid metal conduit (RMC) can serve as an equipment grounding conductor.

(3) Intermediate metal conduit (IMC) can serve as an equipment grounding conductor.

(4) Electrical metallic tubing (EMT) can serve as an equipment grounding conductor.

(5) Listed flexible metal conduit (FMC) can serve as an equipment grounding conductor where: Figure 250–151

a. The raceway terminates in listed fittings.

b. The circuit conductors are protected by an overcurrent device rated 20A or less.

c. The combined length of the flexible conduit in the same ground-fault current path doesn't exceed 6 ft.

d. If flexibility is required to minimize the transmission of vibration from equipment or to provide flexibility for equipment that requires movement after installation, an equipment grounding conductor of the wire type must be installed with the circuit conductors in accordance with 250.102(E), and it must be sized in accordance with 250.122, based on the rating of the circuit overcurrent device. Figure 250–152

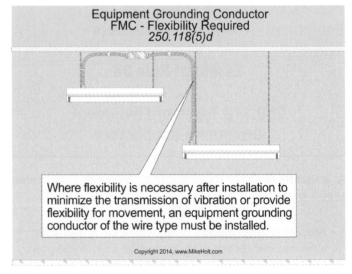

Figure 250–152

(6) Listed liquidtight flexible metal conduit (LFMC) can serve as an equipment grounding conductor where: Figure 250–153

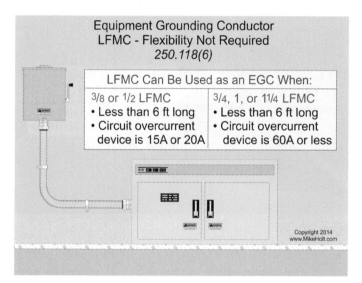

Figure 250–153

a. The raceway terminates in listed fittings.

b. For ⅜ in. through ½ in., the circuit conductors are protected by an overcurrent device rated 20A or less.

c. For ¾ in. through 1¼ in., the circuit conductors are protected by an overcurrent device rated 60A or less.

d. The combined length of the flexible conduit in the same ground-fault current path doesn't exceed 6 ft.

e. If flexibility is required to minimize the transmission of vibration from equipment or to provide flexibility for equipment that requires movement after installation, an equipment grounding conductor of the wire type must be installed with the circuit conductors in accordance with 250.102(E), and it must be sized in accordance with 250.122, based on the rating of the circuit overcurrent device.

(8) The sheath of Type AC cable containing an aluminum bonding strip can serve as an equipment grounding conductor. Figure 250–154

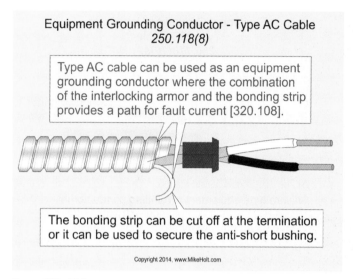

Figure 250–154

Author's Comment:

■ The internal aluminum bonding strip isn't an equipment grounding conductor, but it allows the interlocked armor to serve as an equipment grounding conductor because it reduces the impedance of the armored spirals to ensure that a ground fault will be cleared. It's the aluminum bonding strip in combination with the cable armor that creates the circuit equipment grounding conductor. Once the bonding strip exits the cable, it can be cut off because it no longer serves any purpose.

■ The effective ground-fault current path must be maintained by the use of fittings specifically listed for Type AC cable [320.40]. See 300.12, 300.15, and 320.100.

(9) The copper sheath of Type MI cable can serve as an equipment grounding conductor.

(10) Type MC cable

a. The interlock type cable contains an insulated or uninsulated equipment grounding conductor in compliance with 250.118(1) can serve as an equipment grounding conductor. Figure 250–155

b. The combined metallic sheath and uninsulated equipment grounding/bonding conductor of interlocked metal is listed and identified as an equipment grounding conductor can serve as an equipment grounding conductor. Figure 250–156

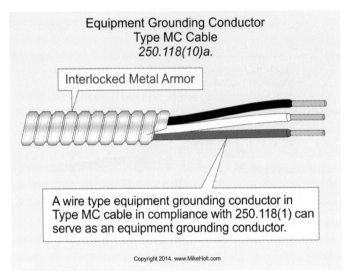

Figure 250–155

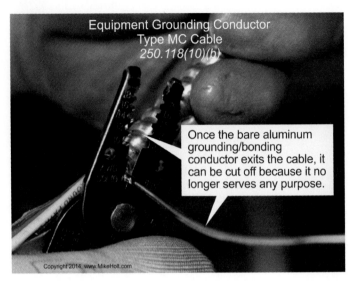

Figure 250–157

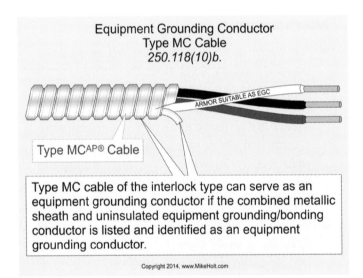

Figure 250–156

Author's Comment:

■ Once the bare aluminum grounding/bonding conductor exits the cable, it can be cut off because it no longer serves any purpose. The effective ground-fault current path must be maintained by the use of fittings specifically listed for Type MC^AP® cable [330.40]. See 300.12, 300.15, and 330.100. Figure 250–157

c. The metallic sheath of the smooth or corrugated tube-type MC cable that's listed and identified as an equipment grounding conductor can serve as an equipment grounding conductor.

(11) Metallic cable trays can serve as an equipment grounding conductor where continuous maintenance and supervision ensure only qualified persons will service the cable tray, with cable tray and fittings identified for grounding and the cable tray, fittings [392.10], and raceways are bonded using bolted mechanical connectors or bonding jumpers sized and installed in accordance with 250.102 [392.60]. Figure 250–158

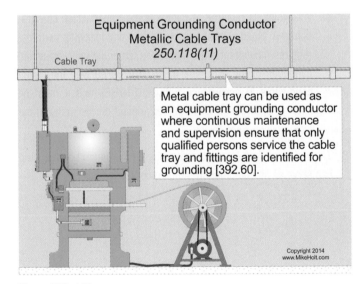

Figure 250–158

(13) Listed electrically continuous metal raceways, such as metal wireways [Article 376] or strut-type channel raceways [384.60] can serve as an equipment grounding conductor.

(14) Surface metal raceways listed for grounding [Article 386] can serve as an equipment grounding conductor.

Essential Rule 39

250.122 Sizing Equipment Grounding Conductor

(A) General. Equipment grounding conductors of the wire type must be sized not smaller than shown in Table 250.122, based on the rating of the circuit overcurrent device; however, the circuit equipment grounding conductor isn't required to be larger than the circuit conductors. Figure 250–159

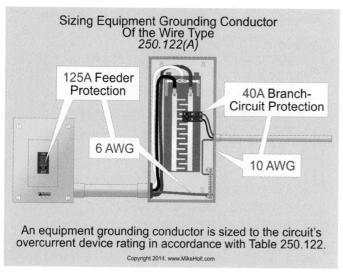

Figure 250–159

(B) Increased in Size. If ungrounded conductors are increased in size from the minimum ampacity that'd be required for the load, wire type equipment grounding conductors must be proportionately increased in size according to the circular mil area of the ungrounded conductors.

Table 250.122 Sizing Equipment Grounding Conductor	
Overcurrent Device Rating	**Copper Conductor**
15A	14 AWG
20A	12 AWG
25A—60A	10 AWG
70A—100A	8 AWG
110A—200A	6 AWG
225A—300A	4 AWG
350A—400A	3 AWG
450A—500A	2 AWG
600A	1 AWG
700A—800A	1/0 AWG
1,000A	2/0 AWG
1,200A	3/0 AWG

Author's Comment:

■ Ungrounded conductors are sometimes increased in size to accommodate conductor voltage drop, harmonic current heating, short-circuit rating, or simply for future capacity.

Question: If the ungrounded conductors for a 40A circuit (with 75°C terminals) are increased in size from 8 AWG to 6 AWG due to voltage drop, the circuit equipment grounding conductor must be increased in size from 10 AWG to _____. Figure 250–160

(a) 10 AWG   (b) 8 AWG   (c) 6 AWG   (d) 4 AWG

Answer: (b) 8 AWG

The circular mil area of 6 AWG is 59 percent more than 8 AWG (26,240 Cmil/16,510 Cmil) [Chapter 9, Table 8].

According to Table 250.122, the circuit equipment grounding conductor for a 40A overcurrent device will be 10 AWG (10,380 Cmil), but the circuit equipment grounding conductor for this circuit must be increased in size by a multiplier of 1.59.

Conductor Size = 10,380 Cmil x 1.59
Conductor Size = 16,504 Cmil
Conductor Size = 8 AWG, Chapter 9, Table 8

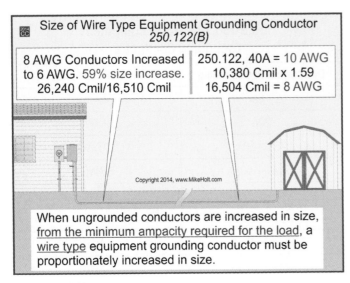

Figure 250–160

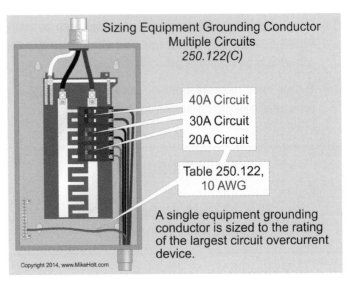

Figure 250–161

Question: *If the ungrounded conductors for a 40A circuit (with 60°C terminals) are increased in size from 8 AWG to 6 AWG due to having four current-carrying conductors in a raceway, the circuit equipment grounding conductor must be increased in size from 10 AWG to _____.*

(a) An increase isn't required   *(b) 8 AWG*
(c) 6 AWG   *(d) 4 AWG*

Answer: *(a) An increase isn't required*

The equipment grounding conductor doesn't need to be increased in size in this example, because the 6 AWG is the smallest size ungrounded conductor allowed by the Code.

8 AWG rated 40A at 60°C x 0.80 = 32A after adjustment factors is too small for the circuit example. 6 AWG rated 55A at 60°C, is required (55A x 0.80 = 44A).

(C) Multiple Circuits. When multiple circuits are installed in the same raceway, cable, or cable tray, one equipment grounding conductor sized in accordance with 250.122, based on the rating of the largest circuit overcurrent device is sufficient. Figure 250–161

(D) Motor Branch Circuits.

(1) General. The equipment grounding conductor of the wire type must be sized in accordance with Table 250.122, based on the rating of the motor circuit branch-circuit short-circuit and ground-fault overcurrent device, but this conductor isn't required to be larger than the circuit conductors [250.122(A)].

Question: *What size equipment grounding conductor is required for a 2 hp, 230V, single-phase motor?* Figure 250–162

(a) 14 AWG   *(b) 12 AWG*   *(c) 10 AWG*   *(d) 8 AWG*

Answer: *(a) 14 AWG*

Step 1: *Determine the branch-circuit conductor size [430.22(A) and Table 310.15(B)(16)]*

2 hp, 230V Motor FLC = 12A [Table 430.248]

12A x 1.25 = 15A, 14 AWG, rated 20A at 75°C [Table 310.15(B)(16)]

Step 2: *Determine the branch-circuit protection [240.6(A), 430.52(C)(1), and Table 430.248]*

12A x 2.50 = 30A

Step 3: *The circuit equipment grounding conductor must be sized to the 30A overcurrent device—10 AWG [Table 250.122], but it's not required to be sized larger than the circuit conductors—14 AWG.*

(F) Parallel Runs. If circuit conductors are installed in parallel in separate raceways or cable as permitted by 310.10(H), an equipment grounding conductor must be installed for each parallel conductor set. The equipment grounding conductor in each raceway or cable must be sized in accordance with Table 250.122, based on the rating of the circuit overcurrent device, but it's not required to be larger than the circuit conductors [250.122(A)]. Figure 250–163

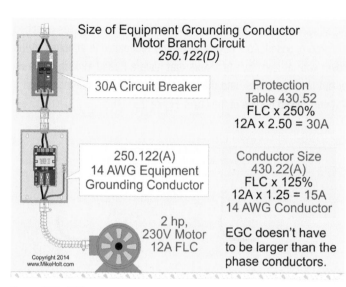

Size of Equipment Grounding Conductor
Motor Branch Circuit
250.122(D)

30A Circuit Breaker

Protection
Table 430.52
FLC x 250%
12A x 2.50 = 30A

250.122(A)
14 AWG Equipment
Grounding Conductor

Conductor Size
430.22(A)
FLC x 125%
12A x 1.25 = 15A
14 AWG Conductor

2 hp,
230V Motor
12A FLC

EGC doesn't have
to be larger than the
phase conductors.

Copyright 2014
www.MikeHolt.com

Figure 250–162

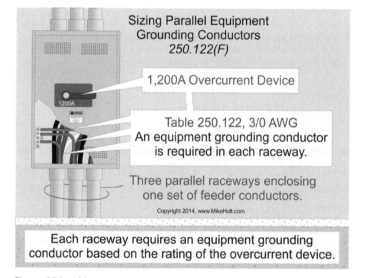

Sizing Parallel Equipment
Grounding Conductors
250.122(F)

1,200A Overcurrent Device

Table 250.122, 3/0 AWG
An equipment grounding conductor
is required in each raceway.

Three parallel raceways enclosing
one set of feeder conductors.

Copyright 2014, www.MikeHolt.com

Each raceway requires an equipment grounding
conductor based on the rating of the overcurrent device.

Figure 250–163

(G) Feeder Tap Conductors. Equipment grounding conductors for feeder taps must be sized in accordance with Table 250.122, based on the ampere rating of the overcurrent device ahead of the feeder, but in no case is it required to be larger than the feeder tap conductors. Figure 250–164

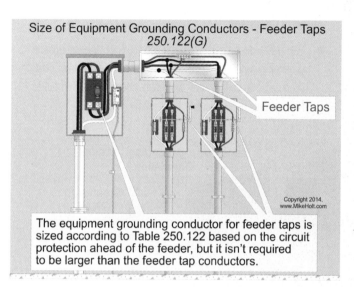

Size of Equipment Grounding Conductors - Feeder Taps
250.122(G)

Feeder Taps

Copyright 2014,
www.MikeHolt.com

The equipment grounding conductor for feeder taps is
sized according to Table 250.122 based on the circuit
protection ahead of the feeder, but it isn't required
to be larger than the feeder tap conductors.

Figure 250–164

Part VII. Methods of Equipment Grounding

Essential Rule 40

250.146 Connecting Receptacle Grounding Terminal to Metal Enclosure

Except as permitted for (A) through (D), an equipment bonding jumper sized in accordance with 250.122, based on the rating of the circuit overcurrent device, must connect the grounding terminal of a receptacle to a metal box. Figure 250–165

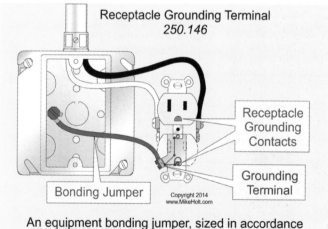

Receptacle Grounding Terminal
250.146

Receptacle
Grounding
Contacts

Grounding
Terminal

Bonding Jumper

Copyright 2014
www.MikeHolt.com

An equipment bonding jumper, sized in accordance
with 250.122, must connect the grounding terminal
of the receptacle to the metal box.

Figure 250–165

Author's Comment:

- The *NEC* doesn't restrict the position of the receptacle grounding terminal; it can be up, down, or sideways. *Code* proposals to specify the mounting position of receptacles have always been rejected. Figure 250–166

An equipment bonding jumper isn't required for receptacles attached to listed exposed work covers when the receptacle is attached to the cover with at least two fasteners that have a thread locking or screw or nut locking means, and the cover mounting holes are located on a flat non-raised portion of the cover. Figure 250–168

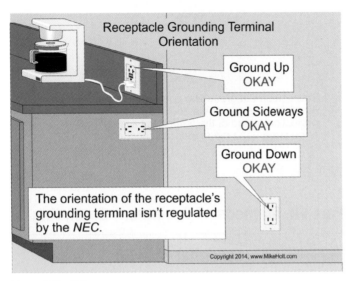

Figure 250–166

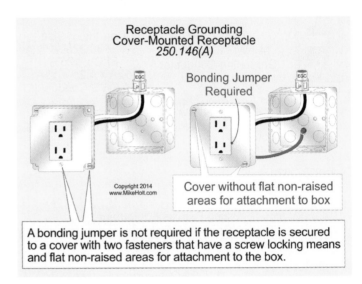

Figure 250–168

(A) Surface-Mounted Box. An equipment bonding jumper from a receptacle to a metal box that's surface mounted isn't required if there's direct metal-to-metal contact between the device yoke and the metal box. To ensure a suitable bonding path between the device yoke and a metal box, at least one of the insulating retaining washers on the yoke screw must be removed. Figure 250–167

(B) Self-Grounding Receptacles. Receptacle yokes listed as self-grounding are designed to establish the equipment bonding between the device yoke and a metal box via the metal mounting screws. Figure 250–169

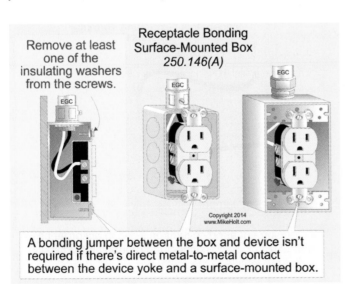

Figure 250–167

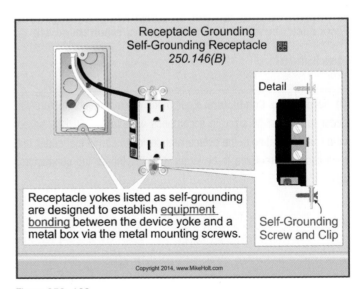

Figure 250–169

(C) Floor Boxes. Listed floor boxes are designed to establish the bonding path between the device yoke and a metal box.

(D) Isolated Ground Receptacles. The grounding terminal of an isolated ground receptacle must be connected to an insulated equipment grounding conductor run with the circuit conductors. Figure 250–170

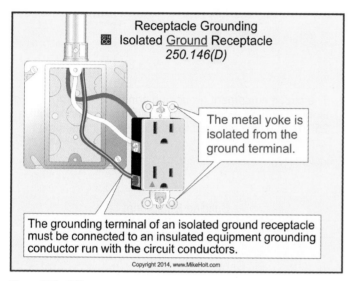

Figure 250–170

The circuit equipment grounding conductor is permitted to pass through panelboards [408.40 Ex], boxes, wireways, or other enclosures without a connection to the enclosure [250.148 Ex].

⚠ **CAUTION:** *Type AC Cable—Type AC cable containing an insulated equipment grounding conductor of the wire type can be used to supply receptacles having insulated grounding terminals because the metal armor of the cable is listed as an equipment grounding conductor [250.118(8)].* Figure 250–171

Type MC Cable—The metal armor sheath of interlocked Type MC cable containing an insulated equipment grounding conductor isn't listed as an equipment grounding conductor. Therefore, this wiring method with a single equipment grounding conductor can't supply an isolated ground receptacle installed in a metal box (because the box isn't connected to an equipment grounding conductor). However, Type MC cable with two insulated equipment grounding conductors is acceptable, since one equipment grounding conductor connects to the metal box and the other to the isolated ground receptacle. See Figure 250–171

The armor assembly of interlocked Type MC$^{AP®}$ cable with a 10 AWG bare aluminum grounding/bonding conductor running just below the metal armor is listed to serve as an equipment grounding conductor in accordance with 250.118(10)(b).

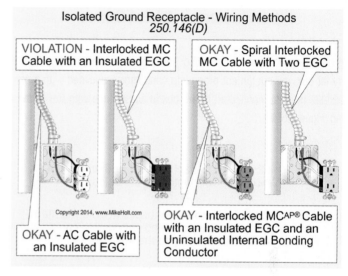

Figure 250–171

Author's Comment:

■ When should an isolated ground receptacle be installed and how should the isolated ground system be designed? These questions are design issues and must not be answered based on the *NEC* alone [90.1(A)]. In most cases, using isolated ground receptacles is a waste of money. For example, IEEE 1100—*Powering and Grounding Electronic Equipment* (Emerald Book) states: "The results from the use of the isolated ground method range from no observable effects, the desired effects, or worse noise conditions than when standard equipment bonding configurations are used to serve electronic load equipment [8.5.3.2]."

■ In reality, few electrical installations truly require an isolated ground system. For those systems that can benefit from an isolated ground system, engineering opinions differ as to what's a proper design. Making matters worse—of those properly designed, few are correctly installed and even fewer are properly maintained. For more information on how to properly ground electronic equipment, go to: www.MikeHolt. com, click on the "Technical" link, and then visit the "Power Quality" page.

Essential Rule 41

250.148 Continuity and Attachment of Equipment Grounding Conductors in Metal Boxes

If circuit conductors are spliced or terminated on equipment within a metal box, the equipment grounding conductor associated with those circuits must be connected to the box in accordance with the following: Figure 250–172

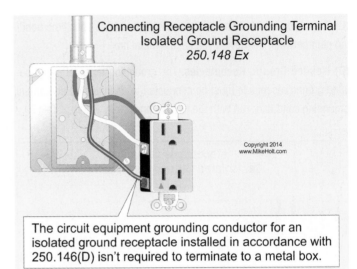

Connecting Receptacle Grounding Terminal
Isolated Ground Receptacle
250.148 Ex

The circuit equipment grounding conductor for an isolated ground receptacle installed in accordance with 250.146(D) isn't required to terminate to a metal box.

Figure 250–173

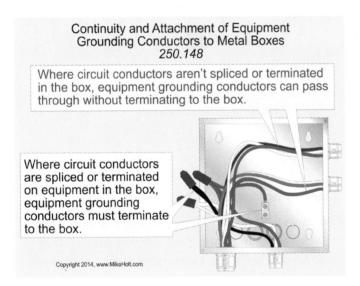

Continuity and Attachment of Equipment
Grounding Conductors to Metal Boxes
250.148

Where circuit conductors aren't spliced or terminated in the box, equipment grounding conductors can pass through without terminating to the box.

Where circuit conductors are spliced or terminated on equipment in the box, equipment grounding conductors must terminate to the box.

Copyright 2014, www.MikeHolt.com

Figure 250–172

Ex: The circuit equipment grounding conductor for an isolated ground receptacle installed in accordance with 250.146(D) isn't required to terminate to a metal box. Figure 250–173

(A) Splicing. Equipment grounding conductors must be spliced together with a device listed for the purpose [110.14(B)]. Figure 250–174

Author's Comment:

■ Wire connectors of any color can be used with equipment grounding conductor splices, but green wire connectors can only be used with equipment grounding conductors since they're only tested for that application.

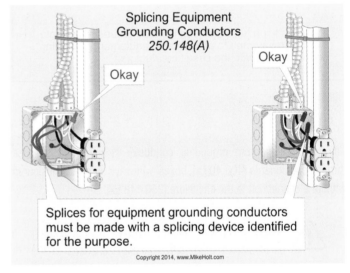

Splicing Equipment
Grounding Conductors
250.148(A)

Okay

Okay

Splices for equipment grounding conductors must be made with a splicing device identified for the purpose.

Copyright 2014, www.MikeHolt.com

Figure 250–174

(B) Grounding Continuity. Equipment grounding conductors must terminate in a manner such that the disconnection or the removal of a receptacle, luminaire, or other device won't interrupt the grounding continuity. Figure 250–175

(C) Metal Boxes. Terminating equipment grounding conductors within metal boxes must be with a grounding screw that's not used for any other purpose, a fitting listed for grounding, or a listed grounding device such as a ground clip. Figure 250–176

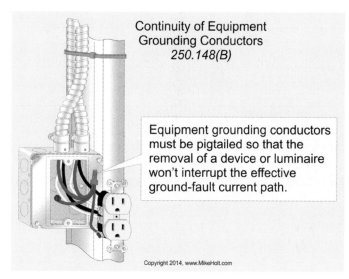

Continuity of Equipment Grounding Conductors
250.148(B)

Equipment grounding conductors must be pigtailed so that the removal of a device or luminaire won't interrupt the effective ground-fault current path.

Copyright 2014, www.MikeHolt.com

Figure 250–175

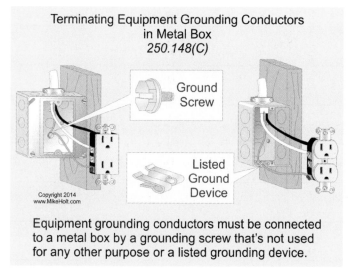

Terminating Equipment Grounding Conductors in Metal Box
250.148(C)

Ground Screw

Listed Ground Device

Copyright 2014 www.MikeHolt.com

Equipment grounding conductors must be connected to a metal box by a grounding screw that's not used for any other purpose or a listed grounding device.

Figure 250–176

Author's Comment:

■ Equipment grounding conductors aren't permitted to terminate to a screw that secures a plaster ring. Figure 250–177

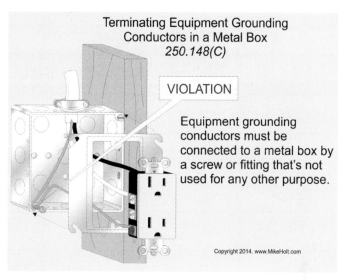

Terminating Equipment Grounding Conductors in a Metal Box
250.148(C)

VIOLATION

Equipment grounding conductors must be connected to a metal box by a screw or fitting that's not used for any other purpose.

Copyright 2014, www.MikeHolt.com

Figure 250–177

Notes

Mike Holt's Illustrated Guide to Essential Rules of the 2014 National Electrical Code

ARTICLE 300

GENERAL REQUIREMENTS FOR WIRING METHODS AND MATERIALS

Introduction to Article 300—General Requirements for Wiring Methods and Materials

Article 300 contains the general requirements for all wiring methods included in the *NEC*. However, the article doesn't apply to communications systems, which are covered in Chapter 8, except when Article 300 is specifically referenced in Chapter 8.

This article is primarily concerned with how to install, route, splice, protect, and secure conductors and raceways. How well you conform to the requirements of Article 300 will generally be evident in the finished work, because many of the requirements tend to determine the appearance of the installation. Because of this, it's often easy to spot Article 300 problems if you're looking for *Code* violations. For example, you can easily see when someone runs an equipment grounding conductor outside a raceway instead of grouping all conductors of a circuit together, as required by 300.3(B).

A good understanding of Article 300 will start you on the path to correctly installing the wiring methods included in Chapter 3. Be sure to carefully consider the accompanying illustrations, and refer to the definitions in Article 100 as needed.

Part I. General

Essential Rule 42

300.5 Underground Installations

(A) Minimum Burial Depths. When cables or raceways are installed underground, they must have a minimum "cover" in accordance with Table 300.5. Figure 300–1

Author's Comment:

- The cover requirements contained in 300.5 don't apply to signaling, communications, and other power-limited wiring systems: Figure 300–2

  □ CATV, 90.3

  □ Class 2 and 3 Circuits, 725.3

  □ Communications Cables and Raceways, 90.3

  □ Fire Alarm Circuits, 760.3

  □ Optical Fiber Cables and Raceways, 770.3

Underground Installations - Minimum Cover Depths
Table 300.5

	UF or USE Cables or Conductors	RMC or IMC	PVC not Encased in Concrete	Residential 15A & 20A GFCI 120V Branch Ckts
Street Driveway Parking Lot	24 in.	24 in.	24 in.	24 in.
Driveways One - Two Family	18 in.	18 in.	18 in.	12 in.
Solid Rock With not Less than 2 in. of Concrete	Raceway Only			Raceway Only
Other Applications	24 in.	6 in.	18 in.	12 in.

Copyright 2014, www.MikeHolt.com

Figure 300–1

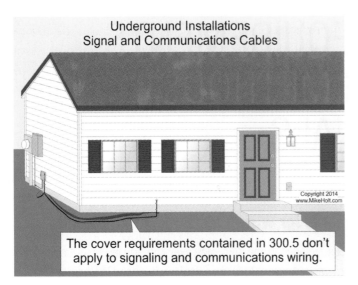

Figure 300–2

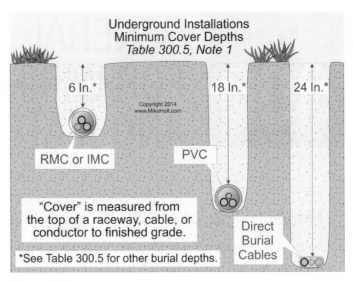

Figure 300–3

Table 300.5 Minimum Cover Requirements in Inches

Location	Buried Cables	Metal Raceway	Nonmetallic Raceway
Under Building	0	0	0
Dwelling Unit	24/12*	6	18
Dwelling Unit Driveway	18/12*	6	18/12*
Under Roadway	24	24	24
Other Locations	24	6	18

*Residential branch circuits rated 120V or less with GFCI protection and maximum overcurrent protection of 20A.

Note: This is a summary of the NEC's Table 300.5. See the table in the NEC for full details.

Note 1 to Table 300.5 defines "Cover" as the distance from the top of the underground cable or raceway to the top surface of finished grade. Figure 300–3

(B) Wet Locations. The interior of enclosures or raceways installed in an underground installation are considered to be a wet location. Cables and insulated conductors installed in underground enclosures or raceways must comply with 310.10(C). Splices within an underground enclosure must be listed as suitable for wet locations [110.14(B)]. Figure 300–4

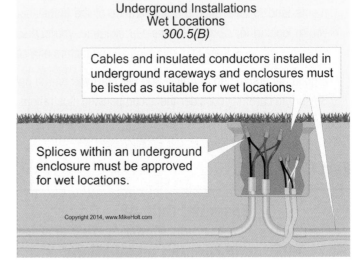

Figure 300–4

Author's Comment:

■ The definition of a "Wet Location" as contained in Article 100, includes installations underground, in concrete slabs in direct contact with the earth, locations subject to saturation with water, and unprotected locations exposed to weather. If raceways are installed in wet locations above grade, the interior of these raceways is also considered to be a wet location [300.9].

(C) Cables and Conductors Under Buildings. Cables and conductors installed under a building must be installed in a raceway that extends past the outside walls of the building. Figure 300–5

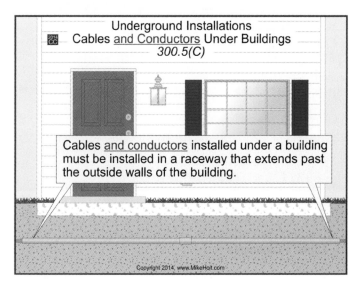

Figure 300–5

Ex 2: Type MC Cable listed for direct burial is permitted under a building without installation in a raceway [330.10(A)(5)]. Figure 300–6

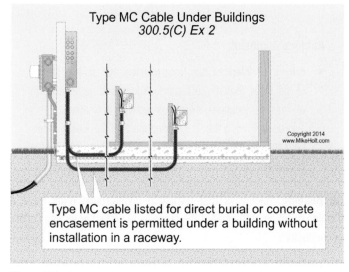

Figure 300–6

(D) Protecting Underground Cables and Conductors. Direct-buried conductors and cables such as Types MC, UF, and USE installed underground must be protected from damage in accordance with (1) through (4).

(1) Emerging from Grade. Direct-buried cables or conductors that emerge from grade must be installed in an enclosure or raceway to protect against physical damage. Protection isn't required to extend more than 18 in. below grade, and protection above ground must extend to a height of not less than 8 ft. Figure 300–7

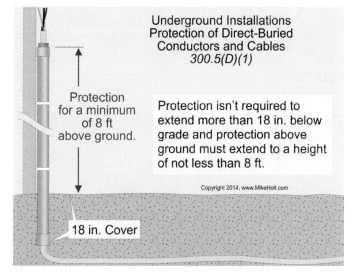

Figure 300–7

(2) Conductors Entering Buildings. Underground conductors and cables that enter a building must be protected to the point of entrance.

(3) Service Conductors. Underground service conductors must have their location identified by a warning ribbon placed in the trench at least 12 in. above the underground conductor installation. Figure 300–8

(E) Underground Splices and Taps. Direct-buried conductors or cables can be spliced or tapped underground without a splice box [300.15(G)], if the splice or tap is made in accordance with 110.14(B). Figure 300–9

(F) Backfill. Backfill material for underground wiring must not damage the underground cable or raceway, or contribute to the corrosion of the metal raceway.

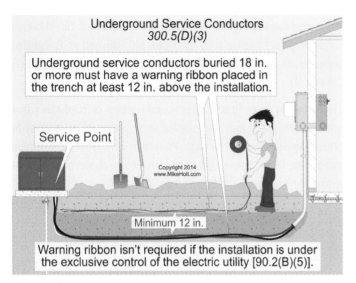

Figure 300–8

Figure 300–10

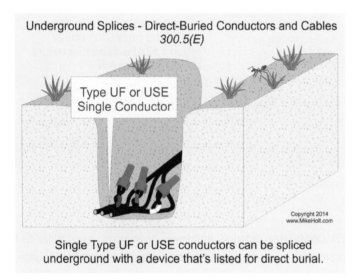

Figure 300–9

Author's Comment:

■ Large rocks, chunks of concrete, steel rods, mesh, and other sharp-edged objects must not be used for backfill material, because they can damage the underground conductors, cables, or raceways.

(G) Raceway Seals. If moisture could enter an underground raceway and contact energized live parts, a seal must be installed at one or both ends of the raceway. Figure 300–10

Author's Comment:

■ This is a common problem for equipment located downhill from the supply, or in underground equipment rooms. See 230.8 for service raceway seals and 300.7(A) for different temperature area seals.

Note: Hazardous explosive gases or vapors make it necessary to seal underground raceways that enter the building in accordance with 501.15.

Author's Comment:

■ It isn't the intent of this Note to imply that sealing fittings of the types required in hazardous locations be installed in unclassified locations, except as required in Chapter 5. This also doesn't imply that the sealing material provides a water-tight seal, but only that it prevents moisture from entering the raceways.

(H) Bushing. Raceways that terminate underground must have a bushing or fitting at the end of the raceway to protect emerging cables or conductors.

(I) Conductors Grouped Together. All underground conductors of the same circuit, including the equipment grounding conductor, must be inside the same raceway, or in close proximity to each other in the same trench. See 300.3(B). Figure 300–11

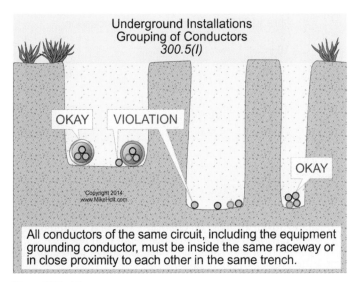

Figure 300–11

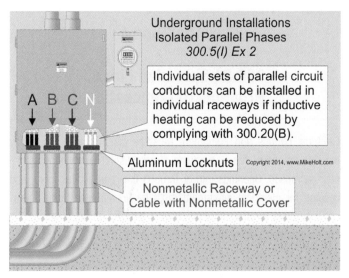

Figure 300–12

Ex 1: Conductors can be installed in parallel in raceways, multiconductor cables, or direct-buried single-conductor cables. Each raceway or multiconductor cable must contain all conductors of the same circuit including the equipment grounding conductor. Each direct-buried single-conductor cable must be located in close proximity in the trench to the other single conductor cables in the same parallel set of conductors, including equipment grounding conductors.

Ex 2: Parallel circuit conductors installed in accordance with 310.10(H) of the same phase or neutral can be installed in underground PVC conduits, if inductive heating at raceway terminations is reduced by the use of aluminum locknuts and cutting a slot between the individual holes through which the conductors pass as required by 300.20(B). Figure 300–12

Author's Comment:

- Installing ungrounded and neutral conductors in different PVC conduits makes it easier to terminate larger parallel sets of conductors, but it'll result in higher levels of electromagnetic fields (EMF).

(J) Earth Movement. Direct-buried conductors, cables, or raceways that are subject to movement by settlement or frost must be arranged to prevent damage to conductors or equipment connected to the wiring.

(K) Directional Boring. Cables or raceways installed using directional boring equipment must be approved by the authority having jurisdiction for this purpose.

Author's Comment:

- Directional boring technology uses a directional drill, which is steered continuously from point "A" to point "B." When the drill head comes out of the earth at point "B," it's replaced with a back-reamer and the duct or raceway being installed is attached to it. The size of the boring rig (hp, torque, and pull-back power) comes into play, along with the types of soil, in determining the type of raceways required. For telecommunications work, multiple poly innerducts are pulled in at one time. At major crossings, such as expressways, railroads, or rivers, outerduct may be installed to create a permanent sleeve for the innerducts.

  "Innerduct" and "outerduct" are terms usually associated with optical fiber cable installations, while "unitduct" comes with factory installed conductors. All of these come in various sizes. Galvanized rigid metal conduit, Schedule 40 and Schedule 80 PVC, HDPE conduit and nonmetallic underground conduit with conductors (NUCC) are common wiring methods used with directional boring installations.

Essential Rule 43

300.21 Spread of Fire or Products of Combustion

Electrical circuits and equipment must be installed in such a way that the spread of fire or products of combustion won't be substantially increased. Openings into or through fire-rated walls, floors, and ceilings for electrical equipment must be fire-stopped using methods approved by the authority having jurisdiction to maintain the fire-resistance rating of the fire-rated assembly. Figure 300–13

Spread of Fire or Products of Combustion
300.21

OKAY

VIOLATION
Firewall

Copyright 2014,
www.MikeHolt.com

Openings into or through fire-rated assemblies must be firestopped using approved methods to maintain the fire-resistance rating.

Figure 300–13

Author's Comment:

■ Fire-stopping materials are listed for the specific types of wiring methods and the construction of the assembly that they penetrate.

Note: Directories of electrical construction materials published by qualified testing laboratories contain listing and installation restrictions necessary to maintain the fire-resistive rating of assemblies. Outlet boxes must have a horizontal separation not less than 24 in. when installed in a fire-rated assembly, unless an outlet box is listed for closer spacing or protected by fire-resistant "putty pads" in accordance with manufacturer's instructions. Figure 300–14

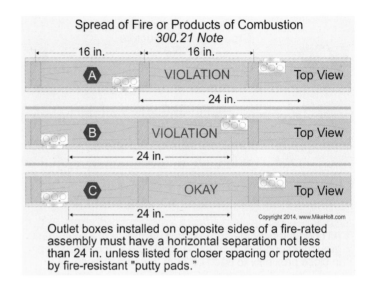

Spread of Fire or Products of Combustion
300.21 Note

16 in. | 16 in.

Ⓐ VIOLATION Top View
24 in.

Ⓑ VIOLATION Top View
24 in.

Ⓒ OKAY Top View
24 in.

Copyright 2014, www.MikeHolt.com

Outlet boxes installed on opposite sides of a fire-rated assembly must have a horizontal separation not less than 24 in. unless listed for closer spacing or protected by fire-resistant "putty pads."

Figure 300–14

Author's Comment:

■ Boxes installed in fire-resistance-rated assemblies must be listed for the purpose. If steel boxes are used, they must be secured to the framing member, so cut-in type boxes aren't permitted (UL White Book, *Guide Information for Electrical Equipment,* www.ul.com/regulators/2008_WhiteBook.pdf).

■ This rule also applies to control, signaling, and communications cables or raceways.

  □ CATV, 820.26
  □ Communications, 800.26
  □ Control and Signaling, 725.25
  □ Fire Alarm, 760.3(A)
  □ Optical Fiber, 770.26
  □ Sound Systems, 640.3(A)

Essential Rule 44

300.22 Wiring in Ducts and Plenums Spaces

Scan the QR code for a video clip of this *Code* rule. See page x for additional products to help you learn.

The provisions of this section apply to the installation and uses of electrical wiring and equipment in ducts used for dust, loose stock, or vapor removal; ducts specifically fabricated for environmental air, and spaces used for environmental air (plenums).

(A) Ducts Used for Dust, Loose Stock, or Vapor. Ducts that transport dust, loose stock, or vapors must not have any wiring method installed within them. Figure 300–15

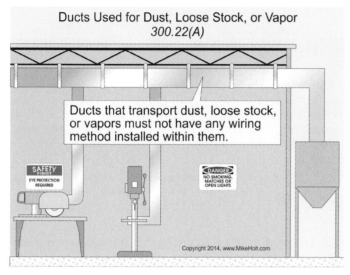

Figure 300–15

(B) Ducts Specifically Fabricated for Environmental Air. If necessary for direct action upon, or sensing of, the contained air, Type MC cable that has a smooth or corrugated impervious metal sheath without an overall nonmetallic covering, electrical metallic tubing, flexible metallic tubing, intermediate metal conduit, or rigid metal conduit without an overall nonmetallic covering can be installed in ducts specifically fabricated to transport environmental air. Flexible metal conduit in lengths not exceeding 4 ft can be used to connect physically adjustable equipment and devices within the fabricated duct.

Equipment is only permitted within the duct specifically fabricated to transport environmental air if necessary for the direct action upon, or sensing of, the contained air. Equipment, devices, and/or illumination are only permitted to be installed in the duct if necessary to facilitate maintenance and repair. Figure 300–16

(C) Other Spaces Used for Environmental Air (Plenums). This section applies to spaces used for air-handling purposes, but not fabricated for environmental air-handling purposes. This requirement doesn't apply to habitable rooms or areas of buildings, the prime purpose of which isn't air handling. Figure 300–17

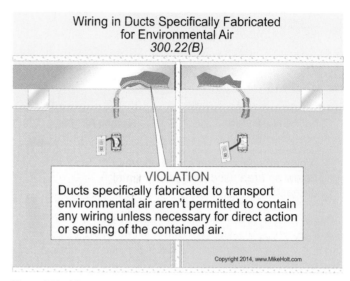

Figure 300–16

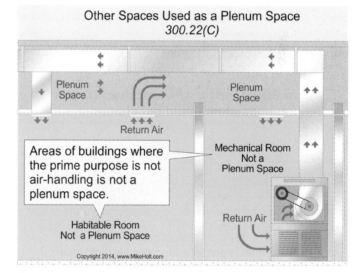

Figure 300–17

Note 1: The spaces above a suspended ceiling or below a raised floor used for environmental air are examples of the type of space to which this section applies. Figure 300–18

Note 2: The phrase "other space used for environmental air (plenums)" correlates with the term "plenum" in NFPA 90A, *Standard for the Installation of Air-Conditioning and Ventilating Systems*, and other mechanical codes where the ceiling is used for return air purposes, as well as some other air-handling spaces.

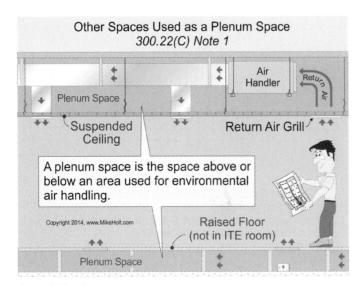

Figure 300–18

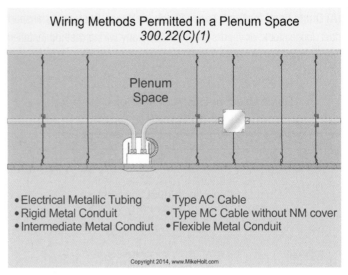

Figure 300–20

Ex: In a dwelling unit, this section doesn't apply to the space between joists or studs where the wiring passes through that space perpendicular to the long dimension of that space. Figure 300–19

Cable ties for securing and supporting must be listed as having adequate fire resistant and low smoke producing characteristics. Figure 300–21

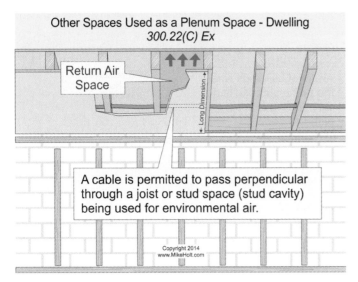

Figure 300–19

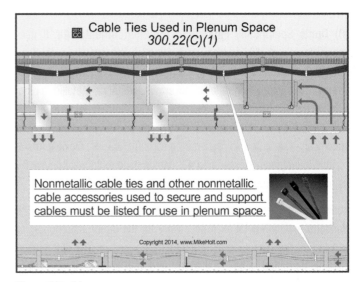

Figure 300–21

(1) Wiring Methods. Electrical metallic tubing, rigid metal conduit, intermediate metal conduit, armored cable, metal-clad cable without a nonmetallic cover, and flexible metal conduit can be installed in plenum spaces. If accessible, surface metal raceways or metal wireways with metal covers can be installed in a plenum space. Figure 300–20

Author's Comment:

■ PVC conduit [Article 352], electrical nonmetallic tubing [Article 362], liquidtight flexible conduit, and nonmetallic cables aren't permitted to be installed in plenum spaces because they give off deadly toxic fumes when burned or superheated.

- Plenum-rated control, signaling, and communications cables and raceways are permitted in plenum spaces: Figure 300–22

  - □ CATV, 820.179(A)
  - □ Communications, 800.21
  - □ Control and Signaling, Table 725.154
  - □ Fire Alarm, 760.7
  - □ Optical Fiber Cables and Raceways, 770.113(C)
  - □ Sound Systems, 640.9(C) and Table 725.154

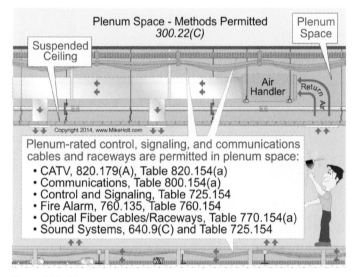

Figure 300–22

- Any wiring method suitable for the condition can be used in a space not used for environmental air-handling purposes. Figure 300–23

(2) Cable Tray Systems.

(a) Metal Cable Tray Systems. Metal cable tray systems can be installed to support the wiring methods and equipment permitted by this section. Figure 300–24

(3) Equipment. Electrical equipment with metal enclosures is permitted to be installed in plenum spaces. Figure 300–25

Figure 300–23

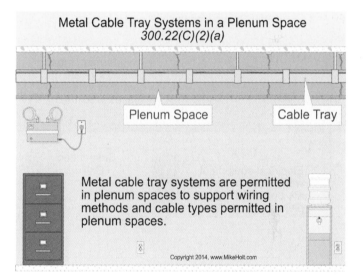

Figure 300–24

Author's Comment:

- Examples of electrical equipment permitted in plenum spaces are air-handlers, junction boxes, and dry-type transformers; however, transformers must not be rated over 50 kVA when located in hollow spaces [450.13(B)]. Figure 300–26

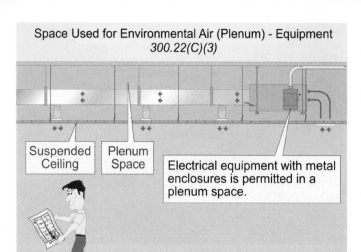

Figure 300–25

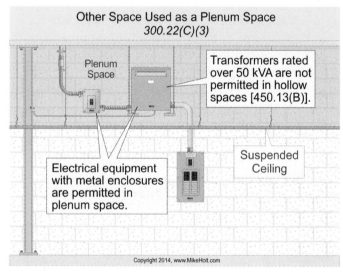

Figure 300–26

(D) Information Technology Equipment. Wiring methods beneath raised floors for information technology equipment can be as permitted in Article 645. Figure 300–27

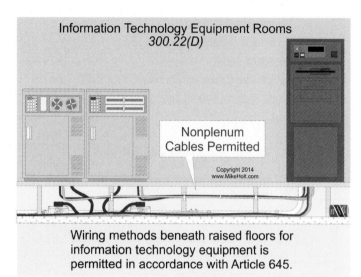

Figure 300–27

Introduction to Article 310—Conductors for General Wiring

This article contains the general requirements for conductors, such as insulation markings, ampacity ratings, and conditions of use. Article 310 doesn't apply to conductors that are part of flexible cords, fixture wires, or to conductors that are an integral part of equipment [90.7 and 300.1(B)].

People often make mistakes in applying the ampacity tables contained in Article 310. If you study the explanations carefully, you'll avoid common errors such as applying Table 310.15(B)(17) when you should be applying Table 310.15(B)(16).

Why so many tables? Why does Table 310.15(B)(17) list the ampacity of 6 THHN as 105 amperes, while Table 310.15(B)(16) lists the same conductor as having an ampacity of only 75 amperes? To answer that, go back to Article 100 and review the definition of ampacity. Notice the phrase "conditions of use." These tables set a maximum current value at which premature failure of the conductor insulation shouldn't occur during normal use, under the conditions described in the tables.

The designations THHN, THHW, RHH, and so on, are insulation types. Every type of insulation has a limit to how much heat it can withstand. When current flows through a conductor, it creates heat. How well the insulation around a conductor can dissipate that heat depends on factors such as whether that conductor is in free air or not. Think about what happens when you put on a sweater, a jacket, and then a coat—all at the same time. You heat up. Your skin can't dissipate heat with all that clothing on nearly as well as it dissipates heat in free air. The same principal applies to conductors.

Conductor insulation also fails with age. That's why we conduct cable testing and take other measures to predict failure and replace certain conductors (for example, feeders or critical equipment conductors) while they're still within design specifications. But conductor insulation failure takes decades under normal use—and it's a maintenance issue. However, if a conductor is forced to exceed the ampacity listed in the appropriate table, and as a result its design temperature is exceeded, insulation failure happens much more rapidly—often catastrophically. Consequently, exceeding the allowable ampacity of a conductor is a serious safety issue.

Part II. Installation

Essential Rule 45

310.15 Conductor Ampacity

 Scan the QR code for a video clip of this *Code* rule. See page x for additional products to help you learn.

Author's Comment:

- According to Article 100, "ampacity" means the maximum current, in amperes, a conductor can carry continuously, where the temperature of the conductor won't be raised in excess of its insulation temperature rating. Figure 310–1

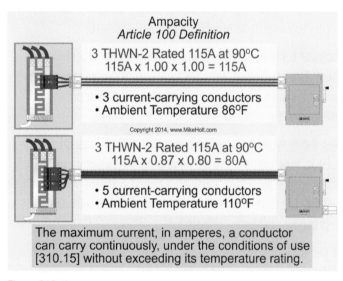

Figure 310–1

(A) General Requirements.

(1) Tables for Engineering Supervision. The ampacity of a conductor can be determined either by using the tables in accordance with 310.15(B), or under engineering supervision as provided in 310.15(C).

> **Note 1:** Ampacities provided by this section don't take voltage drop into consideration. See 210.19(A) Note 4, for branch circuits and 215.2(D) Note 2, for feeders.

(2) Conductor Ampacity—Lower Rating. Where more than one ampacity applies for a given circuit length, the lowest value must be used. Figure 310–2

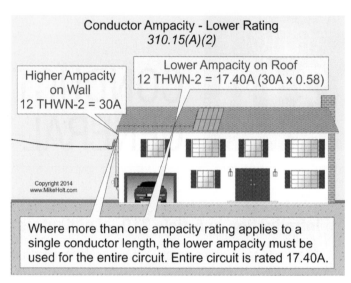

Figure 310–2

Ex: When different ampacities apply to a length of conductor, the higher ampacity is permitted for the entire circuit if the reduced ampacity length doesn't exceed 10 ft and its length doesn't exceed 10 percent of the length of the higher ampacity. Figure 310–3 *and* Figure 310–4

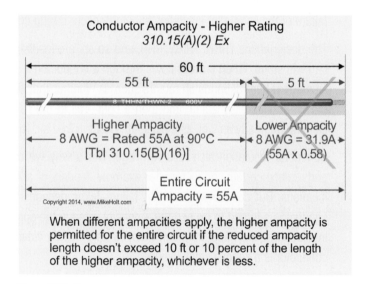

Figure 310–3

(3) Insulation Temperature Limitation. Conductors must not be used where the operating temperature exceeds that designated for the type of insulated conductor involved.

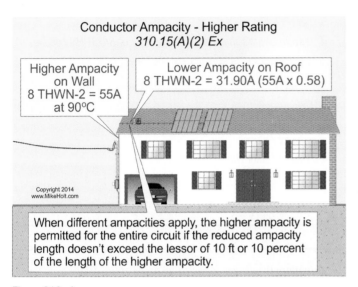

Conductor Ampacity - Higher Rating
310.15(A)(2) Ex

Higher Ampacity on Wall
8 THWN-2 = 55A at 90°C

Lower Ampacity on Roof
8 THWN-2 = 31.90A (55A x 0.58)

When different ampacities apply, the higher ampacity is permitted for the entire circuit if the reduced ampacity length doesn't exceed the lessor of 10 ft or 10 percent of the length of the higher ampacity.

Figure 310–4

Note 1: The insulation temperature rating of a conductor [Table 310.104(A)] is the maximum temperature a conductor can withstand over a prolonged time period without serious degradation. The main factors to consider for conductor operating temperature include:

(1) Ambient temperature may vary along the conductor length as well as from time to time [Table 310.15(B)(2)(a)].

(2) Heat generated internally in the conductor—load current flow.

(3) The rate at which generated heat dissipates into the ambient medium.

(4) Adjacent load-carrying conductors have the effect of raising the ambient temperature and impeding heat dissipation [Table 310.15(B)(3)(a)].

Note 2: See 110.14(C)(1) for the temperature limitation of terminations.

(B) Ampacity Table. The allowable conductor ampacities listed in Table 310.15(B)(16) are based on conditions where the ambient temperature isn't over 86°F, and no more than three current-carrying conductors are bundled together. Figure 310–5

The temperature correction and adjustment factors apply to the conductor ampacity, based on the temperature rating of the conductor insulation in accordance with Table 310.15(B)(16). Figure 310–6

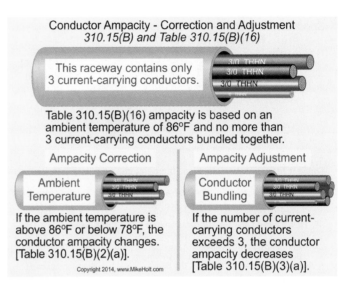

Conductor Ampacity - Correction and Adjustment
310.15(B) and Table 310.15(B)(16)

This raceway contains only 3 current-carrying conductors.

Table 310.15(B)(16) ampacity is based on an ambient temperature of 86°F and no more than 3 current-carrying conductors bundled together.

Ampacity Correction

Ambient Temperature

If the ambient temperature is above 86°F or below 78°F, the conductor ampacity changes. [Table 310.15(B)(2)(a)].

Ampacity Adjustment

Conductor Bundling

If the number of current-carrying conductors exceeds 3, the conductor ampacity decreases [Table 310.15(B)(3)(a)].

Figure 310–5

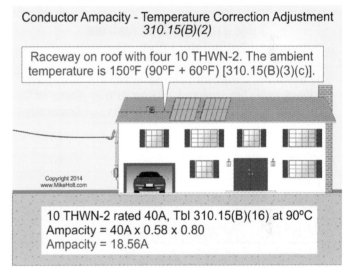

Conductor Ampacity - Temperature Correction Adjustment
310.15(B)(2)

Raceway on roof with four 10 THWN-2. The ambient temperature is 150°F (90°F + 60°F) [310.15(B)(3)(c)].

10 THWN-2 rated 40A, Tbl 310.15(B)(16) at 90°C
Ampacity = 40A x 0.58 x 0.80
Ampacity = 18.56A

Figure 310–6

(2) Conductor Ampacity Ambient Temperature Correction. When conductors are installed in an ambient temperature other than 78°F to 86°F, the ampacities listed in Table 310.15(B)(16) must be corrected in accordance with the multipliers listed in Table 310.15(B)(2)(a). Figure 310–7

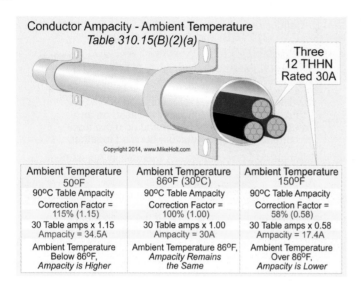

Conductor Ampacity - Ambient Temperature
Table 310.15(B)(2)(a)

Three
12 THHN
Rated 30A

Copyright 2014, www.MikeHolt.com

Ambient Temperature 50°F	Ambient Temperature 86°F (30°C)	Ambient Temperature 150°F
90°C Table Ampacity	90°C Table Ampacity	90°C Table Ampacity
Correction Factor = 115% (1.15)	Correction Factor = 100% (1.00)	Correction Factor = 58% (0.58)
30 Table amps x 1.15 Ampacity = 34.5A	30 Table amps x 1.00 Ampacity = 30A	30 Table amps x 0.58 Ampacity = 17.4A
Ambient Temperature Below 86°F, *Ampacity is Higher*	Ambient Temperature 86°F, *Ampacity Remains the Same*	Ambient Temperature Over 86°F, *Ampacity is Lower*

Figure 310–7

Table 310.15(B)(2)(a) Ambient Temperature Correction

Ambient Temperature °F	Ambient Temperature °C	Correction Factor 75°C Conductors	Correction Factor 90°C Conductors
50 or less	10 or less	1.20	1.15
51–59°F	11–15°C	1.15	1.12
60–68°F	16–20°C	1.11	1.08
69–77°F	21–25°C	1.05	1.04
78–86°F	26–30°C	1.00	1.00
87–95°F	31–35°C	0.94	0.96
96–104°F	36–40°C	0.88	0.91
105–113°F	41–45°C	0.82	0.87
114–122°F	46–50°C	0.75	0.82
123–131°F	51–55°C	0.67	0.76
132–140°F	56–60°C	0.58	0.71
141–149°F	61–65°C	0.47	0.65
150–158°F	66–70°C	0.33	0.58
159–167°F	71–75°C	0.00	0.50
168–176°F	76–80°C	0.00	0.41
177–185°F	81–85°C	0.00	0.29

Question: *What's the corrected ampacity of 3/0 THHN conductors if the ambient temperature is 108°F?*

(a) 173A   *(b) 196A*   *(c) 213A*   *(d) 241A*

Answer: *(b) 196A*

Conductor Ampacity [90°C] = 225A
Correction Factor [Table 310.(B)(2)(a)] = 0.87

Corrected Ampacity = 225A x 0.87
Corrected Ampacity = 196A

Question: *What's the corrected ampacity of 3/0 THWN conductors if the ambient temperature is 108°F?*

(a) 164A   *(b) 196A*   *(c) 213A*   *(d) 241A*

Answer: *(a) 164A*

Conductor Ampacity [75°C] = 200A
Correction Factor [Table 310.(B)(2)(a)] = 0.82

Corrected Ampacity = 200A x 0.82
Corrected Ampacity = 164A

(3) Conductor Ampacity Adjustment.

(a) Four or More Current-Carrying Conductors. Where four or more current-carrying power conductors are in a raceway longer than 24 in. [310.15(B)(3)(a)(3)], or where cables are bundled for a length longer than 24 in., the ampacity of each conductor must be reduced in accordance with Table 310.15(B)(3)(a).

Author's Comment:

■ Conductor ampacity reduction is required when four or more current-carrying conductors are bundled because heat generated by current flow isn't able to dissipate as quickly as when there are three or fewer current-carry conductors. Figure 310–8 and Figure 310–9

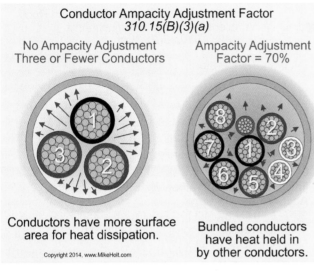

Conductor Ampacity Adjustment Factor
310.15(B)(3)(a)

No Ampacity Adjustment
Three or Fewer Conductors

Conductors have more surface area for heat dissipation.

Ampacity Adjustment
Factor = 70%

Bundled conductors have heat held in by other conductors.

Copyright 2014, www.MikeHolt.com

Figure 310–8

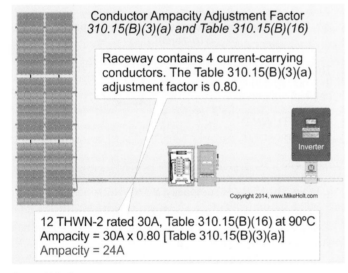

Conductor Ampacity Adjustment Factor
310.15(B)(3)(a) and Table 310.15(B)(16)

Raceway contains 4 current-carrying conductors. The Table 310.15(B)(3)(a) adjustment factor is 0.80.

Inverter

Copyright 2014, www.MikeHolt.com

12 THWN-2 rated 30A, Table 310.15(B)(16) at 90°C
Ampacity = 30A x 0.80 [Table 310.15(B)(3)(a)]
Ampacity = 24A

Figure 310–9

Table 310.15(B)(3)(a) Conductor Ampacity Adjustment for More Than Three Current–Carrying Conductors

Number of Conductors1	Adjustment
4–6	0.80 or 80%
7–9	0.70 or 70%
10–20	0.50 or 50%
21–30	0.45 or 45%
31–40	0.40 or 40%
41 and above	0.35 or 35%

[1]*Number of conductors is the total number of conductors, including spare conductors, including spare conductors, adjusted in accordance with 310.15(B)(5) and (B)(6). It doesn't include conductors that can't be energized at the same time.*

(1) Conductor ampacity adjustment of Table 310.15(B)(3)(a) doesn't apply to conductors installed in cable trays, 392.80 applies.

(2) Conductor ampacity adjustment of Table 310.15(B)(3)(a) doesn't apply to conductors in raceways having a length not exceeding 24 in. Figure 310–10

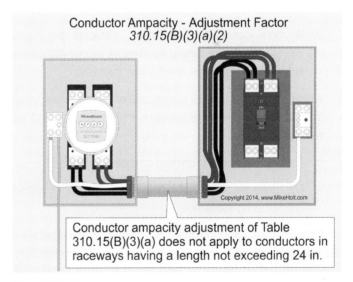

Conductor Ampacity - Adjustment Factor
310.15(B)(3)(a)(2)

Copyright 2014, www.MikeHolt.com

Conductor ampacity adjustment of Table 310.15(B)(3)(a) does not apply to conductors in raceways having a length not exceeding 24 in.

Figure 310–10

(4) Conductor ampacity adjustment of Table 310.15(B)(3)(a) doesn't apply to conductors within Type AC or Type MC cable under the following conditions: Figure 310–11

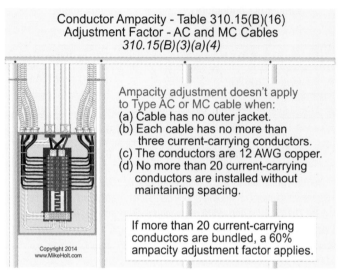

Figure 310–11

a. The cables don't have an outer jacket,

b. Each cable has no more than three current-carrying conductors,

c. The conductors are 12 AWG copper, and

d. No more than 20 current-carrying conductors (ten 2-wire cables or six 3-wire cables) are installed without maintaining spacing for a continuous length longer than 24 in.

(5) Ampacity adjustment of 60 percent applies to conductors within Type AC or Type MC cable without an overall outer jacket under the following conditions:

b. The number of current-carrying conductors exceeds 20.

c. The cables are stacked or bundled longer than 24 in. without spacing being maintained.

(c) Raceways and Cables Exposed to Sunlight on Rooftops. When applying ampacity adjustment correction factors, the ambient temperature adjustment contained in Table 310.15(B)(3)(c) is added to the outdoor ambient temperature for conductors installed in raceways or cables exposed to direct sunlight on or above rooftops to determine the applicable ambient temperature for ampacity correction factors in Table 310.15(B)(2)(a) or Table 310.15(B)(2)(b). Figure 310–12 and Figure 310–13

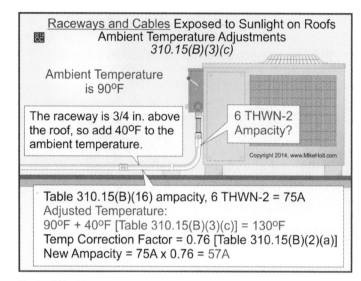

Figure 310–12

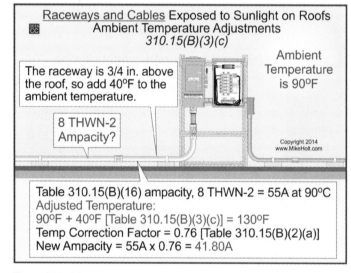

Figure 310–13

Ex: The ampacity adjustment isn't required for conductors that are type XHHW-2.

Note 1: See the *ASHRAE Handbook—Fundamentals* (www.ashrae.org) as a source for the ambient temperatures in various locations.

Note 2: The temperature adders in Table 310.15(B)(3)(c) are based on the measured temperature rise above local climatic ambient temperatures due to sunlight heating.

Table 310.15(B)(3)(c) Ambient Temperature Adder for <u>Raceways or Cables</u> On or Above Rooftops		
Distance of <u>Raceway or Cable</u> Above Roof	C°	F°
0 to ½ in.	33	60
Above ½ in. to 3½ in.	22	40
Above 3½ in. to 12 in.	17	30
Above 12 in. to 36 in.	14	25

Author's Comment:

■ This rule requires the ambient temperature used for ampacity correction to be adjusted where conductors or cables are installed in a raceway or cable on or above a rooftop and the raceway is exposed to direct sunlight. The reasoning is that the air inside raceways and cables that are in direct sunlight is significantly hotter than the surrounding air, and appropriate ampacity corrections must be made in order to comply with 310.10.

(5) Neutral Conductors.

(a) The neutral conductor of a 3-wire, single-phase, 120/240V system, or 4-wire, three-phase, 120/208V or 277/480V wye-connected system, isn't considered a current-carrying conductor for conductor ampacity adjustment of 310.15(B)(3)(a). Figure 310–14

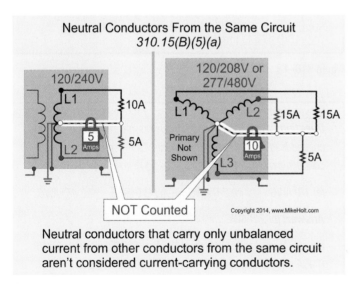

Neutral Conductors From the Same Circuit
310.15(B)(5)(a)

NOT Counted

Neutral conductors that carry only unbalanced current from other conductors from the same circuit aren't considered current-carrying conductors.

Figure 310–14

(b) The neutral conductor of a 3-wire circuit from a 4-wire, three-phase, 120/208V or 277/480V wye-connected system is considered a current-carrying conductor for conductor ampacity adjustment of 310.15(B)(3)(a).

Author's Comment:

■ When a 3-wire circuit is supplied from a 4-wire, three-phase, 120/208V or 277/480V wye-connected system, the neutral conductor carries approximately the same current as the ungrounded conductors. Figure 310–15

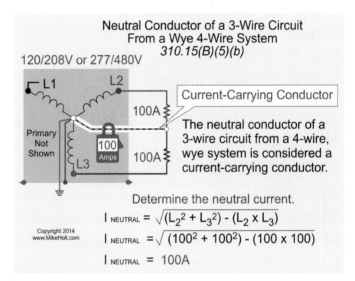

Neutral Conductor of a 3-Wire Circuit From a Wye 4-Wire System
310.15(B)(5)(b)
120/208V or 277/480V

Current-Carrying Conductor

The neutral conductor of a 3-wire circuit from a 4-wire, wye system is considered a current-carrying conductor.

Determine the neutral current.

$I_{NEUTRAL} = \sqrt{(L_2{}^2 + L_3{}^2) - (L_2 \times L_3)}$

$I_{NEUTRAL} = \sqrt{(100^2 + 100^2) - (100 \times 100)}$

$I_{NEUTRAL} = 100A$

Figure 310–15

(c) The neutral conductor of a 4-wire, three-phase, 120/208V or 277/480V wye-connected system is considered a current-carrying conductor for conductor ampacity adjustment of 310.15(B)(3)(a) if more than 50 percent of the neutral load consists of nonlinear loads.

Author's Comment:

■ Nonlinear loads supplied by a 4-wire, three-phase, 120/208V or 277/480V wye-connected system can produce unwanted and potentially hazardous odd triplen harmonic currents (3rd, 9th, 15th, and so on) that can add on the neutral conductor. To prevent fire or equipment damage from excessive harmonic neutral current, the designer should consider increasing the size of the neutral conductor or installing a separate neutral for each phase. For more information, visit .MikeHolt.com, click on the "Technical" link, then the "Power Quality" link. Also see 210.4(A) Note, 220.61 Note 2, and 450.3 Note 2. Figure 310–16

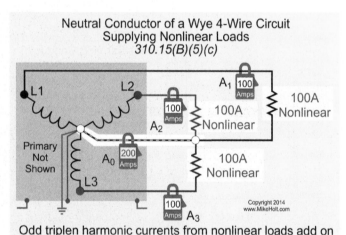

Neutral Conductor of a Wye 4-Wire Circuit Supplying Nonlinear Loads 310.15(B)(5)(c)

Odd triplen harmonic currents from nonlinear loads add on the neutral conductor and the actual current can be twice the ungrounded conductor's current.

Figure 310–16

(6) Grounding Conductors. Grounding and bonding conductors aren't considered current carrying. Figure 310–17

(7) 120/240V, Single-Phase Dwelling Services and Feeders. For one-family dwellings and individual dwelling units of two-family and multifamily dwellings, service and feeder conductors supplied by a single phase, 120/240V system can be sized using 310.15(B)(7)(1) through (4). Figure 310–18

(1) Service conductors supplying the entire load of a one-family dwelling or an individual dwelling unit in a two-family or multi-family dwelling can have an ampacity of 83 percent of the service rating.

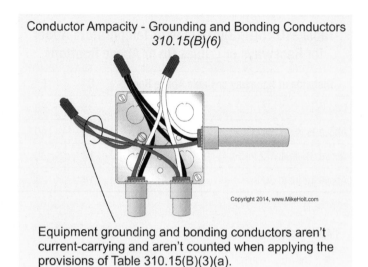

Conductor Ampacity - Grounding and Bonding Conductors 310.15(B)(6)

Equipment grounding and bonding conductors aren't current-carrying and aren't counted when applying the provisions of Table 310.15(B)(3)(a).

Figure 310–17

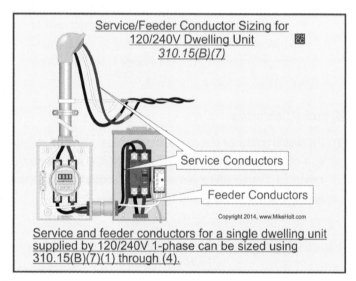

Service/Feeder Conductor Sizing for 120/240V Dwelling Unit 310.15(B)(7)

Service Conductors

Feeder Conductors

Service and feeder conductors for a single dwelling unit supplied by 120/240V 1-phase can be sized using 310.15(B)(7)(1) through (4).

Figure 310–18

Question: What size service conductors are required if the calculated load for a dwelling unit equals 195A, and the service disconnect is rated 200A? Figure 310–19

(a) 1/0 AWG   (b) 2/0 AWG   (c) 3/0 AWG   (d) 4/0 AWG

Answer: (b) 2/0 AWG

Service Conductor: 2/0 AWG rated 175A at 75°C [Table 310.15(B)(16)] (200A rated circuit breaker multiplied by 83% =166A).

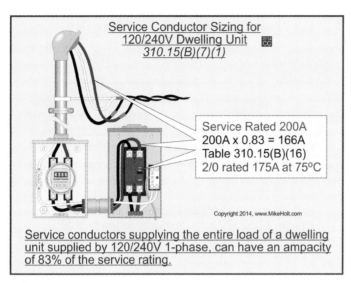

Service Conductor Sizing for
120/240V Dwelling Unit
310.15(B)(7)(1)

Service Rated 200A
200A x 0.83 = 166A
Table 310.15(B)(16)
2/0 rated 175A at 75°C

Copyright 2014, www.MikeHolt.com

Service conductors supplying the entire load of a dwelling unit supplied by 120/240V 1-phase, can have an ampacity of 83% of the service rating.

Figure 310–19

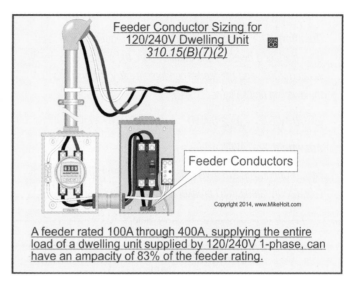

Feeder Conductor Sizing for
120/240V Dwelling Unit
310.15(B)(7)(2)

Feeder Conductors

Copyright 2014, www.MikeHolt.com

A feeder rated 100A through 400A, supplying the entire load of a dwelling unit supplied by 120/240V 1-phase, can have an ampacity of 83% of the feeder rating.

Figure 310–21

Author's Comment:

- 310.15(B)(7) can't be used for service conductors for two-family or multifamily dwelling buildings. Figure 310–20

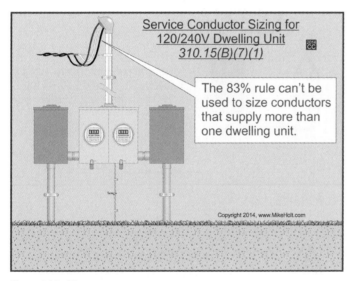

Service Conductor Sizing for
120/240V Dwelling Unit
310.15(B)(7)(1)

The 83% rule can't be used to size conductors that supply more than one dwelling unit.

Copyright 2014, www.MikeHolt.com

Figure 310–20

Author's Comment:

- 310.15B(7)(2) can't be used to size feeder conductors where a feeder doesn't carry the entire load of the dwelling unit. Figure 310–22

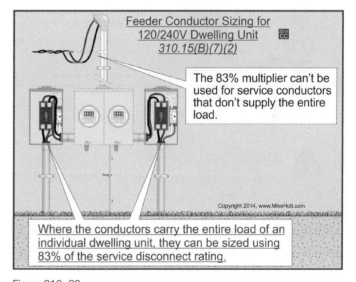

Feeder Conductor Sizing for
120/240V Dwelling Unit
310.15(B)(7)(2)

The 83% multiplier can't be used for service conductors that don't supply the entire load.

Copyright 2014, www.MikeHolt.com

Where the conductors carry the entire load of an individual dwelling unit, they can be sized using 83% of the service disconnect rating.

Figure 310–22

(2) For a feeder rated 100A through 400A, feeder conductors supplying a one-family dwelling, or an individual dwelling unit in a two-family or multifamily dwelling, can have an ampacity of 83 percent of the feeder rating, but only if the feeder supplies the entire load of the dwelling. Figure 310–21

Question: *What size feeder conductors are required if the calculated load for a dwelling unit equals 195A, the service disconnect is rated 200A, and the feeder conductors carry the entire load of the dwelling unit?* Figure 310–23

(a) 1/0 AWG   (b) 2/0 AWG   (c) 3/0 AWG   (d) 4/0 AWG

Answer: *(b) 2/0 AWG*

Feeder Conductor: 2/0 AWG rated 175A at 75°C [Table 310.15(B) (16)] (200A rated circuit breaker multiplied by 83% =166A).

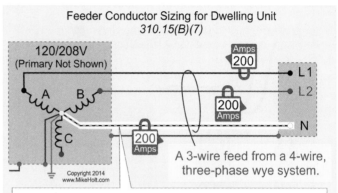

The 83% rule [310.15(B)(7)] doesn't apply to 3-wire, 1-phase, 120/208V circuits, because the neutral conductor in these circuits carries neutral current even when the phases are balanced [310.15(B)(5)(b)].

Figure 310–24

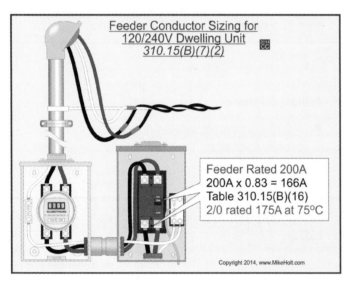

Figure 310–23

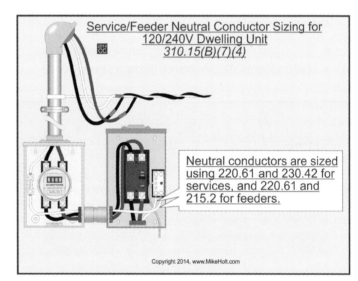

Figure 310–25

⚠ **WARNING:** *310.15(B)(7) doesn't apply to 3-wire service or feeder conductors connected to a three-phase, 120/208V system, because the neutral conductor in these systems always carries neutral current, even when the load on the phases is balanced [310.15(B)(5)(b)]. For more information on this topic, see 220.61(C)(1).* Figure 310–24

(3) Feeders for an individual dwelling unit are never required to be larger than the conductors in 310.15(B)(7)(1) or (2).

(4) Neutral conductors are sized using 220.61 and 230.42 for services and 220.61 and 215.2 for feeders. Figure 310–25

⚠ **CAUTION:** *Because the service neutral conductor is required to serve as the effective ground-fault current path, it must be sized so it can safely carry the maximum fault current likely to be imposed on it [110.10 and 250.4(A)(5)]. This is accomplished by sizing the neutral conductor in accordance with Table 250.102(C), based on the area of the largest ungrounded service conductor [250.24(C)(1)].*

Question: *What size neutral conductor is required if the calculated load for a dwelling unit equals 195A, the maximum unbalanced load is 100A, and the service disconnect is rated 200A with 2/0 AWG conductors?* Figure 310–26

(a) 6 AWG   *(b) 3 AWG*   *(c) 2 AWG*   *(d) 1 AWG*

Answer: *(b) 3 AWG*

Neutral Conductor: 3 AWG is rated 100A at 75°C in accordance with Table 310.15(B)(16), and 310.15(B)(7)(3) doesn't allow for the 83 percent deduction for neutral conductors. In addition, 250.24(C) requires the neutral conductor to be sized no smaller than 4 AWG based on 2/0 AWG service conductors in accordance with Table 250.102(C).

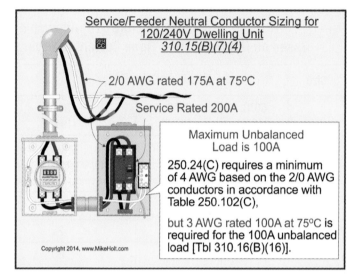

Figure 310–26

Table 310.15(B)(16) Allowable Ampacities of Insulated Conductors
Based on Not More Than Three Current–Carrying Conductors and Ambient Temperature of 30°C (86°F)*

Size	60°C (140°F)	75°C (167°F)	90°C (194°F)	60°C (140°F)	75°C (167°F)	90°C (194°F)	Size
AWG kcmil	TW UF	RHW THHW THW THWN XHHW USE	RHH RHW-2 THHN THHW THW-2 THWN-2 USE-2 XHHW XHHW-2	TW UF	THHN THW THWN XHHW	THHN THW–2 THWN–2 THHW XHHW XHHW–2	AWG kcmil
	Copper			Aluminum/Copper–Clad Aluminum			
14*	15	20	25				14*
12*	20	25	30	15	20	25	12*
10*	30	35	40	25	30	35	10*
8	40	50	55	35	40	45	8
6	55	65	75	40	50	55	6
4	70	85	95	55	65	75	4
3	85	100	115	65	75	85	3
2	95	115	130	75	90	100	2
1	110	130	145	85	100	115	1
1/0	125	150	170	100	120	135	1/0
2/0	145	175	195	115	135	150	2/0
3/0	165	200	225	130	155	175	3/0
4/0	195	230	260	150	180	205	4/0
250	215	255	290	170	205	230	250
300	240	285	320	195	230	260	300
350	260	310	350	210	250	280	350
400	280	335	380	225	270	305	400
500	320	380	430	260	310	350	500

*See 240.4(D)

CABINET AND CUTOUT BOXES

Introduction to Article 312—Cabinet and Cutout Boxes

This article addresses the installation and construction specifications for the items mentioned in its title. In Article 310, we observed that the conditions of use have an effect on the ampacity of a conductor. Likewise, the conditions of use have an effect on the selection and application of cabinet. For example, you can't use just any enclosure in a wet location or in a hazardous location. The conditions of use impose special requirements for these situations.

For all such enclosures, certain requirements apply—regardless of the use. For example, you must cover any openings, protect conductors from abrasion, and allow sufficient bending room for conductors.

Notice that Article 408 covers switchboards and panelboards, with primary emphasis on the interior, or "guts," while the cabinet that'd be used to enclose a panelboard is covered here in Article 312. Therefore you'll find that some important considerations such as wire-bending space at terminals of panelboards are included in this article.

Article 312 covers the installation and construction specifications for cabinets and cutout boxes. [312.1].

Part I. Scope and Installation

Essential Rule 46

312.8 Cabinets and Cutout Boxes Containing Splices, Taps, and Feed-Through Conductors

Cabinets and cutout boxes can be used for conductors feeding through, spliced, or tapping off to other enclosures, switches, or overcurrent devices where all of the following conditions are met:

(1) The total area of the conductors at any cross section doesn't exceed 40 percent of the cross-sectional area of the space. Figure 312–1

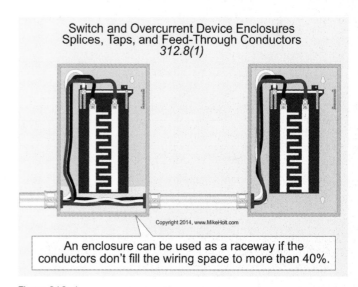

Switch and Overcurrent Device Enclosures
Splices, Taps, and Feed-Through Conductors
312.8(1)

Copyright 2014, www.MikeHolt.com

An enclosure can be used as a raceway if the conductors don't fill the wiring space to more than 40%.

Figure 312–1

(2) The total area of conductors, splices, and taps installed at any cross section doesn't exceed 75 percent of the cross-sectional area of that space. Figure 312–2

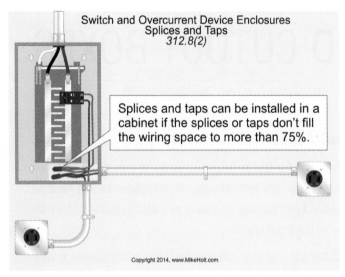

Figure 312–2

(3) A warning label that's not <u>handwritten, must be permanently affixed, be of sufficient durability to withstand the environment involved</u> [110.21(B)] on the cabinet or cutout box identify the location of the disconnecting means for the feed-through conductors. Figure 312–3

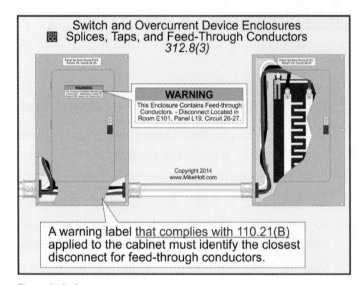

Figure 312–3

ARTICLE 430 — MOTORS, MOTOR CIRCUITS, AND CONTROLLERS

Introduction to Article 430—Motors, Motor Circuits, and Controllers

Article 430 contains the specific rules for conductor sizing, overcurrent protection, control circuit conductors, controllers, and disconnecting means for electric motors. The installation requirements for motor control centers are covered in Part VIII, and air-conditioning and refrigeration equipment are covered in Article 440.

Article 430 is one of the longest articles in the *NEC*. It's also one of the most complex, but motors are also complex equipment. They're electrical and mechanical devices, but what makes motor applications complex is the fact that they're inductive loads with a high-current demand at start-up that's typically six, or more, times the running current. This makes overcurrent protection for motor applications necessarily different from the protection employed for other types of equipment. So don't confuse general overcurrent protection with motor protection—you must calculate and apply them differently using the rules in Article 430.

You might be uncomfortable with the allowances for overcurrent protection found in this article, such as protecting a 10 AWG conductor with a 60A overcurrent protection device, but as you learn to understand how motor protection works, you'll understand why these allowances aren't only safe, but necessary.

Part II. Conductor Size

Essential Rule 47

430.22 Single Motor Conductor Size

Conductors to a single motor must be sized not less than 125 percent of the motor FLC rating as listed in Table 430.247 Direct-Current Motors, Table 430.248 Single-Phase Motors, or Table 430.250 Three-Phase Motors. Figure 430–1

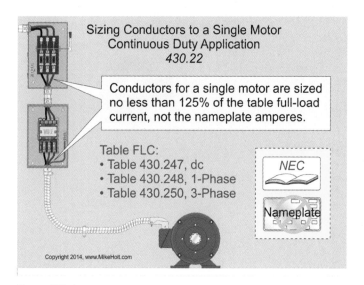

Sizing Conductors to a Single Motor
Continuous Duty Application
430.22

Conductors for a single motor are sized no less than 125% of the table full-load current, not the nameplate amperes.

Table FLC:
- Table 430.247, dc
- Table 430.248, 1-Phase
- Table 430.250, 3-Phase

NEC

Nameplate

Copyright 2014, www.MikeHolt.com

Figure 430–1

Question: What size branch-circuit conductor is required for a 7½ hp, 230V, three-phase motor with 75°C terminals? Figure 430–2

(a) 14 AWG   (b) 12 AWG   (c) 10 AWG   (d) 8 AWG

Answer: (c) 10 AWG

Motor FLC = 22A [Table 430.250]

Conductor's Size = 22A x 1.25
Conductor's Size = 27.50A, 10 AWG, rated 35A at 75°C
[Table 310.15(B)(16)]

Note: The branch-circuit short-circuit and ground-fault protection device using an inverse time breaker is sized at 60A according to 430.52(C)(1) Ex 1:

Circuit Protection = 22A x 2.50
Circuit Protection = 55A, next size up 60A [240.6(A)]

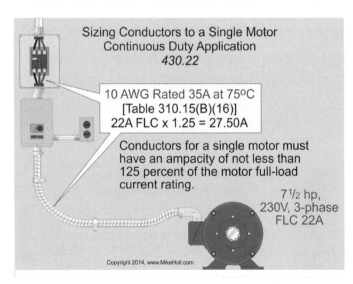

Figure 430–2

Part IV. Branch-Circuit Short-Circuit and Ground-Fault Protection

Essential Rule 48

430.52 Branch-Circuit Short-Circuit and Ground-Fault Protection

(A) General. The motor branch-circuit short-circuit and ground-fault protective device must comply with 430.52(B) and 430.52(C).

(B) All Motors. A motor branch-circuit short-circuit and ground-fault protective device must be capable of carrying the motor's starting current.

(C) Rating or Setting.

(1) Table 430.52. Each motor branch circuit must be protected against short circuit and ground faults by a protective device sized no greater than the following percentages listed in Table 430.52.

Table 430.52			
Motor Type	Nontime Delay	Dual-Element Fuse	Inverse Time Breaker
Wound Rotor	150%	150%	150%
Direct Current	150%	150%	150%
All Other Motors	300%	175%	250%

Question: What size conductor and inverse time circuit breaker are required for a 2 hp, 230V, single-phase motor with 75°C terminals? Figure 430–3

(a) 14 AWG, 30A breaker   (b) 14 AWG, 35A breaker
(c) 14 AWG, 40A breaker   (d) 14 AWG, 45A breaker

Answer: (a) 14 AWG, 30A breaker

Step 1: Determine the branch-circuit conductor [Table 310.15(B)(16), 430.22, and Table 430.248]:

12A x 1.25 = 15A, 14 AWG, rated 20A at 75°C
[Table 310.15(B)(16)]

Step 2: Determine the branch-circuit protection [240.6(A), 430.52(C)(1), and Table 430.248]:

12A x 2.50 = 30A

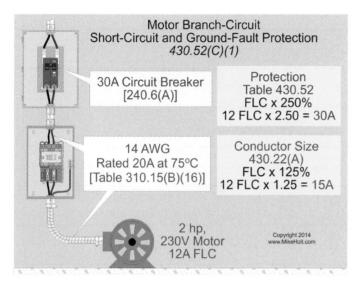

Figure 430–3

Author's Comment:

■ I know it bothers many in the electrical industry to see a 14 AWG conductor protected by a 30A circuit breaker, but branch-circuit conductors are protected against overloads by the overload device, which is sized between 115 and 125 percent of the motor nameplate current rating [430.32]. The small conductor rule contained in 240.4(D) which limits 15A protection for 14 AWG doesn't apply to motor circuit protection. See 240.4(D) and 240.4(G).

Ex 1: If the motor short-circuit and ground-fault protective device values derived from Table 430.52 don't correspond with the standard overcurrent device ratings listed in 240.6(A), the next higher overcurrent device rating can be used. Figure 430–4

Question: *What size conductor and inverse time circuit breaker are required for a 7½ hp, 230V, three-phase motor with 75°C terminals?* Figure 430–5

(a) 10 AWG, 50A breaker (b) 10 AWG, 60A breaker
(c) a or b (d) none of these

Answer: *(b) 10 AWG, 60A breaker*

Step 1: *Determine the branch-circuit conductor [Table 310.15(B)(16), 430.22, and Table 430.250]:*

22A x 1.25 = 27.50A, 10 AWG, rated 35A at 75°C [Table 310.15(B)(16)]

Step 2: *Determine the branch-circuit protection [240.6(A), 430.52(C)(1) Ex 1, and Table 430.250]:*

22A x 2.50 = 55A, next size up = 60A

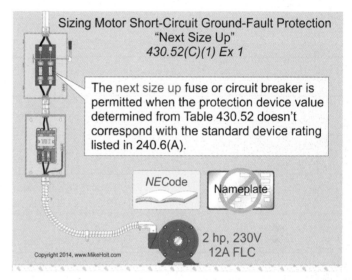

Figure 430–4

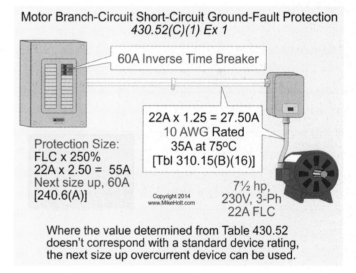

Where the value determined from Table 430.52 doesn't correspond with a standard device rating, the next size up overcurrent device can be used.

Figure 430–5

Mike Holt's Illustrated Guide to Essential Rules of the 2014 National Electrical Code

ARTICLE 450 TRANSFORMERS

Introduction to Article 450—Transformers

Article 450 opens by saying, "This article covers the installation of all transformers." Then it lists eight exceptions. So what does Article 450 really cover? Essentially, it covers power transformers and most kinds of lighting transformers.

A major concern with transformers is preventing overheating. The *Code* doesn't completely address this issue. Article 90 explains that the *NEC* isn't a design manual, and it assumes that the person using the *Code* has a certain level of expertise. Proper transformer selection is an important part of preventing it from overheating.

The *NEC* assumes you've already selected a transformer suitable to the load characteristics. For the *Code* to tell you how to do that would push it into the realm of a design manual. Article 450 then takes you to the next logical step—providing overcurrent protection and the proper connections. But this article doesn't stop there; 450.9 provides ventilation requirements, and 450.13 contains accessibility requirements.

Part I of Article 450 contains the general requirements such as guarding, marking, and accessibility, Part II contains the requirements for different types of transformers, and Part III covers transformer vaults.

Part I. General

Essential Rule 49

450.3 Overcurrent Protection

Note 2: Nonlinear loads on 4-wire, wye-connected secondary wiring can increase heat in a transformer without operating the primary overcurrent device. Figure 450–1

(B) Overcurrent Protection for Transformers Not Over 600V. The primary winding of a transformer must be protected against overcurrent in accordance with the percentages listed in Table 450.3(B) and all applicable notes.

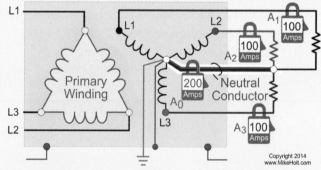

Transformer Overheating - Harmonic Current
450.3 Note 2

In 3-phase, 4-wire delta/wye transformers, odd triplen harmonic currents from nonlinear loads can cause excessive heating of the primary winding.

Figure 450–1

Table 450.3(B) Primary Protection Only

Primary Current Rating	Maximum Protection
9A or More	125%, see Table Note 1
Less Than 9A	167%
Less Than 2A	300%

Note 1. *If 125 percent of the primary current doesn't correspond to a standard rating of a fuse or nonadjustable circuit breaker, the next higher rating is permitted [240.6(A)].*

Question: *What's the primary overcurrent device rating and conductor size required for a 45 kVA, three-phase, 480V transformer that's fully loaded? The terminals are rated 75°C. Figure 450–2*

(a) 8 AWG, 40A   *(b) 6 AWG, 50A*
(c) 6 AWG, 60A   *(d) 4 AWG, 70A*

Answer: *(d) 4 AWG, 70A*

Step 1: *Determine the primary current:*

$$I = VA/(E \times 1.732)$$

I = 45,000 VA/(480V x 1.732)
I = 54A

Step 2: *Determine the primary overcurrent device rating [240.6(A)]:*

54A x 1.25 = 68A, next size up 70A, Table 450.3(B), Table Note 1

Step 3: *The primary conductor must be sized to carry 54A continuously (54A x 1.25 = 68A) [215.2(A)(1)] and be protected by a 70A overcurrent device [240.4(B)]. A 4 AWG conductor rated 85A at 75°C meets all of the requirements [110.14(C)(1) and 310.15(B)(16)].*

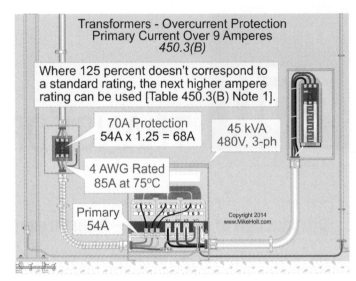

Figure 450–2

Essential Rule 50

450.14 Disconnecting Means

A disconnect is required to disconnect all transformer ungrounded primary conductors, unless the transformer is Class 2 or Class 3. The disconnect must be located within sight of the transformer, unless the location of the disconnect is field marked on the transformer and the disconnect is lockable, <u>as described in 110.25</u>. Figure 450–3 and Figure 450–4

Author's Comment:

- Within sight means that it's visible and not more than 50 ft from one to the other [Article 100].

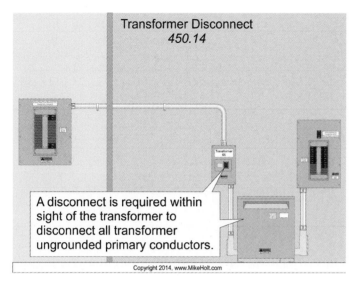

Figure 450–3

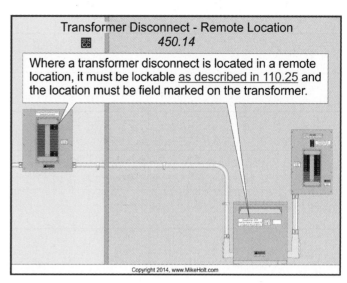

Figure 450–4

PRACTICE QUESTIONS FOR THE ESSENTIAL RULES OF THE *NEC*

Please use the 2014 *Code* book to answer the following questions.

Article 90. Introduction to the *NEC*

1. The *NEC* is _____.

   (a) intended to be a design manual
   (b) meant to be used as an instruction guide for untrained persons
   (c) for the practical safeguarding of persons and property
   (d) published by the Bureau of Standards

2. The *Code* isn't intended as a design specification standard or instruction manual for untrained persons.

   (a) True
   (b) False

3. Compliance with the provisions of the *NEC* will result in _____.

   (a) good electrical service
   (b) an efficient electrical system
   (c) an electrical system essentially free from hazard
   (d) all of these

4. The *Code* contains provisions considered necessary for safety, which will not necessarily result in _____.

   (a) efficient use
   (b) convenience
   (c) good service or future expansion of electrical use
   (d) all of these

5. Hazards often occur because of _____.

   (a) overloading of wiring systems by methods or usage not in conformity with the *NEC*
   (b) initial wiring not providing for increases in the use of electricity
   (c) a and b
   (d) none of these

6. The following systems shall be installed in accordance with the *NEC* requirements:

   (a) signaling conductors, equipment, and raceways
   (b) communications conductors, equipment, and raceways
   (c) electrical conductors, equipment, and raceways
   (d) all of these

7. The *NEC* applies to the installation of _____.

    (a) electrical conductors and equipment within or on public and private buildings
    (b) outside conductors and equipment on the premises
    (c) optical fiber cables and raceways
    (d) all of these

8. This *Code* covers the installation of _____ for public and private premises, including buildings, structures, mobile homes, recreational vehicles, and floating buildings.

    (a) optical fiber cables
    (b) electrical equipment
    (c) raceways
    (d) all of these

9. The *NEC* does not cover electrical installations in ships, watercraft, railway rolling stock, aircraft, or automotive vehicles.

    (a) True
    (b) False

10. The *Code* covers underground mine installations and self-propelled mobile surface mining machinery and its attendant electrical trailing cable.

    (a) True
    (b) False

11. Installations of communications equipment that are under the exclusive control of communications utilities, and located outdoors or in building spaces used exclusively for such installations _____ covered by the *NEC*.

    (a) are
    (b) are sometimes
    (c) are not
    (d) may be

12. Electric utilities may include entities that install, operate, and maintain _____.

    (a) communications systems (telephone, CATV, Internet, satellite, or data services)
    (b) electric supply systems (generation, transmission, or distribution systems)
    (c) local area network wiring on the premises
    (d) a or b

13. Utilities may be subject to compliance with codes and standards covering their regulated activities as adopted under governmental law or regulation.

    (a) True
    (b) False

14. The *NEC* does not apply to electric utility-owned wiring and equipment _____.

    (a) installed by an electrical contractor
    (b) installed on public property
    (c) consisting of service drops or service laterals
    (d) in a utility office building

15. Utilities may include entities that are designated or recognized by governmental law or regulation by public service/utility commissions.

    (a) True
    (b) False

16. Chapters 1 through 4 of the *NEC* apply _____.

    (a) generally to all electrical installations
    (b) only to special occupancies and conditions
    (c) only to special equipment and material
    (d) all of these

17. Communications wiring such as telephone, antenna, and CATV wiring within a building shall not be required to comply with the installation requirements of Chapters 1 through 7, except where specifically referenced in Chapter 8.

    (a) True
    (b) False

18. The material located in the *NEC* Annexes are part of the requirements of the *Code* and shall be complied with.

    (a) True
    (b) False

19. The authority having jurisdiction shall not be allowed to enforce any requirements of Chapter 7 (Special Conditions) or Chapter 8 (Communications Systems).

    (a) True
    (b) False

20. The _____ has the responsibility for deciding on the approval of equipment and materials.

    (a) manufacturer
    (b) authority having jurisdiction
    (c) testing agency
    (d) none of these

21. By special permission, the authority having jurisdiction may waive specific requirements in this *Code* where it is assured that equivalent objectives can be achieved by establishing and maintaining effective safety.

    (a) True
    (b) False

22. The authority having jurisdiction has the responsibility for _____.

    (a) making interpretations of rules
    (b) deciding upon the approval of equipment and materials
    (c) waiving specific requirements in the *Code* and permitting alternate methods and material if safety is maintained
    (d) all of these

23. If the *NEC* requires new products that are not yet available at the time a new edition is adopted, the _____ may permit the use of the products that comply with the most recent previous edition of the *Code* adopted by that jurisdiction.

    (a) electrical engineer
    (b) master electrician
    (c) authority having jurisdiction
    (d) permit holder

24. Factory-installed _____ wiring of listed equipment need not be inspected at the time of installation of the equipment, except to detect alterations or damage.

    (a) external
    (b) associated
    (c) internal
    (d) all of these

Article 110. Requirements for Electrical Installations

1. In judging equipment for approval, considerations such as the following shall be evaluated:

    (a) mechanical strength
    (b) wire-bending space
    (c) arcing effects
    (d) all of these

2. Listed or labeled equipment shall be installed and used in accordance with any instructions included in the listing or labeling.

    (a) True
    (b) False

3. Conductor terminal and splicing devices must be _____ for the conductor material and they must be properly installed and used.

    (a) listed
    (b) approved
    (c) identified
    (d) all of these

4. Connectors and terminals for conductors more finely stranded than Class B and Class C, as shown in Table 10 of Chapter 9, must be _____ for the specific conductor class or classes.

    (a) listed
    (b) approved
    (c) identified
    (d) all of these

5. Many terminations and equipment are either marked with _____, or have that information included in the product's installation instructions.

    (a) an etching tool
    (b) a removable label
    (c) a tightening torque
    (d) the manufacturer's initials

6. Connection of conductors to terminal parts shall ensure a thoroughly good connection without damaging the conductors and shall be made by means of _____.

   (a) solder lugs
   (b) pressure connectors
   (c) splices to flexible leads
   (d) any of these

7. Connection by means of wire-binding screws, studs, or nuts having upturned lugs or the equivalent shall be permitted for _____ or smaller conductors.

   (a) 12 AWG
   (b) 10 AWG
   (c) 8 AWG
   (d) 6 AWG

8. Soldered splices shall first be spliced or joined so as to be mechanically and electrically secure without solder and then be soldered.

   (a) True
   (b) False

9. The temperature rating associated with the ampacity of a _____ shall be selected and coordinated so as not to exceed the lowest temperature rating of any connected termination, conductor, or device.

   (a) terminal
   (b) conductor
   (c) device
   (d) all of these

10. Conductor ampacity shall be determined using the _____ column of Table 310.15(B)(16) for circuits rated 100A or less or marked for 14 AWG through 1 AWG conductors, unless the equipment terminals are listed for use with conductors that have higher temperature ratings.

    (a) 30°C
    (b) 60°C
    (c) 75°C
    (d) 90°C

11. For circuits rated 100A or less, when the equipment terminals are listed for use with 75°C conductors, the _____ column of Table 310.15(B)(16) shall be used to determine the ampacity of THHN conductors.

    (a) 30°C
    (b) 60°C
    (c) 75°C
    (d) 90°C

12. Conductors shall have their ampacity determined using the _____ column of Table 310.15(B)(16) for circuits rated over 100A, or marked for conductors larger than 1 AWG, unless the equipment terminals are listed for use with higher temperature-rated conductors.

    (a) 30°C
    (b) 60°C
    (c) 75°C
    (d) 90°C

13. Separately installed pressure connectors shall be used with conductors at the _____ not exceeding the ampacity at the listed and identified temperature rating of the connector.

    (a) voltages
    (b) temperatures
    (c) listings
    (d) ampacities

14. Electrical equipment such as switchboards, switchgear, panelboards, industrial control panels, meter socket enclosures, and motor control centers, that are in other than dwelling units, and are likely to require _____ while energized, shall be field or factory marked to warn qualified persons of potential electric arc flash hazards.

    (a) examination
    (b) adjustment
    (c) servicing or maintenance
    (d) any of these

15. _____ in other than dwelling units must be legibly field marked with the maximum available fault current, including the date the fault-current calculation was performed and be of sufficient durability to withstand the environment involved.

    (a) Service equipment
    (b) Sub panels
    (c) Motor control centers
    (d) all of these

16. When modifications to the electrical installation affect the maximum available fault current at the service, the maximum available fault current shall be verified or _____ as necessary to ensure the service equipment ratings are sufficient for the maximum available fault current at the line terminals of the equipment.

    (a) recalculated
    (b) increased
    (c) decreased
    (d) adjusted

17. Field markings of maximum available fault current at a service are not required in industrial installations where conditions of maintenance and supervision ensure that only qualified persons service the equipment.

    (a) True
    (b) False

18. Access and _____ shall be provided and maintained about all electrical equipment to permit ready and safe operation and maintenance of such equipment.

    (a) ventilation
    (b) cleanliness
    (c) circulation
    (d) working space

19. A minimum working space depth of _____ to live parts operating at 277 volts-to-ground is required where there are exposed live parts on one side and no live or grounded parts on the other side.

    (a) 2 ft
    (b) 3 ft
    (c) 4 ft
    (d) 6 ft

20. The minimum working space on a circuit that is 120 volts-to-ground, with exposed live parts on one side and no live or grounded parts on the other side of the working space, is _____.

    (a) 1 ft
    (b) 3 ft
    (c) 4 ft
    (d) 6 ft

21. Concrete, brick, or tile walls are considered _____, as applied to working space requirements.

    (a) inconsequential
    (b) in the way
    (c) grounded
    (d) none of these

22. The required working space for access to live parts operating at 300 volts-to-ground, where there are exposed live parts on one side and grounded parts on the other side, is _____.

    (a) 3 ft
    (b) 3½ ft
    (c) 4 ft
    (d) 4½ ft

23. The required working space for access to live parts operating at 300 volts-to-ground, where there are exposed live parts on both sides of the workspace is _____.

    (a) 3 ft
    (b) 3½ ft
    (c) 4 ft
    (d) 4½ ft

24. Working space distances for enclosed live parts shall be measured from the _____ of equipment or apparatus, if the live parts are enclosed.

    (a) enclosure
    (b) opening
    (c) a or b
    (d) none of these

25. The working space in front of the electric equipment shall not be less than _____ wide, or the width of the equipment, whichever is greater.

    (a) 15 in.
    (b) 30 in.
    (c) 40 in.
    (d) 60 in.

26. Equipment associated with the electrical installation can be located above or below other electrical equipment within their working space when the associated equipment does not extend more than _____ from the front of the electrical equipment.

    (a) 3 in.
    (b) 6 in.
    (c) 12 in.
    (d) 30 in.

27. The minimum height of working spaces about electrical equipment, switchboards, panelboards, or motor control centers operating at 600V, nominal, or less and likely to require examination, adjustment, servicing, or maintenance while energized shall be 6½ ft or the height of the equipment, whichever is greater, except for service equipment or panelboards in existing dwelling units that do not exceed 200A.

    (a) True
    (b) False

28. Working space shall not be used for _____.

    (a) storage
    (b) raceways
    (c) lighting
    (d) accessibility

29. When normally enclosed live parts are exposed for inspection or servicing, the working space, if in a passageway or general open space, shall be suitably _____.

    (a) accessible
    (b) guarded
    (c) open
    (d) enclosed

30. For equipment rated 1,200A or more and over 6 ft wide that contains overcurrent devices, switching devices, or control devices, there shall be one entrance to and egress from the required working space not less than 24 in. wide and _____ high at each end of the working space.

    (a) 5½ ft
    (b) 6 ft
    (c) 6½ ft
    (d) any of these

31. For equipment rated 800A or more that contains overcurrent devices, switching devices, or control devices; and where the entrance to the working space has a personnel door less than 25 ft from the working space, the door shall _____.

    (a) open either in or out with simple pressure and shall not have any lock
    (b) open in the direction of egress and be equipped with listed panic hardware
    (c) be equipped with a locking means
    (d) be equipped with an electronic opener

32. Illumination shall be provided for all working spaces about service equipment, switchboards, switchgear, panelboards, and motor control centers _____.

    (a) over 600V
    (b) located indoors
    (c) rated 1,200A or more
    (d) using automatic means of control

33. All switchboards, panelboards, and motor control centers shall be _____.

    (a) located in dedicated spaces
    (b) protected from damage
    (c) in weatherproof enclosures
    (d) a and b

34. The minimum height of dedicated equipment space for motor control centers installed indoors is _____ above the enclosure, or to the structural ceiling, whichever is lower.

    (a) 3 ft
    (b) 5 ft
    (c) 6 ft
    (d) 6½ ft

35. For indoor installations, heating, cooling, or ventilating equipment shall not be installed in the dedicated space above a panelboard or switchboard.

    (a) True
    (b) False

36. The dedicated equipment space for electrical equipment that is required for panelboards installed indoors is measured from the floor to a height of _____ above the equipment, or to the structural ceiling, whichever is lower.

    (a) 3 ft
    (b) 6 ft
    (c) 12 ft
    (d) 30 ft

37. The dedicated space above a panelboard extends to a dropped or suspended ceiling, which is considered a structural ceiling.

    (a) True
    (b) False

38. Electrical equipment rooms or enclosures housing electrical apparatus that are controlled by a lock(s) shall be considered _____ to qualified persons.

    (a) readily accessible
    (b) accessible
    (c) available
    (d) none of these

Article 210. Branch Circuits

1. A three-phase, 4-wire, _____ power system used to supply power to nonlinear loads may necessitate that the power system design allow for the possibility of high harmonic currents on the neutral conductor.

    (a) wye-connected
    (b) delta-connected
    (c) wye/delta-connected
    (d) none of these

2. Each multiwire branch circuit shall be provided with a means that will simultaneously disconnect all _____ conductors at the point where the branch circuit originates.

    (a) circuit
    (b) grounded
    (c) grounding
    (d) ungrounded

3. Multiwire branch circuits shall _____.

    (a) supply only line-to-neutral loads
    (b) not be permitted in dwelling units
    (c) have their conductors originate from different panelboards
    (d) none of these

4. The ungrounded and grounded conductors of each _____ shall be grouped by wire ties or similar means at the panelboard or other point of origination.

    (a) branch circuit
    (b) multiwire branch circuit
    (c) feeder circuit
    (d) service-entrance conductor

5. Where more than one nominal voltage system supplies branch circuits in a building, each _____ conductor of a branch circuit shall be identified by phase and system at all termination, connection, and splice points.

    (a) grounded
    (b) ungrounded
    (c) grounding
    (d) all of these

6. The GFCI protection required by 210.8(A), (B), (C), and (D) must be _____.

    (a) the circuit breaker type only
    (b) accessible
    (c) readily accessible
    (d) concealed

7. All 15A and 20A, 125V receptacles installed in bathrooms of _____ shall have ground-fault circuit-interrupter (GFCI) protection for personnel.

   (a) guest rooms in hotels/motels
   (b) dwelling units
   (c) office buildings
   (d) all of these

8. GFCI protection shall be provided for all 15A and 20A, 125V receptacles installed in a dwelling unit _____.

   (a) attic
   (b) garage
   (c) laundry room
   (d) all of these

9. GFCI protection shall be provided for all 15A and 20A, 125V receptacles in dwelling unit accessory buildings that have a floor located at or below grade level not intended as _____ and limited to storage areas, work areas, or similar use.

   (a) habitable rooms
   (b) finished space
   (c) a or b
   (d) none of these

10. All 15A and 20A, 125V receptacles located outdoors of dwelling units, including receptacles installed under the eaves of roofs, must be GFCI protected except for a receptacle that's supplied by a branch circuit dedicated to _____ if the receptacle isn't readily accessible and the equipment or receptacle has ground-fault protection of equipment (GFPE) [426.28 or 427.22].

    (a) electric snow-melting or deicing equipment
    (b) pipeline and vessel heating equipment
    (c) holiday decorative lighting
    (d) a or b

11. All 15A and 20A, 125V receptacles installed in crawl spaces at or below grade level of dwelling units shall have GFCI protection.

    (a) True
    (b) False

12. All 15A and 20A, 125V receptacles installed in _____ of dwelling units shall have GFCI protection.

    (a) unfinished attics
    (b) finished attics
    (c) unfinished basements and crawl spaces
    (d) finished basements

13. GFCI protection shall be provided for all 15A and 20A, 125V receptacles _____ in dwelling unit kitchens.

    (a) installed to serve the countertop surfaces
    (b) within 6 ft of the sink
    (c) for all receptacles
    (d) that are readily accessible

14. GFCI protection shall be provided for all 15A and 20A, 125V receptacles installed within 6 ft of all dwelling unit sinks located in _____.

    (a) laundry rooms
    (b) bathrooms
    (c) dens
    (d) all of these

15. All 15A and 20A, 125V receptacles installed in dwelling unit boathouses shall have GFCI protection.

    (a) True
    (b) False

16. All 15A and 20A, 125V receptacles _____ of commercial occupancies shall have GFCI protection.

    (a) in bathrooms
    (b) on rooftops
    (c) in kitchens
    (d) all of these

17. In other than dwelling units, GFCI protection shall be provided for all outdoor 15A and 20A, 125V receptacles.

    (a) True
    (b) False

18. All 15A and 20A, 125V receptacles located outdoors or on rooftops in locations other than dwelling units must be GFCI protected except for a receptacle that's supplied by a branch circuit dedicated to _____ if the receptacle isn't readily accessible and the equipment or receptacle has ground-fault protection of equipment (GFPE) [426.28 and 427.22].

    (a) electric snow-melting or deicing equipment
    (b) pipeline and vessel heating equipment
    (c) holiday decorative lighting
    (d) a or b

19. In other than dwelling locations, GFCI protection is required in _____.

    (a) indoor wet locations
    (b) locker rooms with associated showering facilities
    (c) garages, service bays, and similar areas other than vehicle exhibition halls and showrooms
    (d) all of these

20. All 15A and 20A, 125V receptacles installed within 6 ft of the outside edge of a sink in locations other than dwelling units must be _____.

    (a) AFCI protected
    (b) GFCI protected
    (c) tamperproof
    (d) a and b

21. In industrial laboratories, 15A and 20A, 125V receptacles within 6 ft. of a sink used to supply equipment where removal of power would introduce a greater hazard aren't required to be GFCI protected.

    (a) True
    (b) False

22. 15A and 20A, 125V receptacles located in patient bed locations of general care or critical care areas of health care facilities, other than those covered by 210.8(B)(1), aren't required to be GFCI protected.

    (a) True
    (b) False

23. All 15A and 20A, 125V receptacles installed indoors, in other than dwelling units, in wet locations must be GFCI protected.

    (a) True
    (b) False

24. All 15A and 20A, 125V receptacles installed in locker rooms with associated showering facilities must be GFCI protected.

    (a) True
    (b) False

25. All 15A and 20A, 125V receptacles installed in other than dwelling unit garages, service bays, and similar areas where _____ is/are to be used must be GFCI protected, unless located in vehicle exhibition halls and showrooms.

    (a) electrical diagnostic equipment
    (b) electrical hand tools
    (c) portable lighting equipment
    (d) all of these

26. Ground-fault circuit-interrupter protection shall be provided for outlets not exceeding 240V that supply boat hoists installed in dwelling unit locations.

    (a) True
    (b) False

27. Two or more _____ small-appliance branch circuits shall be provided to supply power for receptacle outlets in the dwelling unit kitchen, dining room, breakfast room, pantry, or similar dining areas.

    (a) 15A
    (b) 20A
    (c) 30A
    (d) either 20A or 30A

28. There shall be a minimum of one _____ branch circuit for the laundry outlet(s) required by 210.52(F).

    (a) 15A
    (b) 20A
    (c) 30A
    (d) b and c

29. An individual 20A branch circuit can supply a single dwelling unit bathroom for receptacle outlet(s) and other equipment within the same bathroom.

    (a) True
    (b) False

30. All 15A or 20A, 120V branch circuits that supply outlets or devices in dwelling unit kitchens, family rooms, dining rooms, living rooms, parlors, libraries, dens, bedrooms, sunrooms, recreation rooms, closets, hallways, laundry areas, or similar rooms or areas shall be AFCI protected by a listed arc-fault circuit interrupter.

    (a) True
    (b) False

31. Where branch circuit wiring in a dwelling unit is modified, replaced, or extended in any of the areas specified in 210.12(A), the branch circuit must be protected by _____.

    (a) a listed combination AFCI located at the origin of the branch circuit
    (b) a listed outlet branch-circuit AFCI located at the first receptacle outlet of the existing branch circuit
    (c) a GFCI circuit breaker or receptacle
    (d) a or b

32. The recommended maximum total voltage drop on branch-circuit conductors is _____ percent.

    (a) 2
    (b) 3
    (c) 4
    (d) 6

33. Where a branch circuit supplies continuous loads, or any combination of continuous and noncontinuous loads, the rating of the overcurrent device shall not be less than the noncontinuous load plus 125 percent of the continuous load.

    (a) True
    (b) False

Article 225. Outside Branch Circuits and Feeders

1. The disconnecting means for a building supplied by a feeder shall be installed at a(n) _____ location.

    (a) accessible
    (b) readily accessible
    (c) outdoor
    (d) indoor

2. Where documented safe switching procedures are established and maintained and the installation is monitored by _____ individuals, the disconnecting means for a building supplied by a feeder can be located elsewhere on the premises.

    (a) maintenance
    (b) management
    (c) service
    (d) qualified

Article 230. Services

1. There shall be no more than _____ disconnects installed for each service or for each set of service-entrance conductors as permitted in 230.2 and 230.40.

    (a) two
    (b) four
    (c) six
    (d) eight

2. When the service contains two to six service disconnecting means, they shall be _____.

    (a) the same size
    (b) grouped
    (c) in the same enclosure
    (d) none of these

3. The additional service disconnecting means for fire pumps, emergency systems, legally required standby, or optional standby services, shall be installed remote from the one to six service disconnecting means for normal service to minimize the possibility of _____ interruption of supply.

    (a) intentional
    (b) accidental
    (c) simultaneous
    (d) prolonged

4. In a multiple-occupancy building, each occupant shall have access to the occupant's _____.

    (a) service disconnecting means
    (b) service drops
    (c) distribution transformer
    (d) lateral conductors

5. In a multiple-occupancy building where electric service and electrical maintenance are provided by the building management under continuous building management supervision, the service disconnecting means can be accessible to authorized _____ only.

    (a) inspectors
    (b) tenants
    (c) management personnel
    (d) qualified persons

Article 240. Overcurrent Protection

1. Conductor overload protection shall not be required where the interruption of the _____ would create a hazard, such as in a material-handling magnet circuit or fire pump circuit. However, short-circuit protection is required.

    (a) circuit
    (b) line
    (c) phase
    (d) system

2. The next higher standard rating overcurrent device above the ampacity of the ungrounded conductors being protected shall be permitted to be used, provided the _____.

    (a) conductors are not part of a branch circuit supplying more than one receptacle for cord-and-plug-connected portable loads
    (b) ampacity of the conductors doesn't correspond with the standard ampere rating of a fuse or circuit breaker
    (c) next higher standard rating selected doesn't exceed 800A
    (d) all of these

3. If the circuit's overcurrent device exceeds _____, the conductor ampacity must have a rating not less than the rating of the overcurrent device.

    (a) 800A
    (b) 1,000A
    (c) 1,200A
    (d) 2,000A

4. Overcurrent protection shall not exceed _____.

    (a) 15A for 14 AWG copper
    (b) 20A for 12 AWG copper
    (c) 30A for 10 AWG copper
    (d) all of these

Article 250. Grounding and Bonding

Part I. General

1. A conductor installed on the supply side of a service or within a service equipment enclosure, or for a separately derived system, to ensure the electrical conductivity between metal parts required to be electrically connected is known as the _____.

    (a) supply-side bonding jumper
    (b) ungrounded conductor
    (c) the electrical supply source
    (d) grounding electrode conductor

2. Grounded electrical systems shall be connected to earth in a manner that will _____.

   (a) limit voltages due to lightning, line surges, or unintentional contact with higher-voltage lines
   (b) stabilize the voltage-to-ground during normal operation
   (c) facilitate overcurrent device operation in case of ground faults
   (d) a and b

3. An important consideration for limiting imposed voltage on electrical systems is to remember that bonding and grounding electrode conductors shouldn't be any longer than necessary and unnecessary bends and loops should be avoided.

   (a) True
   (b) False

4. For grounded systems, normally noncurrent-carrying conductive materials enclosing electrical conductors or equipment shall be connected to earth so as to limit the voltage-to-ground on these materials.

   (a) True
   (b) False

5. For grounded systems, normally noncurrent-carrying conductive materials enclosing electrical conductors or equipment, or forming part of such equipment, shall be connected together and to the _____ to establish an effective ground-fault current path.

   (a) ground
   (b) earth
   (c) electrical supply source
   (d) none of these

6. In grounded systems, normally noncurrent-carrying electrically conductive materials that are likely to become energized shall be _____ in a manner that establishes an effective ground-fault current path.

   (a) connected together
   (b) connected to the electrical supply source
   (c) connected to the closest grounded conductor
   (d) a and b

7. For grounded systems, electrical equipment and other electrically conductive material likely to become energized, shall be installed in a manner that creates a _____ from any point on the wiring system where a ground fault may occur to the electrical supply source.

   (a) circuit facilitating the operation of the overcurrent device
   (b) low-impedance circuit
   (c) circuit capable of safely carrying the ground-fault current likely to be imposed on it
   (d) all of these

8. For grounded systems, electrical equipment and electrically conductive material likely to become energized, shall be installed in a manner that creates a low-impedance circuit capable of safely carrying the maximum ground-fault current likely to be imposed on it from where a ground fault may occur to the _____.

   (a) ground
   (b) earth
   (c) electrical supply source
   (d) none of these

9. For grounded systems, the earth is considered an effective ground-fault current path.

   (a) True
   (b) False

10. For ungrounded systems, noncurrent-carrying conductive materials enclosing electrical conductors or equipment shall be connected to the _____ in a manner that will limit the voltage imposed by lightning or unintentional contact with higher-voltage lines.

    (a) ground
    (b) earth
    (c) electrical supply source
    (d) none of these

11. For ungrounded systems, noncurrent-carrying conductive materials enclosing electrical conductors or equipment, or forming part of such equipment, shall be connected together and to the supply system equipment in a manner that creates a low-impedance path for ground-fault current that is capable of carrying _____.

    (a) the maximum branch-circuit current
    (b) at least twice the maximum ground-fault current
    (c) the maximum fault current likely to be imposed on it
    (d) the equivalent to the main service rating

12. Electrically conductive materials that are likely to _____ in ungrounded systems shall be connected together and to the supply system grounded equipment in a manner that creates a low-impedance path for ground-fault current that is capable of carrying the maximum fault current likely to be imposed on it.

    (a) become energized
    (b) require service
    (c) be removed
    (d) be coated with paint or nonconductive materials

13. In ungrounded systems, electrical equipment, wiring, and other electrically conductive material likely to become energized shall be installed in a manner that creates a low-impedance circuit from any point on the wiring system to the electrical supply source to facilitate the operation of overcurrent devices should a(n) _____ fault from a different phase occur on the wiring system.

    (a) isolated ground
    (b) second ground
    (c) arc
    (d) high impedance

14. The grounding of electrical systems, circuit conductors, surge arresters, surge-protective devices, and conductive normally noncurrent-carrying metal parts of equipment shall be installed and arranged in a manner that will prevent objectionable current.

    (a) True
    (b) False

15. Temporary currents resulting from abnormal conditions, such as ground faults, are not considered to be objectionable currents.

    (a) True
    (b) False

16. Currents that introduce noise or data errors in electronic equipment are considered objectionable currents in the context of 250.6(d) of the *NEC*.

    (a) True
    (b) False

Part II. System Grounding

1. The grounding electrode conductor shall be connected to the grounded service conductor at the _____.

    (a) load end of the service drop
    (b) load end of the service lateral
    (c) service disconnecting means
    (d) any of these

2. Where the main bonding jumper is installed from the grounded conductor terminal bar to the equipment grounding terminal bar in service equipment, the _____ conductor is permitted to be connected to the equipment grounding terminal bar.

    (a) grounding
    (b) grounded
    (c) grounding electrode
    (d) none of these

3. For a grounded system, an unspliced _____ shall be used to connect the equipment grounding conductor(s) and the service disconnecting means to the grounded conductor of the system within the enclosure for each service disconnect.

    (a) grounding electrode
    (b) main bonding jumper
    (c) busbar
    (d) insulated copper conductor

4. Where an alternating-current system operating at 1,000V or less is grounded at any point, the _____ conductor(s) shall be routed with the ungrounded conductors to each service disconnecting means and shall be connected to each disconnecting means grounded conductor(s) terminal or bus.

    (a) ungrounded
    (b) grounded
    (c) grounding
    (d) none of these

5. The grounded conductor of an alternating-current system operating at 1,000V or less shall be routed with the ungrounded conductors and connected to each disconnecting means grounded conductor terminal or bus, which is then connected to the service disconnecting means enclosure via a(n) _____ that's installed between the service neutral conductor and the service disconnecting means enclosure.

    (a) equipment bonding conductor
    (b) main bonding jumper
    (c) grounding electrode
    (d) intersystem bonding terminal

6. The grounded conductor brought to service equipment shall be routed with the phase conductors and shall not be smaller than specified in Table _____ when the service-entrance conductors are 1,100 kcmil copper and smaller.

    (a) 250.102(C)(1)
    (b) 250.122
    (c) 310.16
    (d) 430.52

7. When service-entrance conductors exceed 1,100 kcmil for copper, the required grounded conductor for the service shall be sized not less than _____ percent of the circular mil area of the largest set of ungrounded service-entrance conductor(s).

    (a) 9
    (b) 11
    (c) 12½
    (d) 15

8. Where service-entrance phase conductors are installed in parallel in two or more raceways, the size of the grounded conductor in each raceway shall be based on the total circular mil area of the parallel ungrounded service-entrance conductors in the raceway, sized in accordance with 250.24(C)(1), but not smaller than _____.

    (a) 1/0 AWG
    (b) 2/0 AWG
    (c) 3/0 AWG
    (d) 4/0 AWG

9. A grounding electrode conductor, sized in accordance with 250.66, shall be used to connect the equipment grounding conductors, the service-equipment enclosures, and, where the system is grounded, the grounded service conductor to the grounding electrode(s).

    (a) True
    (b) False

10. A grounded conductor shall not be connected to normally noncurrent-carrying metal parts of equipment on the _____ side of the system bonding jumper of a separately derived system except as otherwise permitted in Article 250.

    (a) supply
    (b) grounded
    (c) high-voltage
    (d) load

11. An unspliced _____ that is sized based on the derived phase conductors shall be used to connect the grounded conductor and the supply-side bonding jumper, or the equipment grounding conductor, or both, at a separately derived system.

    (a) system bonding jumper
    (b) equipment grounding conductor
    (c) grounded conductor
    (d) grounding electrode conductor

12. The connection of the system bonding jumper for a separately derived system shall be made _____ on the separately derived system from the source to the first system disconnecting means or overcurrent device.

    (a) in at least two locations
    (b) in every location that the grounded conductor is present
    (c) at any single point
    (d) none of these

13. Where a supply-side bonding jumper of the wire type is run with the derived phase conductors from the source of a separately derived system to the first disconnecting means, it shall be sized in accordance with 250.102(C), based on _____.

    (a) the size of the primary conductors
    (b) the size of the secondary overcurrent protection
    (c) the size of the derived ungrounded conductors
    (d) one third the size of the primary grounded conductor

14. The grounding electrode for a separately derived system shall be as near as practicable to, and preferably in the same area as, the grounding electrode conductor connection to the system.

    (a) True
    (b) False

15. For a single separately derived system, the grounding electrode conductor connects the grounded conductor of the derived system to the grounding electrode at the same point on the separately derived system where the _____ is connected.

    (a) metering equipment
    (b) transfer switch
    (c) system bonding jumper
    (d) largest circuit breaker

16. The grounding electrode conductor for a single separately derived system is used to connect the grounded conductor of the derived system to the grounding electrode.

    (a) True
    (b) False

17. Grounding electrode conductor taps from a separately derived system to a common grounding electrode conductor are permitted when a building or structure has multiple separately derived systems, provided that the taps terminate at the same point as the system bonding jumper.

    (a) True
    (b) False

18. The common grounding electrode conductor installed for multiple separately derived systems shall not be smaller than _____ copper when using a wire-type conductor.

    (a) 1/0 AWG
    (b) 2/0 AWG
    (c) 3/0 AWG
    (d) 4/0 AWG

19. Each tap conductor to a common grounding electrode conductor for multiple separately derived systems shall be sized in accordance with _____, based on the derived ungrounded conductors of the separately derived system it serves.

    (a) 250.66
    (b) 250.118
    (c) 250.122
    (d) 310.15

20. Tap connections to a common grounding electrode conductor for multiple separately derived systems shall be made at an accessible location by _____.

    (a) a connector listed as grounding and bonding equipment
    (b) listed connections to aluminum or copper busbars
    (c) the exothermic welding process
    (d) any of these

21. Tap connections to a common grounding electrode conductor for multiple separately derived systems may be made to a copper or aluminum busbar that is _____.

    (a) smaller than ¼ in. x 4 in.
    (b) not smaller than ¼ in. x 2 in.
    (c) not smaller than ½ in. x 2 in.
    (d) a and c

22. In an area served by a separately derived system, the _____ shall be connected to the grounded conductor of the separately derived system.

    (a) structural steel
    (b) metal piping
    (c) metal building skin
    (d) a and b

23. A grounding electrode shall be required if a building or structure is supplied by a feeder.

    (a) True
    (b) False

24. A grounding electrode at a separate building or structure shall be required where one multiwire branch circuit serves the building or structure.

    (a) True
    (b) False

25. When supplying a grounded system at a separate building or structure, an equipment grounding conductor shall be run with the supply conductors and connected to the building or structure disconnecting means.

    (a) True
    (b) False

26. For a separate building or structure supplied by a feeder or branch circuit, the grounded conductor can serve as the ground-fault return path for the building/structure disconnecting means for existing installations made in compliance with previous editions of the *Code* as long as the installation continues to meet the condition(s) that _____.

    (a) there are no continuous metallic paths between buildings and structures
    (b) ground-fault protection of equipment isn't installed on the supply side of the feeder
    (c) the neutral conductor is sized no smaller than the larger required by 220.61 or 250.122
    (d) all of these

27. For a separate building or structure supplied by a separately derived system when overcurrent protection is provided where the conductors originate, the supply conductors must contain a(n) _____.

    (a) equipment grounding conductor
    (b) copper conductors only
    (c) GFI protection for the feeder
    (d) all of these

28. For a separate building or structure supplied by a separately derived system when overcurrent protection isn't provided for the supply conductors to the building/structure as permitted by 240.21(C)(4), the installation must be _____ in accordance with 250.30(A).

    (a) AFCI protected
    (b) grounded and bonded
    (c) isolated
    (d) all of these

29. The size of the grounding electrode conductor for a building or structure supplied by a feeder shall not be smaller than that identified in _____, based on the largest ungrounded supply conductor.

    (a) 250.66
    (b) 250.122
    (c) Table 310.15(B)(16)
    (d) none of these

30. The frame of a portable generator shall not be required to be connected to a(n) _____ if the generator only supplies equipment mounted on the generator, or cord-and-plug connected equipment using receptacles mounted on the generator, or both.

    (a) grounding electrode
    (b) grounded conductor
    (c) ungrounded conductor
    (d) equipment grounding conductor

31. The frame of a vehicle-mounted generator shall not be required to be connected to a(n) _____ if the generator only supplies equipment mounted on the vehicle or cord-and-plug connected equipment, using receptacles mounted on the vehicle.

    (a) grounding electrode
    (b) grounded conductor
    (c) ungrounded conductor
    (d) equipment grounding conductor

Part III. Grounding Electrode System and Grounding Electrode Conductor

1. Concrete-encased electrodes of _____ shall not be required to be part of the grounding electrode system where the steel reinforcing bars or rods aren't accessible for use without disturbing the concrete.

   (a) hazardous (classified) locations
   (b) health care facilities
   (c) existing buildings or structures
   (d) agricultural buildings with equipotential planes

2. In order for a metal underground water pipe to be used as a grounding electrode, it shall be in direct contact with the earth for _____.

   (a) 5 ft
   (b) 10 ft or more
   (c) less than 10 ft
   (d) 20 ft or more

3. The metal frame of a building shall be considered a grounding electrode where one of the *NEC*-prescribed methods for connection of the metal frame to earth has been met.

   (a) True
   (b) False

4. A bare 4 AWG copper conductor installed horizontally near the bottom or vertically, and within that portion of a concrete foundation or footing that is in direct contact with the earth can be used as a grounding electrode when the conductor is at least _____ ft in length.

   (a) 10
   (b) 15
   (c) 20
   (d) 25

5. An electrode encased by at least 2 in. of concrete, located horizontally near the bottom or vertically and within that portion of a concrete foundation or footing that is in direct contact with the earth, shall be permitted as a grounding electrode when it consists of _____.

   (a) at least 20 ft of ½ in. or larger steel reinforcing bars or rods
   (b) at least 20 ft of bare copper conductor of 4 AWG or larger
   (c) a or b
   (d) none of these

6. Reinforcing bars for use as a concrete-encased electrode can be bonded together by the usual steel tie wires or other effective means.

   (a) True
   (b) False

7. Where more than one concrete-encased electrode is present at a building or structure, it shall be permitted to connect to only one of them.

   (a) True
   (b) False

8. A ground ring encircling the building or structure can be used as a grounding electrode when _____.

   (a) the ring is in direct contact with the earth
   (b) the ring consists of at least 20 ft of bare copper conductor
   (c) the bare copper conductor is not smaller than 2 AWG
   (d) all of these

9. Grounding electrodes of the rod type less than _____ in diameter shall be listed.

   (a) ½ in.
   (b) ⅝ in.
   (c) ¾ in.
   (d) none of these

10. A buried iron or steel plate used as a grounding electrode shall expose not less than _____ of surface area to exterior soil.

    (a) 2 sq ft
    (b) 4 sq ft
    (c) 9 sq ft
    (d) 10 sq ft

11. Local metal underground systems or structures such as _____ are permitted to serve as grounding electrodes.

    (a) piping systems
    (b) underground tanks
    (c) underground metal well casings that are not bonded to a metal water pipe
    (d) all of these

12. _____ shall not be used as grounding electrodes.

    (a) Metal underground gas piping systems
    (b) Aluminum
    (c) Metal well casings
    (d) a and b

13. Where practicable, rod, pipe, and plate electrodes shall be installed _____.

    (a) directly below the electrical meter
    (b) on the north side of the building
    (c) below permanent moisture level
    (d) all of these

14. Where the resistance-to-ground of 25 ohms or less is not achieved for a single rod electrode, _____.

    (a) other means besides electrodes shall be used in order to provide grounding
    (b) the single rod electrode shall be supplemented by one additional electrode
    (c) no additional electrodes are required
    (d) none of these

15. Two or more grounding electrodes bonded together are considered a single grounding electrode system.

    (a) True
    (b) False

16. Where a metal underground water pipe is used as a grounding electrode, the continuity of the grounding path or the bonding connection to interior piping shall not rely on _____ and similar equipment.

    (a) bonding jumpers
    (b) water meters or filtering devices
    (c) grounding clamps
    (d) all of these

17. Where the supplemental electrode is a rod, that portion of the bonding jumper that is the sole connection to the supplemental grounding electrode shall not be required to be larger than _____ AWG copper.

    (a) 8
    (b) 6
    (c) 4
    (d) 1

18. When a ground ring is used as a grounding electrode, it shall be buried at a depth below the earth's surface of not less than _____.

    (a) 18 in.
    (b) 24 in.
    (c) 30 in.
    (d) 8 ft

19. Ground rod electrodes shall be installed so that at least _____ of the length is in contact with the soil.

    (a) 5 ft
    (b) 8 ft
    (c) one-half
    (d) 80 percent

20. The upper end of a ground rod electrode shall be _____ ground level unless the aboveground end and the grounding electrode conductor attachment are protected against physical damage.

    (a) above
    (b) flush with
    (c) below
    (d) b or c

21. Where rock bottom is encountered when driving a ground rod at an angle up to 45 degrees, the electrode can be buried in a trench that is at least _____ deep.

    (a) 18 in.
    (b) 30 in.
    (c) 4 ft
    (d) 8 ft

22. Where used outside, aluminum or copper-clad aluminum grounding electrode conductors shall not be terminated within _____ of the earth.

    (a) 6 in.
    (b) 12 in.
    (c) 15 in.
    (d) 18 in.

23. Bare aluminum or copper-clad aluminum grounding electrode conductors shall not be used where in direct contact with _____ or where subject to corrosive conditions.

    (a) masonry or the earth
    (b) bare copper conductors
    (c) wooden framing members
    (d) all of these

24. Grounding electrode conductors _____ and larger that are not subject to physical damage can be run exposed along the surface of the building construction if it is securely fastened to the construction.

    (a) 10 AWG
    (b) 8 AWG
    (c) 6 AWG
    (d) 4 AWG

25. Grounding electrode conductors smaller than _____ shall be in rigid metal conduit, IMC, PVC conduit, electrical metallic tubing, or cable armor.

    (a) 10 AWG
    (b) 8 AWG
    (c) 6 AWG
    (d) 4 AWG

26. Grounding electrode conductors shall be installed in one continuous length without a splice or joint, unless spliced by _____.

    (a) connecting together sections of a busbar
    (b) irreversible compression-type connectors listed as grounding and bonding equipment
    (c) the exothermic welding process
    (d) any of these

27. Where service equipment consists of more than one enclosure, grounding electrode conductor connections shall be permitted to be _____.

    (a) multiple individual grounding electrode conductors
    (b) one grounding electrode conductor at a common location
    (c) a common grounding electrode conductor and taps
    (d) any of these

28. Ferrous metal raceways and enclosures for grounding electrode conductors shall be electrically continuous from the point of attachment to cabinets or equipment to the grounding electrode.

    (a) True
    (b) False

29. A grounding electrode conductor shall be permitted to be run to any convenient grounding electrode available in the grounding electrode system where the other electrode(s), if any, is connected by bonding jumpers in accordance with 250.53(C).

    (a) True
    (b) False

30. A service consisting of 12 AWG service-entrance conductors requires a grounding electrode conductor sized no less than _____.

    (a) 10 AWG
    (b) 8 AWG
    (c) 6 AWG
    (d) 4 AWG

31. The largest size grounding electrode conductor required is _____ copper.

    (a) 6 AWG
    (b) 1/0 AWG
    (c) 3/0 AWG
    (d) 250 kcmil

32. What size copper grounding electrode conductor is required for a service that has three sets of 600 kcmil copper conductors per phase?

    (a) 1 AWG
    (b) 1/0 AWG
    (c) 2/0 AWG
    (d) 3/0 AWG

33. In an ac system, the size of the grounding electrode conductor to a concrete-encased electrode shall not be required to be larger than a(n) _____ copper conductor.

    (a) 10 AWG
    (b) 8 AWG
    (c) 6 AWG
    (d) 4 AWG

Part V. Bonding

1. The normally noncurrent-carrying metal parts of service equipment, such as _____, shall be bonded together.

    (a) service raceways or service cable armor
    (b) service equipment enclosures containing service conductors, including meter fittings, boxes, or the like, interposed in the service raceway or armor
    (c) service cable trays
    (d) all of these

2. Bonding jumpers for service raceways shall be used around impaired connections such as _____.

    (a) oversized concentric knockouts
    (b) oversized eccentric knockouts
    (c) reducing washers
    (d) any of these

3. Electrical continuity at service equipment, service raceways, and service conductor enclosures shall be ensured by _____.

    (a) bonding equipment to the grounded service conductor
    (b) connections utilizing threaded couplings on enclosures, if made up wrenchtight
    (c) other listed bonding devices, such as bonding-type locknuts, bushings, or bushings with bonding jumpers
    (d) any of these

4. Service raceways threaded into metal service equipment such as bosses (hubs) are considered to be effectively _____ to the service metal enclosure.

    (a) attached
    (b) bonded
    (c) grounded
    (d) none of these

5. Service metal raceways and metal-clad cables are considered effectively bonded when using threadless couplings and connectors that are _____.

    (a) nonmetallic
    (b) made up tight
    (c) sealed
    (d) classified

6. A means external to enclosures for connecting intersystem _____ conductors shall be provided at service equipment or metering equipment enclosure and disconnecting means of buildings or structures supplied by a feeder.

    (a) bonding
    (b) ungrounded
    (c) secondary
    (d) a and b

7. The intersystem bonding termination shall _____.

   (a) be accessible for connection and inspection
   (b) consist of a set of terminals with the capacity for connection of not less than three intersystem bonding conductors
   (c) not interfere with opening the enclosure for a service, building/ structure disconnecting means, or metering equipment
   (d) all of these

8. The intersystem bonding termination shall _____.

   (a) be securely mounted and electrically connected to service equipment, the meter enclosure, or exposed nonflexible metallic service raceway, or be mounted at one of these enclosures and be connected to the enclosure or grounding electrode conductor with a minimum 6 AWG copper conductor
   (b) be securely mounted to the building/structure disconnecting means, or be mounted at the disconnecting means and be connected to the metallic enclosure or grounding electrode conductor with a minimum 6 AWG copper conductor
   (c) have terminals that are listed as grounding and bonding equipment
   (d) all of these

9. At existing buildings or structures, an intersystem bonding termination is not required if other acceptable means of bonding exits. An external accessible means for bonding communications systems together can be by the use of a(n) _____.

   (a) nonflexible metallic raceway
   (b) exposed grounding electrode conductor
   (c) connection to a grounded raceway or equipment approved by the authority having jurisdiction
   (d) any of these

10. For circuits over 250 volts-to-ground, electrical continuity can be maintained between a box or enclosure where no oversized, concentric or eccentric knockouts are encountered, and a metal conduit by _____.

    (a) threadless fittings for cables with metal sheaths
    (b) double locknuts on threaded conduit (one inside and one outside the box or enclosure)
    (c) fittings that have shoulders that seat firmly against the box with a locknut on the inside or listed fittings
    (d) all of these

11. Metal water piping system(s) shall be bonded to the _____.

    (a) grounded conductor at the service
    (b) service equipment enclosure
    (c) equipment grounding bar or bus at any panelboard within a single occupancy building
    (d) a or b

12. The bonding jumper used to bond the metal water piping system shall be sized in accordance with _____.

    (a) Table 250.66
    (b) Table 250.122
    (c) Table 310.15(B)(16)
    (d) Table 310.15(B)(6)

13. Where isolated metal water piping systems are installed in a multiple-occupancy building, the water pipes can be bonded with bonding jumpers sized in accordance with Table 250.122, based on the size of the _____.

    (a) service-entrance conductors
    (b) feeder conductors
    (c) rating of the service equipment overcurrent device
    (d) rating of the overcurrent device supplying the occupancy

14. A building or structure shall have the interior metal water piping system bonded with a conductor sized in accordance with _____.

    (a) Table 250.66
    (b) Table 250.122
    (c) Table 310.15(B)(16)
    (d) none of these

15. Metal gas piping shall be considered bonded by the equipment grounding conductor for the circuit that is likely to energize the piping.

    (a) True
    (b) False

16. Exposed structural metal interconnected to form a metal building frame that is not intentionally grounded and is likely to become energized, shall be bonded to the _____.

    (a) service equipment enclosure or building disconnecting means
    (b) grounded conductor at the service
    (c) grounding electrode conductor where of sufficient size
    (d) any of these

Part VI. Equipment Grounding and Equipment Grounding Conductors

1. Listed FMC can be used as the equipment grounding conductor if the length in any ground return path does not exceed 6 ft and the circuit conductors contained in the conduit are protected by overcurrent devices rated at _____ or less.

    (a) 15A
    (b) 20A
    (c) 30A
    (d) 60A

2. Listed FMC and LFMC shall contain an equipment grounding conductor if the raceway is installed for the reason of _____.

    (a) physical protection
    (b) flexibility after installation
    (c) minimizing transmission of vibration from equipment
    (d) b or c

3. The *Code* requires the installation of an equipment grounding conductor of the wire type in _____.

    (a) rigid metal conduit (RMC)
    (b) intermediate metal conduit (IMC)
    (c) electrical metallic tubing (EMT)
    (d) listed flexible metal conduit over 6 ft in length

4. Listed liquidtight flexible metal conduit (LFMC) is acceptable as an equipment grounding conductor when it terminates in listed fittings and is protected by an overcurrent device rated 60A or less for trade sizes 3⁄8 through ½.

    (a) True
    (b) False

5. The armor of Type AC cable containing an aluminum bonding strip is recognized by the *NEC* as an equipment grounding conductor.

    (a) True
    (b) False

6. Type MC cable provides an effective ground-fault current path and is recognized by the *NEC* as an equipment grounding conductor when _____.

    (a) it contains an insulated or uninsulated equipment grounding conductor in compliance with 250.118(1)
    (b) the combined metallic sheath and uninsulated equipment grounding/bonding conductor of interlocked metal tape–type MC cable is listed and identified as an equipment grounding conductor
    (c) only when it is hospital grade Type MC cable
    (d) a or b

7. The equipment grounding conductor shall not be required to be larger than the circuit conductors.

    (a) True
    (b) False

8. When ungrounded circuit conductors are increased in size from the minimum size that has sufficient ampacity for the intended installation, the equipment grounding conductor must be proportionately increased in size according to the _____ of the ungrounded conductors.

    (a) ampacity
    (b) circular mil area
    (c) diameter
    (d) none of these

9. When a single equipment grounding conductor is used for multiple circuits in the same raceway, cable, or cable tray, the single equipment grounding conductor shall be sized according to the _____.

    (a) combined rating of all the overcurrent devices
    (b) largest overcurrent device of the multiple circuits
    (c) combined rating of all the loads
    (d) any of these

10. Equipment grounding conductors for motor branch circuits shall be sized in accordance with Table 250.122, based on the rating of the _____ device.

    (a) motor overload
    (b) motor over-temperature
    (c) branch-circuit short-circuit and ground-fault protective
    (d) feeder overcurrent protection

11. Where conductors are run in parallel in multiple raceways or cables and include an EGC of the wire type, the equipment grounding conductor must be installed in parallel in each raceway or cable, sized in compliance with 250.122.

    (a) True
    (b) False

12. Equipment grounding conductors for feeder taps are not required to be larger than the tap conductors.

    (a) True
    (b) False

Part VII. Methods of Equipment Grounding

1. A(n) _____ shall be used to connect the grounding terminal of a grounding-type receptacle to a grounded box.

    (a) equipment bonding jumper
    (b) grounded conductor jumper
    (c) a or b
    (d) a and b

2. Where the box is mounted on the surface, direct metal-to-metal contact between the device yoke and the box shall be permitted to ground the receptacle to the box if at least _____ of the insulating washers of the receptacle is (are) removed.

    (a) one
    (b) two
    (c) three
    (d) none of these

3. A listed exposed work cover can be the grounding and bonding means when the device is attached to the cover with at least _____ permanent fastener(s) and the cover mounting holes are located on a non-raised portion of the cover.

    (a) one
    (b) two
    (c) three
    (d) none of these

4. Receptacle yokes designed and _____ as self-grounding can, in conjunction with the supporting screws, establish the equipment bonding between the device yoke and a flush-type box.

    (a) approved
    (b) advertised
    (c) listed
    (d) installed

5. The receptacle grounding terminal of an isolated ground receptacle shall be connected to a(n) _____ equipment grounding conductor run with the circuit conductors.

    (a) insulated
    (b) covered
    (c) bare
    (d) solid

6. Where circuit conductors are spliced or terminated on equipment within a box, any equipment grounding conductors associated with those circuit conductors shall be connected to the box with devices suitable for the use.

    (a) True
    (b) False

7. The arrangement of grounding connections shall be such that the disconnection or the removal of a receptacle, luminaire, or other device fed from the box does not interrupt the grounding continuity.

    (a) True
    (b) False

8. A connection between equipment grounding conductors and a metal box shall be by _____.

   (a) a grounding screw used for no other purpose
   (b) equipment listed for grounding
   (c) a listed grounding device
   (d) any of these

Article 300. General Requirements for Wiring Methods and Materials

1. What is the minimum cover requirement for direct burial Type UF cable installed outdoors that supplies a 120V, 30A circuit?

   (a) 6 in.
   (b) 12 in.
   (c) 18 in.
   (d) 24 in.

2. Rigid metal conduit that is directly buried outdoors shall have at least _____ in. of cover.

   (a) 6
   (b) 12
   (c) 18
   (d) 24

3. When installing PVC conduit underground without concrete cover, there shall be a minimum of _____ in. of cover.

   (a) 6
   (b) 12
   (c) 18
   (d) 22

4. What's the minimum cover requirement for Type UF cable supplying power to a 120V, 15A GFCI-protected circuit outdoors under a driveway of a one-family dwelling?

   (a) 6 in.
   (b) 12 in.
   (c) 16 in.
   (d) 24 in.

5. Type UF cable used with a 24V landscape lighting system can have a minimum cover of _____ in.

   (a) 6
   (b) 12
   (c) 18
   (d) 24

6. _____ is defined as the area between the top of direct-burial cable and the top surface of the finished grade.

   (a) Notch
   (b) Cover
   (c) Gap
   (d) none of these

7. The interior of underground raceways shall be considered a _____ location.

   (a) wet
   (b) dry
   (c) damp
   (d) corrosive

8. Type MC Cable listed for _____ is permitted to be installed underground under a building without installation in a raceway.

   (a) direct burial
   (b) damp and wet locations
   (c) rough service
   (d) b and c

9. Where direct-buried conductors and cables emerge from grade, they shall be protected by enclosures or raceways to a point at least _____ ft above finished grade.

   (a) 3
   (b) 6
   (c) 8
   (d) 10

10. Direct-buried service conductors that are not encased in concrete and that are buried 18 in. or more below grade shall have their location identified by a warning ribbon placed in the trench at least _____ in. above the underground installation.

    (a) 6
    (b) 10
    (c) 12
    (d) 18

11. Direct-buried conductors or cables can be spliced or tapped without the use of splice boxes when the splice or tap is made in accordance with 110.14(B).

    (a) True
    (b) False

12. Backfill used for underground wiring shall not _____.

    (a) damage the wiring method
    (b) prevent compaction of the fill
    (c) contribute to the corrosion of the raceway
    (d) all of these

13. Conduits or raceways through which moisture may contact live parts shall be _____ at either or both ends.

    (a) sealed
    (b) plugged
    (c) bushed
    (d) a or b

14. When installing direct-buried cables, a _____ shall be used at the end of a conduit that terminates underground.

    (a) splice kit
    (b) terminal fitting
    (c) bushing
    (d) b or c

15. All conductors of the same circuit shall be _____, unless otherwise specifically permitted in the *Code*.

    (a) in the same raceway or cable
    (b) in close proximity in the same trench
    (c) the same size
    (d) a or b

16. Each direct-buried single conductor cable must be located _____ in the trench to the other single conductor cables in the same parallel set of conductors, including equipment grounding conductors.

    (a) perpendicular
    (b) bundled together
    (c) in close proximity
    (d) spaced apart

17. Direct-buried conductors, cables, or raceways, which are subject to movement by settlement or frost, shall be arranged to prevent damage to the _____ or to equipment connected to the raceways.

    (a) siding of the building mounted on
    (b) landscaping around the cable or raceway
    (c) enclosed conductors
    (d) expansion fitting

18. Cables or raceways installed using directional boring equipment shall be _____ for this purpose.

    (a) marked
    (b) listed
    (c) labeled
    (d) approved

19. Electrical installations in hollow spaces, vertical shafts, and ventilation or air-handling ducts shall be made so that the possible spread of fire or products of combustion is not _____.

    (a) substantially increased
    (b) allowed
    (c) inherent
    (d) possible

20. Openings around electrical penetrations into or through fire-resistant-rated walls, partitions, floors, or ceilings shall _____ to maintain the fire-resistance rating.

    (a) be documented
    (b) not be permitted
    (c) be firestopped using approved methods
    (d) be enlarged

21. No wiring of any type shall be installed in ducts used to transport _____.

    (a) dust
    (b) flammable vapors
    (c) loose stock
    (d) all of these

22. Equipment and devices shall only be permitted within ducts or plenum chambers specifically fabricated to transport environmental air if necessary for their direct action upon, or sensing of, the _____.

    (a) contained air
    (b) air quality
    (c) air temperature
    (d) none of these

23. The space above a hung ceiling used for environmental air-handling purposes is an example of _____, and the wiring limitations of _____ apply.

    (a) a specifically fabricated duct used for environmental air, 300.22(B)
    (b) other space used for environmental air (plenum), 300.22(C)
    (c) a supply duct used for environmental air, 300.22(B)
    (d) none of these

24. Wiring methods permitted in the ceiling areas used for environmental air include _____.

    (a) electrical metallic tubing
    (b) FMC of any length
    (c) RMC without an overall nonmetallic covering
    (d) all of these

25. _____ shall be permitted to support the wiring methods and equipment permitted to be used in other spaces used for environmental air (plenum).

    (a) Metal cable tray systems
    (b) Nonmetallic wireways
    (c) PVC conduit
    (d) Surface nonmetallic raceways

26. Electrical equipment with _____ and having adequate fire-resistant and low-smoke-producing characteristics can be installed within an air-handling space (plenum).

    (a) a metal enclosure
    (b) a nonmetallic enclosure listed for use within an air-handling (plenum) space
    (c) any type of enclosure
    (d) a or b

Article 310. Conductors for General Wiring

1. The _____ rating of a conductor is the maximum temperature, at any location along its length, which the conductor can withstand over a prolonged period of time without serious degradation.

    (a) ambient
    (b) temperature
    (c) maximum withstand
    (d) short-circuit

2. There are four principal determinants of conductor operating temperature, one of which is _____ generated internally in the conductor as the result of load current flow, including fundamental and harmonic currents.

    (a) friction
    (b) magnetism
    (c) heat
    (d) none of these

3. The ampacities listed in 310.15 do not take _____ into consideration.

    (a) continuous loads
    (b) voltage drop
    (c) insulation
    (d) wet locations

4. The ampacity of a conductor can be different along the length of the conductor. The higher ampacity can be used beyond the point of transition for a distance of no more than _____ ft, or no more than _____ percent of the circuit length figured at the higher ampacity, whichever is less.

   (a) 10, 10
   (b) 10, 20
   (c) 15, 15
   (d) 20, 10

5. Each current-carrying conductor of a paralleled set of conductors shall be counted as a current-carrying conductor for the purpose of applying the adjustment factors of 310.15(B)(3)(a).

   (a) True
   (b) False

6. Where six current-carrying conductors are run in the same conduit or cable, the ampacity of each conductor shall be adjusted by a factor of _____ percent.

   (a) 40
   (b) 60
   (c) 80
   (d) 90

7. Conductor adjustment factors shall not apply to conductors in raceways having a length not exceeding _____ in.

   (a) 12
   (b) 24
   (c) 36
   (d) 48

8. The ampacity adjustment factors of Table 310.15(B)(3)(a) do not apply to Type AC or Type MC cable without an overall outer jacket, if which of the following conditions are met?

   (a) Each cable has not more than three current-carrying conductors.
   (b) The conductors are 12 AWG copper.
   (c) No more than 20 current-carrying conductors are installed without maintaining spacing.
   (d) all of these

9. Where conductors are installed in raceways or cables exposed to direct sunlight on or above rooftops, the ambient temperature shall be increased by _____ where the conduits are less than ½ in. from the rooftop.

   (a) 30°F
   (b) 40°F
   (c) 50°F
   (d) 60°F

10. When bare conductors are installed with insulated conductors, their ampacities shall be limited to _____.

   (a) 60°C
   (b) 75°C
   (c) 90°C
   (d) the lowest temperature rating for any of the insulated conductors

11. A(n) _____ conductor that carries only the unbalanced current from other conductors of the same circuit shall not be required to be counted when applying the provisions of 310.15(B)(3)(a).

   (a) neutral
   (b) ungrounded
   (c) grounding
   (d) none of these

12. On a three-phase, 4-wire, wye circuit, where the major portion of the load consists of nonlinear loads, the neutral conductor shall be counted when applying 310.15(B)(3)(a) adjustment factors.

   (a) True
   (b) False

13. When determining the number of current-carrying conductors, a grounding or bonding conductor shall not be counted when applying the provisions of 310.15(B)(3)(a).

   (a) True
   (b) False

Article 312. Cabinets and Cutout Boxes

1. Enclosures for switches or overcurrent devices are allowed to have conductors feeding through where the wiring space at any cross section is not filled to more than _____ percent of the cross-sectional area of the space.

    (a) 20
    (b) 30
    (c) 40
    (d) 60

2. Cabinets, cutout boxes, and meter socket enclosures can be used for conductors feeding through, spliced, or tapping off to other enclosures, switches, or overcurrent devices where _____.

    (a) the total area of the conductors at any cross section doesn't exceed 40 percent of the cross-sectional area of the space
    (b) the total area of conductors, splices, and taps installed at any cross section doesn't exceed 75 percent of the cross-sectional area of that space
    (c) a warning label on the enclosure identifies the closest disconnecting means for any feed-through conductors
    (d) all of these

Article 430. Motors, Motor Circuits, and Controllers

1. Branch-circuit conductors supplying a single continuous-duty motor shall have an ampacity not less than _____ rating.

    (a) 125 percent of the motor's nameplate current
    (b) 125 percent of the motor's full-load current rating as determined by 430.6(A)(1)
    (c) 125 percent of the motor's full locked-rotor
    (d) 80 percent of the motor's full-load current

2. The motor branch-circuit short-circuit and ground-fault protective device shall be capable of carrying the _____ current of the motor.

    (a) varying
    (b) starting
    (c) running
    (d) continuous

3. The maximum rating or setting of an inverse time breaker used as the motor branch-circuit short-circuit and ground-fault protective device for a single-phase motor is _____ percent of the full-load current given in Table 430.248.

    (a) 125
    (b) 175
    (c) 250
    (d) 300

4. Where the motor short-circuit and ground-fault protection devices determined by Table 430.52 do not correspond to the standard sizes or ratings, a higher rating that does not exceed the next higher standard ampere rating shall be permitted.

    (a) True
    (b) False

Article 450. Transformers

1. The primary overcurrent protection for a transformer rated 1,000V, nominal, or less, with no secondary protection and having a primary current rating of over 9A must be set at not more than _____ percent.

   (a) 125
   (b) 167
   (c) 200
   (d) 300

2. A secondary tie of a transformer is a circuit operating at _____, nominal, or less, between phases that connects two power sources or power-supply points.

   (a) 600V
   (b) 1,000V
   (c) 12,000V
   (d) 35,000V

3. For transformers, other than Class 2 and Class 3, a means is required to disconnect all transformer ungrounded primary conductors. The disconnecting means must be located within sight of the transformer unless the disconnect _____.

   (a) location is field marked on the transformer
   (b) is lockable in accordance with 110.25
   (c) is nonfusible
   (d) a and b

Take Your Training to the next level & Save 25%

2014 Detailed Code Library

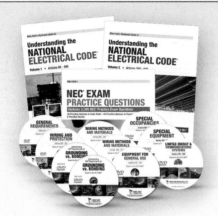

There isn't a better way to learn the Code than Mike's Detailed Code Library.

Understanding the National Electrical Code® Volume 1 textbook
Understanding the National Electrical Code® Volume 2 textbook
NEC® Exam Practice Questions workbook
General Requirements DVD
Wiring and Protection DVD
Grounding vs. Bonding (2 DVDs)
Wiring Methods and Materials (2 DVDs)
Equipment for General Use DVD
Special Occupancies DVD
Special Equipment DVD
Limited Energy and Communications Systems DVD

Product Code: 14DECODVD   List Price: $569.00   Now only $426.75

Electrical Estimating DVD Package

Mike Holt's Electrical Estimating DVD Program will give you the skills and the knowledge to get more jobs and to make sure that those jobs will be profitable. This program will also give you a comprehensive understanding of the Estimating process as well as a review of how Electrical Estimating Software can improve your process.

Electrical Estimating textbook
Estimating versus Bidding DVD
The Estimating Process DVD
The Practical Application DVD
About Estimating Software DVD

Product Code: EST2DVD   List Price: $299.00   Now only $224.25

Business Management Skills DVD Package

This Management Skills Workbook with corresponding DVD is a no nonsense approach to management. You'll be able to create a customized strategic plan to move your business to the next level! Subjects include Business Management, Financial Management, Job Management, and Labor Management.

Business Management Skills textbook
Business Management Skills DVD

Product Code: BMSKD   List Price: $109.00   Now only $81.75

Call Now 888.NEC.CODE (632.2633)

Mike Holt Enterprises, Inc.

All prices and availability are subject to change